AF560035

MATTHEW ARNOLD

MATTHEW ARNOLD

—A CRITICAL STUDY—

C. David

ANMOL PUBLICATIONS PVT. LTD.
NEW DELHI - 110 002 (INDIA)

ANMOL PUBLICATIONS PVT. LTD.
H.O.: 4374/4B, Ansari Road, Darya Ganj,
New Delhi-110 002 (India)
Ph.: 23278000, 23261597
B.O.: No. 1015, Ist Main Road, BSK IIIrd Stage
IIIrd Phase, IIIrd Block
Bangalore - 560 085 (India)
Visit us at: www.anmolpublications.com

Matthew A, nold

First Published, 2007

ISBN 81-261-3102-0

PRINTED IN INDIA

Printed at Mehra Offset Press, Delhi.

Contents

Preface

Matthew Arnold (1822 - 88) was a great English poet, essayist and literary critic, noted particularly for his poems **Soharab and Rustam** and **Dover Beach**, and for his **Essays in Criticism** and **Culture and Anarchy**.

So far many books have been written on Matthew Arnold and many researches have been carried out on his works at different universities. This book is an attempt in direction of portraying him analytically from different angles. Besides his biographical sketch, his literary achievements, a critique of his works is presented, which is penned competently by many different scholars of repute.

Hopefully, this will serve as an ideal reference-cum-helpbook to students, and teachers of English literature.

In fact, the book is substantially based on the work of various experts of literature, the entire credit for this ought go to the original contributors. We express our deep sense of gratitude to them all. We received guidance, inspiration and assistance from various quarters while compiling the material for this work. We are deeply beholden to them all. Last but not the least, we are thankful Mr. J.L. Kumar, Managing Director, Anmol Publications Pvt. Ltd., New Delhi for bringing out this book elegantly within shortest possible time.

—*Editor*

1

Matthew Arnold: An Overview

It is not pretended, in this study, to minimise the extent of other influences than French on Matthew Arnold's thought and art. His classical training, most important of these, played its assured role in Arnold's life; supplying ballast and balance to his intellectual formation, the good taste and judgment which nearly always mark his serious pronouncements, and, lastly, the rich humanity and sense of beauty that are the gifts of the ancient world to the new.

Of his debt to Wordsworth, in whose shadow he grew, to Byron, to Gray, to all his English predecessors, we cannot say much here. Nor of his German interests—literary, social and theological—is it here in our province to speak; unless perhaps to wonder how much in fact Arnold was owing here, to a literature and a society whose language he never possessed with the sureness and intimacy of the French. An early interest in Carlyle, later disavowed, seems to have made him first acquainted with Goethe, for whom he formed an enthusiasm which grew to veneration with the years, but which never had on him the definite influence of a leading ideal. He read and translated Schiller; Heine he first derided and came to appreciate only in later life. It was probably the German habit of loose unrhymed lines that influenced him in his first poetic experiments, but here the example of the classics may also have had its role to play. And, finally, the German religious criticism which he absorbed came to him chiefly through the medium of the French who, as we shall see, gave the whole subject a turn and a beauty and a conviction which the ponderous Dutch and German volumes had been powerless to impart.

THE MAN

The trustees who, in December 1827, elected Thomas Arnold, at the age of thirty-two, to the headmastership of Rugby had been assured by one of his supporters that he would, if appointed, change the face of education all through the public schools of England. This he was indeed to do. At that time, Eton, under Keate, was an atrocious despotism, devoted to pedantry and often close to anarchy; but Rugby, under Arnold, was rapidly to become the earliest of the modern public schools and to serve as an example for the rest. Arnold achieved this result partly by administrative and curricular reforms. He gave a good share of responsibility for the government of the school to the sixth-form boys; he improved the status of the assistant masters; and he added modern history, modern languages, and mathematics—all, admittedly, in small quantities—to the regular classical course of study. But his triumph was due above all to his personal qualities, to his energy and determination. He succeeded in teaching the school subjects to the senior boys in such a way as at one and the same time to turn out good classical scholars, to awaken their historical imaginations, and to instruct them in politics and Christian ethics. Both in these lessons and in his impressive sermons in the school chapel—in fact, in all his dealings with Rugby—he had a clearly conceived end in view: to make the school a centre of what he believed to be genuinely Christian training. Never, in fact, would he tolerate any suggestion that education might be divorced from religion.

Possessed by a profound sense of the sinfulness of human nature, especially in childhood, Arnold was a strict disciplinarian. He demanded from his pupils a high standard of conduct and of moral thoughtfulness, and he let slip no opportunity of impressing upon them, and upon the members of his sixth form in particular, the gravity of their responsibilities. His younger pupils found him a stern, aloof, and awe-inspiring figure. But the older boys, having learned to make allowance for his shyness and his quick temper, came to know him better and to regard him with affection, pride, and reverence.

A few of them, however, allowed their responsibilities as members of his community to weigh much too heavily upon them. Thus, Arthur Hugh Clough, one of his favourite pupils, could write at the age of seventeen, 'I verily believe my whole being is soaked through with the wishing and hoping and striving to do the school good.' Youth ought surely to be encouraged to carry itself more lightly than this. Arnold, inculcating moral earnestness, quite forgot, as one of his admirers pointed out, that it was God Almighty's intention that there should exist between childhood and manhood the natural production known as a boy. On most of Arnold's pupils the effect of this oversight must have been slight enough-and not altogether harmful, either. But on an intelligent, scrupulous, and anxious youth such as Clough the effect could be lasting and disabling. It is not fanciful to relate to it the fatigued joylessness of Clough's maturity.

Clough himself seems to have suspected something of the kind. His *Dipsychus* is a poem dramatizing the dilemma of one torn between the promptings of a tender conscience and those of a worldly wisdom. The 'Epilogue' to it consists of a prose dialogue between the poet and his uncle, who holds that his nephew's generation is too scrupulous and too pious. 'It's all Arnold's doing; he spoilt the public schools . . . Not that I mean that the old schools were perfect, any more than we old boys that were there. But whatever else they were or did, they certainly were in harmony with the world, and they certainly did not disqualify the country's youth for after-life and the country's service.' He brushes aside his nephew's protest and goes on to describe the Rugby product as 'a sort of hobbadi-hoy cherub, too big to be innocent, and too simple for anything else. They're full of the notion of the world being so wicked and of their taking a higher line, as they call it. I only fear they'll never take any line at all.' When the nephew tries to excuse Arnold, the uncle exclaims, 'Why, my dear boy, how often have I not heard from you, how he used to attack offences, not as offences—the right view—against discipline, but as sin, heinous guilt, I don't know what beside! Why didn't he flog them and hold his tongue? Flog them he did, but why preach?' In reply, the nephew invokes the spirit of the age. 'If he did err in this way, sir, which I hardly think, I ascribe it to the spirit of the time. The real cause of the evil you complain of, which to a certain extent I admit, was, I take it, the religious movement of the last century, beginning with Wesleyanism, and culminating at last in Puseyism. This over-excitation of the religious sense, resulting in this irrational, almost animal irritability of consciences, was, in many ways, as foreign to Arnold as it is proper to . . .' The uncle is bored, however, and the conversation ends. Obviously, the uncle's views were not Clough's. But they were held by many men at that time; and Clough evidently felt that there might be some truth in them.

Arnold's move to Rugby in August 1828 detached him from the village where he had lived since shortly before his marriage to Mary Penrose eight years earlier. This village was Laleham, on the Thames between Staines and Chertsey, about eighteen miles above London. Here he had at first conducted a small private school in partnership with his brother-in-law; subsequently, he had concentrated upon coaching a few senior boys—not more than about nine at a time—for the university. Just before leaving for Rugby, he had expressed the fear that he would there miss the 'absolute play', the gymnastics and bathing, which he had enjoyed with these youths. Still worse was the fact that the midland countryside was less varied and attractive than that of the Thames valley, which he loved. After he was installed at Rugby, he explained his distaste for the view eastwards from there by asserting that in that direction there was nothing fine between the observer and the Ural mountains!

His passion for natural scenery was, indeed, Arnold's strongest aesthetic emotion. Despite his warm admiration for Wordsworth, both as a man and as a writer, his taste in poetry was narrow. Nor did he write it with any skill; years later, his son Matthew remarked sadly on seeing a specimen of his verse: 'Ah, my poor father! he had many excellencies, but he was not a poet.' He himself admitted his insensibility to painting and music. His passion for natural scenery, however, was one of the great forces in his life. In alliance with his devotion to history, it led him to spend his holidays travelling not only in England but also in France, Italy, Spain, Switzerland, and Germany—his elder children accompanying him on some of his later Continental tours; and in 1832 it led him to acquire Fox How, a small estate near Ambleside, within easy reach of the Wordsworths.

(Indeed, the poet himself helped him to obtain it.) Here, among the mountains and streams he loved, he and his family began to spend the school holidays. Before long, the grey stone house there had become their true home.

A letter which he wrote during Matthew's last year at school gives a glimpse of them engaged in winter sports during one of these holidays. ' Wordsworth is remarkably well, and we see him daily; and moreover, Rydal Lake is frozen as hard as a rock, and my nine children, and I with them, were all over it to-day, to our great delight. Four of my boys skait. Walter is trundled in his wheelbarrow, and my daughters and I slide, for I am afraid that I am too old to learn to skait now. My wife walks to Ambleside to get the letters, and then goes round to meet us as we come from the Lake.'

Arnold was an enthusiastic walker. He and his wife would set out almost daily from their Rugby home, she riding on a small, quiet pony, preferably a grey one, while he strode along beside her at over four miles an hour, talking freely on history and politics as he did so. When, in the Lake District, a larger party set out, his activities were more various: he comforted any children who might tumble, encouraged those who lagged behind, and was throughout a cheerful and judicious guide. He took a keen pleasure in wild flowers; towards the end of his life he was to speak of 'the deep delight with which I look at wood anemones or wood sorrel'.

Arnold loved to join in his children's games. During the summer holiday of 1835, which had to be spent partly at Rugby itself, he greatly enjoyed cricketing with Matthew and his brothers 'on the very cricket ground of the "eleven," that is, of the best players in the school, on which, when the school is assembled, no profane person may encroach'. Those who had known him only at Rugby, and who were unaware of such vacation escapades as this, were often surprised on first witnessing his tenderness and playfulness in the home circle. Presumably they expected the great headmaster, with his intense moral fervour, to be a solemn domestic tyrant. And, though their error was grotesque, there is no doubt that Arnold was a formidable parent. The moral strenuousness and the severity which enabled him successfully to evolve, from the English public school, a more intelligent and more conscientious, if occasionally more priggish, product must have been evident likewise in his home. But equally evident must have been the vigorous enjoyment of living, the boyish good spirits, and the prompt sympathy recorded by those who knew him more intimately.

He was not merely a headmaster and a parent, however. He was also an eager and lively participant in the political and religious controversies of his time. 'I must write a pamphlet in the holidays,' he told his sister during one crisis in public affairs, 'or I shall burst.' His outlook was Liberal. Politically, he supported Catholic Emancipation and Parliamentary Reform and sympathized with the moderate French Revolution of 1830. In religious matters, his Liberalism was so marked that the more dogmatic young J.H. Newman could ask with some asperity, 'But is he a Christian?' and Wordsworth, confiding to Henry Crabb Robinson that he loved Arnold, could add that he was 'a good man, & an admirable schoolmaster, but . . . would make a desperate bad bishop'. His Liberalism exposed him more than once to violent Tory abuse; and it would not be surprising to learn that in consequence his senior pupils' attachment to him grew even stronger.

Arnold was indebted to Samuel Taylor Coleridge more than to anyone else for his views on Church and State. I think', he said, 'with all his faults old Sam was more of a great man than any one who has lived within the four seas in my memory. It is refreshing to see such a union of the highest philosophy and poetry, with so full a knowledge, on so many points at least, of particular facts.' Following Burke, Coleridge had insisted that the state, in addition to its negative function of protecting the individual from undue interference by his fellows, had the positive duty of humanizing and civilizing its members. His defence of the established church rested upon his conviction that in its ideal form an endowed 'clerisy' was the organ by which the state fulfilled its educational and spiritual responsibilities.

Arnold amplified these doctrines and, since he was above all a practical man, strove actively to realize, both in his own tiny province of Rugby and in England as a whole, that ideal of a highly disciplined Christian community to which they seemed to him to point. He persuaded the trustees, in 1831, to allow him to be school chaplain as well as headmaster; in the outside world, similarly, he insisted upon the absolute identity of the church and the state. For was not the highest welfare of man the aim of both? The state could not accomplish this without the wisdom and goodness of the church, nor the church without the sovereign power of the state. The two societies were, or ought to be, one. Utilitarians and others who favoured a merely secular state earned his loathing; so, too, did the Tractarians, with their priestly claim that the church was wholly independent of the secular power. Against such as these, Arnold laboured for the abolition of all distinction between spiritual and secular, for the complete identification of Christian with political society.

But the actual established church was the church of only a portion of the population; outside it, there was a vast body of dissenters. If it was to become a truly national church, a truly effective society for putting down moral evil, making its spiritual influence felt even in spheres hitherto held to be purely secular, it had to be made more comprehensive. This it could become if its doctrine were reduced to that which is acceptable to all Christians, if its constitution were made more democratic, and if the various services of the sects were all conducted, at different hours, in the same parish churches. By these means, virtually the whole population could be brought into the one fold, and Christianity could become the recognized basis of citizenship.

It is evident that the author of these proposals regarded creeds and rituals as of less importance than good deeds. In his eyes, Christianity was above all a system for disseminating morality. Indeed, he defined religion as 'nothing more nor less than a system directing and influencing our conduct, principles, and feelings, and professing to do this with sovereign authority, and most efficacious influence'. This being so, he was not frightened by the German Biblical criticism of which, thanks partly to 'old Sam', he became aware rather earlier than most English scholars. For his faith was not based upon intellectual beliefs such as criticism might undermine.

Arnold's willing acknowledgment of the sovereign power of a state which should be also in its spiritual aspect the national church anticipates his son's elevation of the state above the social classes which he saw competing for supremacy. His wish to unite the Christian sects in a comprehensive established church and his conviction that religion is predominantly morality are likewise echoed and developed in Matthew Arnold's works. But, even when they are engaged in similar undertakings, the tone of the two men's writings is widely different. Father and son may share certain debating tricks—for example, the telling reiteration of an opponent's word or phrase—but whereas the son's tone is bantering and ironical the father's is earnest and urgent. This is well seen in the following passage (originally contributed to a Sheffield newspaper), in which Thomas Arnold follows Coleridge in stressing society's responsibility for humanizing and civilizing its members and anticipates Matthew's persistent concern with the total human perfection of his fellows:

> A man sets up a factory, and wants hands: I beseech you, Sir, to observe the very expressions that are used, for they are all significant. What he wants of his fellow creatures is the loan of their hands;—of their heads and hearts he thinks nothing. These

> hands are attached to certain mouths and bodies which must be fed and lodged: but this must be done as cheaply as possible;—and accordingly, up starts a miserable row of houses, built where ground is cheapest, that is, where it is least generally desirable to get it;—built as close as possible, to have the more of them on a given space, and for the same reason without any sort of garden or outlet attached to them, because the comfort and enjoyment of the human being is quite independent of the serviceableness of his hands. But further, Sir, these hands are not only attached to mouths and bodies, but to reasonable minds and immortal souls. The mouths and bodies must be provided for, however miserably, because without them the hands cannot work; but the minds and souls go utterly unregarded. And is this any other than a national crime, a crime in the civil government, a crime in the church, a crime in all the wealthy and intelligent part of the English people, that while hands have been multiplying so enormously during the last forty years in every corner of the kingdom, no greater efforts have been made to provide for the welfare of the human beings who have multiplied with them; beings born not for time only but for eternity [?] (*Letters on the Social Condition of the Operative Classes, X*).

Matthew Arnold, then, inherited both the profound respect for the idea of the state and the Broad Church liberalism of his father. Very largely from the same source, no doubt, he acquired his taste for travel and his love of the countryside in general and of mountains and streams in particular. But he was no mere docile heir. The characteristic difference in tone of the two men's writing is indicative of important differences in character and personality. These should become evident later.

In 1841, Thomas Arnold was offered the Regius Professorship of Modern History at his old university, Oxford. No public reward or honour could have been so welcome to him, and he accepted it with joy. 'I caught at any opportunity of being connected again with Oxford;' he wrote to a friend whom he had known as an undergraduate, 'and the visions of Bagley Wood and Shotover rose upon me with an irresistible charm.' Moreover, there were the Tractarians, with their glorification of priestcraft, to be combated. His intention was to resign the headmastership of Rugby at the end of 1842 and to retire to Fox How, making his professorial visits to Oxford from there. But these plans were never to be carried out. In the summer of 1842, he died suddenly from an attack of *angina pectoris*, a disease apparently inherited from his father and transmitted to his son Matthew.

His widow, who outlived him by thirty-one years, made Fox How her home for the remainder of her life. Five years his senior, Mary Arnold was a charming, sympathetic, and intelligent woman devoted to her husband during his life and to his memory after his death. Yet this devotion did not result in her binding herself immovably to his opinions. 'She had a clearness and fairness of mind,' wrote Matthew in reply to a letter of condolence, 'an interest in things, and a power of appreciating what might not be in her own line, which were very remarkable, and which remained with her to the very end of her life.' Her reception of her son's *Literature and Dogma* (1873) seemed to him to testify to an openmindedness quite astonishing in a woman past eighty; it was also characteristic of one who remained to the end in close contact with contemporary thought. During her earlier years at Fox How she was a great favourite of the Wordsworths; after the poet's death, she was one of the only three persons who could tempt the aged Crabb Robinson as far afield as the Lake District. Matthew's weekly letters to her are those of a correspondent who knew that he could count upon her full comprehension over the whole range of his interests.

Mrs. Arnold's family was large; and, of the ten children born to Thomas Arnold and herself, five sons and four daughters reached adult life. Matthew, born on 24. December 1822, was their second child. He was a year younger than Jane, who was to become his favourite sister and the first reader, or hearer, of his poems. Jane, an intelligent girl, evidently inherited her father's spirit and determination. As a child of three, she refused on one occasion to curtsy to her mother, 'persisting in her disobedience for two hours in spite of the corner and other tokens of our displeasure, her little heart swelling with pride'. This behaviour made her father consider, rather ponderously, 'how truly pride is our original and besetting sin from the first'. The incident foreshadowed a severer conflict. Shortly before his death, Jane contracted what he thought an imprudent engagement with one of his assistant masters, and he felt obliged to forbid it. Despite this early attachment and its frustration, Jane had from 1850 onwards a very happy married life. Her husband was W. E. Forster, a manufacturer of Quaker upbringing who became a respected Liberal politician and is remembered for his important Education Act of 1870. In 1849, Matthew had acknowledged Jane's 'passionate hopes' and ardour in his poem 'Resignation', which he had dedicated to her as 'Fausta'. Throughout his life, she remained, as 'K', one of his favourite correspondents. 'You and Clough are, I believe,' he assured her in 1859, 'the two people I in my heart care most to please by what I write.' His letters to her contain many friendly messages to a well-liked brother-in-law.

Matthew spent much of his early childhood at Laleham. The large old red-brick house with the wide lawn flanked by cedars was his home until his father took up his appointment at Rugby. Two years after this move, Matthew returned to the district of his birth in order to begin his formal education under the uncle with whom his father had once worked. During all this time there was developing in him that love of the Thames valley which he never lost. Visiting Laleham in early manhood, he recorded with pleasure that he 'found the stream with the old volume, width, shine, rapid fulness, "kempshott,"[1] and swans, unchanged and unequalled, to my partial and remembering eyes at least'.

His father, too, had a hand in his early education, teaching Latin to Jane, Matthew, and Thomas, the third child. But a fresh stage was reached when, at the age of thirteen, Matthew was sent to Winchester, his father's old school. He stayed there only one year. In August 1837, after a holiday with his parents in Paris and other places in northern France, he was transferred to Rugby, where he remained until 1841.

Glimpses of Matthew during his schooldays reveal a child who is recognizably the father of the man. At Winchester, he coolly informed the headmaster that he found the work quite light; not surprisingly, he paid dearly for the pleasure of this remark at the hands of his indignant fellows. At Rugby, where he was seen to be 'very reserved' and known as 'Lofty Mat', his mockery is said to have been directed on at least one occasion, and without its victim's knowledge, upon Dr. Arnold himself. For even as a boy Matthew did not permit himself to appear too much in earnest. His flippancy worried his parents. 'Matt likes general society,' said his father, 'and flitters about from flower to flower, but is not apt to fix.' With an austere literalness, his father tried to restrain his lively sallies. Even so, a neighbour had to record in a letter that, although to her the sons seemed delightful boys, Mrs. Arnold felt that they were not all that 'their Father's children ought to be' and that they did not exhibit 'the sobriety of mind and manliness of character she had a right to expect from their training. Matt's passion for fishing is as strong as Henry Fletcher's. He is not to be allowed to go to College unless he shows a more decided sense of duty in his school work the next half year.'

Matthew's passion for fishing lasted long. But in spite of it his school work must have improved; for in the autumn of 1841, after a holiday with his father and his brother Tom in the south of France and the Pyrenees, he entered Balliol College, Oxford, as a classical scholar. Here his activities were in part such as ought not to have surprised those who knew his athletic father. They may, however, have surprised those who remembered the small boy whose parents had been worried by his ill-health and by the clumsiness which had resulted from his having had his legs in irons for nearly two years. He went out with the harriers. He achieved a leap over the Wadham railings which was long known to many who remained ignorant of his books. He boated on the Cherwell and elsewhere. Above all, he found time to wander in the Cumnor hills with his particular friends Clough and Theodore Walrond and his own brother Tom.

During the vacations, he walked, boated, and skated in the Lake District. There he saw a good deal of Wordsworth, knowing well how to draw out the old poet in conversation. Those who found it strange that the eldest son of the practical and prosaic headmaster should win the poetry prize at Oxford, as previously at Rugby, may have been tempted to ascribe his success to the influence of the Poet Laureate. But Matthew was in many ways an unexpected product of the Arnold home.

At Fox How, the young people produced a family magazine. Comments in this make it clear that the eldest son was something of a dandy, elegant and supercilious. Jane was responsible for a ballad about a 'fine young

Oxford gentleman' who 'wears an eye-glass round his neck hung by a silken string':

> Eau de Mille Fleurs, Eau de Cologne and twenty eaux beside Rowland's Odonto, scented soaps, jostle his books aside.

At Oxford, Matthew was quite a social lion and worried his more scrupulous friends, and particularly the old Rugbeians among them, by his jaunty demeanour, his affectations, and his idleness. While allowing himself filially to echo Dr. Arnold's liberalism in the headquarters of Newman, he evidently wished to avoid seeming too much his father's son, even to the extent of flaunting tastes and attitudes directly opposed to those of his parents. One of his contemporaries years later described him as having been:

> So full of power, yet blithe and debonair, Rallying his friends with pleasant banter gay, Or half a-dream chaunting with jaunty air Great words of Goethe, catch of Béranger.

His friends appreciated his cheerfulness, geniality, and kindliness; but they had their fears. 'Our friend Matt', wrote one of them while they were both still undergraduates, 'utters as many absurdities as ever, with as grave a face, and I am afraid wastes his time considerably, which I deeply regret, but advice does not go for much with him, and perhaps I am not well qualified to give it.' Perhaps Matt resented it, too. At all events, when they went together on a trip to Devonshire in 1843, the same friend reported that they arrived only 'after sundry displays of the most consummate coolness on the part of our friend Matt, who pleasantly induced a belief into the passengers of the coach that I was a poor mad gentleman, and that he was my keeper'.

At length it began to appear that the indolent Matthew might not only fail to reach the first class but even drop below the second class in his degree examination. In July 1844, he retired to Patterdale in the Lake District to read for it under Clough's supervision. But before long Clough was reporting to a correspondent: 'For this evening, Mat is away; a party of Oxford visitants from

Ambleside and Grasmere came over last night to spend the weekly holiday; hospitalities were required, slowdoms to be borne with: so Mat improvised a necessity to visit his Penates, and left the *onus entertainendi* upon me, departing after Morning Services . . . I left Liverpool last Monday; slept at Fox How. Mrs. Arnold was well and kind, but somewhat anxious about Mat . . . Mat has.done something this week, but this foolish walk today will lose him all tomorrow I have no doubt . . . I am painfully coerced to my work by the assurance that should I relax in the least my yoke-fellow would at once come to a dead stop.' Things were no better ten days later: ' Matt has gone out fishing, when he ought properly to be working, it being nearly four o'clock . . . it has, however, come on to rain furiously; so Walrond, who is working sedulously at Herodotus, and I, who am writing to you, rejoice to think that he will get a good wetting.' Three weeks before the examinations began in the autumn of the same year, he became very diligent. 'I think', wrote Clough, 'he is destined for second; this is above his deserts certainly, but I do not think he can drop below it, and one would not be surprised if he rose above it in spite of all his ignorance.' A week later, he repeated this forecast, adding, 'May he also tread in my steps next Easter!'

This is precisely what Arnold did. Like Clough three years earlier, he redeemed his second as an undergraduate at Balliol by a fellowship at Oriel. During the months of waiting, Wordsworth, whose own college career at St. John's, Cambridge, had been undistinguished, is said to have taken him under his special protection. Arnold spent the time teaching the lower fifth form at Rugby under Dr. Tait, his father's successor. Evidently his mischievous sense of fun was not damped down either by his recent rebuff or by his current labours. At a masters' meeting, Tait observed that strict Calvinism devoted thousands of mankind to be eternally—. He paused. Obligingly, Arnold supplied the word which the headmaster's delicacy had prevented him from uttering: 'Damned!' A burlesque examination of conscience follows his report of this incident to Clough.

Among his younger colleagues at Rugby was one whom the respectable and censorious accused of dressing with an unseemly gaiety and of riding to hounds in term time. Nevertheless, he had been made a housemaster. Calling on him one day, Arnold found him conducting with trepidation his first entertainment of parents, a breakfast with a staid couple who had entrusted their son to his care. No doubt, the parents were pleased to meet the eldest son of the late headmaster, a tall, graceful young man with a strong face but a languid manner and with whiskers and wavy hair as black as coal. He sat down at the table with them but fastidiously waved aside the dishes which their host offered to him. 'No thank you, my darling,' he said casually, 'I've just bitten off the tails of those three bull-pups of yours, and that does take the edge off one's appetite.' Revelling in the resultant consternation, he went on: 'By the way, I had a look at that mare of yours when I was in the stable. I'd advise you to have her vetted before you ride her to hounds again.'

In the summer of the year in which he was elected to the fellowship, Arnold visited the Isle of Man with his mother and his sister Jane. In the summer of the following year, 1846, he went further afield. At Oxford, during the regular Sunday morning breakfasts in Clough's rooms, Clough himself, Walrond, and the two Arnolds had, of course, discussed everything under the sun. But they had concerned themselves particularly with George Sand, of whom Clough and more especially Arnold were passionate devotees. Her novels breathed a spirit of emancipation; and there was an enjoyable defiance of conventional susceptibilities involved in preferring them to the edifying works of Mrs. Trimmer or Hannah More. In 1846, Arnold determined to see the George Sand country and, if possible, to meet the authoress herself. By rail and stage-coach he made his way to Boussac in the centre of France. Recalling, thirty years later, his visit to her Château of Nohant, he wrote:

From Boussac I addressed to Madame Sand the sort of letter of which she must in her lifetime have had scores, a letter conveying to her, in bad French, the homage of a youthful and enthusiastic foreigner who had read her works with delight. She received the infliction good-naturedly, for on my return to La Châtre I found a message left at the inn by a servant from Nohant that Madame Sand would be glad to see me if I called. The midday breakfast at Nohant was not yet over when I reached the house, and I found a large party assembled. I entered with some trepidation, as well I might, considering how I had got there; but the simplicity of Madame Sand's manner put me at ease in a moment. She named some of those present; amongst them were her son and daughter, the Maurice and Solange so familiar to us from her books, and Chopin with his wonderful eyes. There was at that time nothing astonishing in Madame Sand's appearance. She was not in man's clothes, she wore a sort of costume not impossible, I should think (although on these matters I speak with hesitation), to members of the fair sex at this hour amongst ourselves, as an out-door dress for the country or for Scotland. She made me sit by her and poured out for me the insipid and depressing beverage, boisson fade et mélancolique, as Balzac called it, for which English people are thought abroad to be always thirsting,—tea. She conversed of the country through which I had been wandering, of the Berry peasants and their mode of life, of Switzerland whither I was going; she touched politely, by a few questions and remarks, upon England and things and persons English,—upon Oxford and Cambridge, Byron, Bulwer. As she spoke, her eyes, head, bearing, were all of them striking; but the main impression she made was an impression of what I have already mentioned,—of simplicity, frank, cordial simplicity. After breakfast she led the way into the garden, asked me a few kind questions about myself and my plans, gathered a flower or two and gave them to me, shook hands heartily at the gate, and I saw her no more. (*Mixed Essays*, 'George Sand'.)

On George Sand, Arnold made the effect of a young Milton on his travels, *'l'effet d'un Milton jeune et voyageant'*. Did he perhaps tell her more about his 'plans' than was known to most of his English acquaintances, to whom his first volume of poems two and a half years later came as something of a surprise?

It has been plausibly conjectured that they must also have talked, in connection with Switzerland, of Étienne Pivert de Senancour, who had died during that year, and who was admired by both of them as the author of *Obermann*. This work, a series of letters written from the solitude of the Bernese Oberland and treating almost entirely of nature and of the human soul, was valued by Arnold for its profound inwardness, its austere sincerity, its delicate feeling for nature, and its melancholy eloquence. It expressed the real du siècle and related it correctly to those forces in contemporary life which tended to promote it.

Arnold must have wished to see the various places associated with Obermann; and when he did visit them the countryside charmed him for life. But he did not go to Switzerland at once. Instead, he returned to England.

In London, he had his first sight of the great French tragic actress, Élisa Rachel, in the part of Hermione. He became immediately an enthusiastic admirer of her art and followed her to Paris. Arriving there on 29 December 1846, he saw her in Corneille *Polyeucte* on the same evening and attended every one of the ten or more performances she gave during his stay of slightly over six weeks. He found time also for French lessons, for dancing, and for visits to other theatres. His love of play-going was to remain with him for life. But no other actress, not even Sarah Bernhardt, was ever to rival 'the divine Rachel' in his estimation.

Back at Oxford, he must have seemed as much of an exquisite, as mannered and as conceited, as ever. Clough reported: ' Matt is full of Parisianism; Theatres in general, and Rachel in special: he enters the room with a chanson of Béranger's on his lips—for the sake of French words almost conscious of tune: his carriage shows him in fancy parading the Rue de Rivoli; and his hair is guiltless of English scissors: he breakfasts at 12, and never dines in Hall, and in the week or 8 days rather (for 2 Sundays must be included) he has been to Chapel once.' In addition to these un-English habits, he had brought back some notable waistcoats. Another contemporary, who must first have seen him at about this time, remembered him as a handsome young man, 'strong and manly, yet full of dreams and schemes. His Olympian manners began even at Oxford; there was no harm in them . . . The very sound of his voice and the wave of his arm were Jovelike.'

In the spring of the same year, 1847, he became private secretary to Lord Lansdowne, the influential Whig statesman. The appointment made Tom apprehensive, presumably because he felt that it might accentuate his brother's worldliness. Certainly, Matthew had now to live in the metropolis; and there he mixed freely with wealthy, talented, and sophisticated people. When his sister Mary visited him in London in 1849, and his mother in 1850, they seem to have feared that his social engagements would leave him little time to see them. If so, they were pleased to discover their mistake; and Mrs. Arnold found her son affectionate and 'unspoiled by his being so much sought after'. He was well liked by Lord Lansdowne.

Naturally he still gave himself airs. In his letters he refers to himself and his chief as 'me and my man'. He was still drawn to 'the life without'. A shopping-street was the best place in which to consider the question of the format of a projected volume of poems by two friends. He was still a dandy. Crabb Robinson enjoyed having him to breakfast, finding him 'a very gentlemanly young man, with a slight tinge of the fop that does no harm when blended with talents, good nature & high spirits'. Charlotte Brontë, however, took a sterner view. Meeting Arnold at Fox How, she found his appearance striking and prepossessing but was displeased by his 'seeming foppery' until she discerned beneath it a real modesty and 'some genuine intellectual aspirations'. On this occasion, Arnold talked at length with both Charlotte Brontë and Harriet Martineau 'and sent the lions roaring to their dens at half-past nine'. Clearly, the young man who had in the previous year spoken of the 'Flibbertigibbet, fanatical, twinkling expression' of his godfather, John Keble, had still not learned to revere the famous.

If a chanson of Béranger's made an effective addition to an English dandy's ensemble, and if it was possible to shock the unco' guid by praising George Sand, it must not be supposed that such considerations exhausted the value of these writers for the young Arnold. Béranger expressed an epicureanism which in certain moods he found highly congenial. George Sand voiced a cry of agony and revolt, a trust in nature and beauty, and an aspiration towards a purged and renewed human society with which, too, he could sympathize. Senancour was, for his romantic melancholy, still closer to him than either of these.

Nor was his interest in modern literature confined to that written in French. He acknowledged Wordsworth's healing power, his ability to bring men back into contact with natural things. While his admiration for Byron had slightly diminished since he had written his Rugby and Oxford prize poems, he was still deeply stirred by the passionate and titanic defiance of eternal law uttered by the poet whom Goethe had represented as Euphorion in the second part of *Faust*. Goethe himself he already recognized as the greatest of the modern in his wise, profound, and comprehensive criticism of life.

Forty years later, recalling the voices which had most charmed him during his Oxford days, he spoke of the salutary novelty of the large, liberal view of human life in Goethe *Wilhelm Meister* to the Englishman of that time; but he went on to say that what had then moved him most deeply had been its poetry, its eloquence. Carlyle's, too, had been an eloquent voice, until he had so sorely strained and abused it. Early in 1848, discussing a recent article by Carlyle, Arnold could couple an admission of the commonplace nature of the thoughts with warm praise for 'the style and feeling by which the beloved man appears'. Eighteen months later, however, Carlyle seemed to him a moral desperado; and ten years later still his eloquence was 'that regular Carlylean strain which we all know by heart and which the clear-headed among us have so utter a contempt for'. The third of the influential voices had been that of Emerson, and Arnold always retained his high regard for a sage whose service to the human spirit he could compare with that of Marcus Aurelius. The last voice had been that of one of the four people from whom Arnold, reviewing in middle life the whole of his development and not merely his Oxford years, was conscious of 'having learnt—a very different thing from merely receiving a strong impression—learnt habits, methods, ruling ideas, which are constantly with me; and the four are—Goethe, Wordsworth, SainteBeuve, and yourself'. John Henry Newman, the recipient of this tribute, had been a leader of the party in Oxford which Arnold's father had detested for its glorification of priestcraft. Nevertheless, he so charmed his opponent's son that towards the end of his life Arnold could write:

> Forty years ago he was in the very prime of life; he was close at hand to us at Oxford; he was preaching in St. Mary's pulpit every Sunday; he seemed about to transform and to renew what was for us the most national and natural institution in the world, the Church of England. Who could resist the charm of that spiritual apparition, gliding in the dim afternoon light through the aisles of St. Mary's, rising into the pulpit, and then, in the most entrancing of voices, breaking the silence with words and thoughts which were a religious music,—subtle, sweet, mournful? . . . Or, if we followed him back to his seclusion at Littlemore, that dreary village by the London road, and to the house of retreat and the church which he built there, . . . who could resist him there either, welcoming back to the severe joys of churchfellowship, and of daily worship and prayer, the firstlings of a generation which had well-nigh forgotten them? (*Discourses in America*, 'Emerson'.)

Arnold was not the only old Rugbeian to feel Newman's charm. But in him the influence showed itself not in the acceptance of a more completely Catholic doctrine but in the development of certain habits of mind. A contemporary reviewer perceived something of this when he said years later that Newman and Arnold were alike as prose-writers in their luminous, urbane, delicately expressed dogmatism and in their irony which tended to run into caricature.

The young man who was receiving and pondering these influences, who at Oxford attended the meetings of the Decade, a debating society which counted among its members Benjamin Jowett, Arthur Stanley, and Clough, and who in 1850 could report that amid much other reading he had been studying Spinoza and finding his atmosphere positive and vivifying, was clearly more than the fop he chose to seem. The same may be said of the correspondent who urged upon Clough one of the greatest of the Hindu scriptures, the *Bhagavad Gita* or 'Lord's Song'. In part, Arnold's dandyism was the product of youthful exuberance; some of the stories told to illustrate it refer to mere practical jokes. Moreover, it served to demonstrate his independence of his father. A third motive, perhaps more important than either of these, is traceable in the letters which he wrote to his friends, and above all to Clough, during this period.

Clough, nearly four years his senior, had entered Rugby in 1829. He had been a gentle, sensitive, affectionate, and highly intelligent boy of rather delicate health. His parents were living in America; and Dr. Arnold had soon become not only a schoolmaster but also in many ways a father to him. On his side, the homeless Clough had grown somewhat too deeply attached to his school and its headmaster, with the result that his natural scrupulousness had been greatly over-stimulated. Academically, he had made excellent progress, and in 1837 he had gone up to Oxford accompanied by the very highest hopes and expectations of all who knew him. These he was to disappoint, though not in any spectacular fashion.

At this time Oxford was profoundly disturbed by the Tractarian movement. In the resultant atmosphere of restless religious speculation, Clough became puzzled, bewildered, and unsettled. His failure to secure a first in his degree examination in 1841 was a natural, though unexpected, consequence, which he redeemed a few months later when he was elected to an Oriel fellowship. By this time Arnold had come up from Rugby, and Clough's schoolboy acquaintance with him quickly ripened into a warm adult friendship. At the Sunday morning breakfasts in his rooms and at the meetings of the Decade, Clough could be voluble, buoyant, brilliant. 'I can talk tremendous!' he once admitted. His friends acknowledged his charm. At the same time, he was still the anxious, scrupulous soul whom the Tractarian controversies had so shaken; and in 1848 he resigned his fellowship because he could not sincerely subscribe to the Thirty-nine Articles of the Church of England. After a continental tour which led him to Paris during the Revolution of 1848 and to Rome during its siege by the French in 1849, he returned to England to take up the post of Principal of University Hall, London—a nonsectarian residence for students which Arnold characteristically nicknamed 'Doubting Castle'. In 1852 he resigned this post. There followed a nine-month search for suitable employment in America, after which he settled down to an examinership in the Education Office in London. In 1859 his health began to fail. Further extensive travels could not restore it, and in 1861 an attack of malaria at Florence hastened his death.

During Arnold's years at Oxford and at Lansdowne House, Clough was his closest friend. Thereafter, for the last ten years of Clough's life, they remained on good terms, though without the old intimacy. As young men, they shared many interests. They were ambitious to prove themselves poets, and they were enthusiastic classicists. They delighted to explore together the countryside around Oxford. They were keenly interested in social and political problems.

Clough, indeed, was something of a radical. At all events, Arnold could address a letter in 1848 to 'Citizen Clough, Oriel Lyceum, Oxford' and by so doing give him a nickname which stuck to him for months. Despite this teasing, Arnold went some distance in political sympathy with his friend, though not, he insisted, so far as to delude himself with unrealizable hopes. The millennium, he assured Clough, wouldn't come this bout. At Lansdowne House, his interest in public affairs was being greatly stimulated. He had every opportunity there of keeping himself well informed and was accustomed to report and to discuss the latest news in his letters. Those to Clough during the early part of 1848 contain a running commentary on events in France. In this connection Arnold was led to speak for the first but by no means for the last time of the '*wide and deepspread intelligence*' which 'makes the French seem to themselves in the van of Europe'. When the poet Lamartine achieved a brief political eminence, his remarks were in a lighter vein. 'My man [i.e., Lord Lansdowne] remarks that Poets should hold up their heads now a Poet is at the head of France. More clergyman than Poet, tho: and a good deal of cambric handkerchief about that. No Parson Adams.'

Domestic affairs interested him, too. He went to hear the speakers at the Chartist convention in the spring of 1848 and was much struck by their ability. He had no doubt that he was living in a time of social revolution and that, as he told his mother, 'hereditary peerage and eldest sonship and immense properties' could not last much longer. At the same time, the state of the English masses was such that he could not without some apprehension regard the prospect of their asserting themselves. On the Irish problem, his views were already close to those which he advanced at length later in life.

But, if Clough and he agreed politically 'like two lambs in a world of wolves', Arnold could not accept the view of poetry which Clough's work seemed to him to embody. Admittedly, Clough's sincerity was unmistakable. It was evident that he was striving to get breast to breast with reality. But in Arnold's opinion this effort cost him too much. There was a 'deficiency of the beautiful' in his poems. For all their wealth and depth of matter, they were without that naturalness, that absolute propriety of form which is essential to poetry. They were the products too exclusively of a profound thinker's attempts to get to the bottom of things, 'to solve the Universe', and too little of a genuine artist's desire to group things perfectly. They excited curiosity and reflection rather than pleasure. In fact, Clough was 'a mere d——d depth hunter'.

Not that Tennyson, a very different poet, was any better. In 1847 Arnold yawned at his dawdling with the painted shell of the Universe. Evidently a poet's true path was flanked by contrasting perils. On the one hand, there was the danger that he might with Clough achieve profundity at the price of failing in beauty; on the other, there was the danger that he might with Tennyson achieve beauty of a kind by consenting to a trifling fragmentariness.

'Not deep the poet sees, but wide' ('Resignation'). His true aim was to see life steadily and see it whole and, thanks to this comprehensive vision, to achieve in his work a perfect grouping of objects. Hence Arnold's groan, 'For me you may often hear my sinews cracking under the effort to unite matter . . .' Hence, too, his rueful admission, 'Composition, in the painter's sense-that is the devil.'

The task was indeed especially difficult in the nineteenth century. In order to avoid a Tennysonian fragmentariness, the poet had to begin with 'an Idea of the world . . . or . . . at least with isolated ideas'. If, however, in his search for such an Idea, he tried conscientiously to take account of all that was known and thought in so complex and disunited an age as his own, he might only too easily lapse like Clough into earnest bewilderment and dispirited doubt. In such a frame of mind, he might retain the sincerity requisite for verse like Clough's; but he would very likely lose the creative ardour requisite for poetry such as Arnold hoped to write.

Probably Arnold suspected that his own creative ardour was not of the fiercest; and certainly he could not claim to be himself exempt from the preoccupations, doubts, and anxieties which so weighed upon Clough. On the contrary, his first volume of poems was to show him deeply affected by them. Nor was Clough the only member of his set whom he saw plunging and bellowing in the Time Stream. They were most of them, old Rugbeians and others, strenuously engaged in solving the Universe. If they had their way they would in the ordinary course of friendship over-stimulate a similar activity in himself. And might not that be the end of his poetic impulse?

By some means, they had to be kept at a slight distance; and Arnold's dandyism was the means chosen. Pococurantism, abhorred and denounced by the father, became to all appearances the son's creed. He flaunted a nonchalant indifference to the serious concerns of his associates. So much so that even as an undergraduate he had on one occasion to write in defence of his procedure:

> It is difficult for me to know in what terms to express myself after your last letter, so completely is it penetrated with that unfortunate error as to my want of interest in my friends which you say they have begun to attribute to me. It is an old subject which I need not discuss over again with you. The accusation, as you say, is not true. I laugh too much and they make one's laughter mean too much. However, the result is that when one wishes to be serious one cannot but fear a half suspicion on one's friends' parts that one is laughing, and, so, the difficulty gets worse and worse.

Five years later, during the Lansdowne House period, he was even more apprehensive of the threat to his creative spontaneity and assured himself with uncharacteristic harshness, 'Yes . . . something tells me I can, if need be, at last dispense with them all, even with him [*i.e.*, Clough]'. He subsequently admitted to Clough that at this time he had had a strong disposition to mental seclusion, and to the elimination of all influences which, he felt, troubled without advancing him; and he continued:

> You ask me in what I think or have thought you going wrong: in this: that you would never take your assiette as something determined final and unchangeable for you and proceed to work away on the basis of that: but were always poking and patching and cobbling at the assiette itself—could never finally, as it seemed—'resolve to be thyself'—but were looking for this and that experience, and doubting whether you ought not to adopt this or that mode of being of persons qui ne vous valaient pas because it might possibly be nearer the truth than your own: you had no reason for thinking it *was*, but it *might* be—and so you would try to adapt yourself to it. You have I am convinced lost infinite time in this way: it is what I call your morbid conscientiousness—you are the most conscientious man I ever knew: but on some lines morbidly so, and it spoils your action.

Late in the same year, 1853, he repeated the charge: 'You certainly do not seem to me sufficiently to desire and earnestly strive towards—assured knowledge-activity—happiness. You are too content to *fluctuate*-to be ever learning, never coming to the knowledge of the truth. This is why, with you, I feel it necessary to stiffen myself—and hold fast my rudder.'Clough's own recognition of this failing in himself is shown by his allowing the Spirit to deride Dipsychus in such lines as:

> Methinks I see you,
> Through everlasting limbos of void time,

> Twirling and twiddling ineffectively,
> And indeterminately swaying for ever. (II, vi.)

On the other hand, Arnold's severity was that of one who knew himself to be in some degree guilty of the offence he was castigating but who was determined that if possible anxious speculation should not be allowed to sap either his creative vitality as an artist or his strength of purpose as a man.

So his friends had to bear with his dandyism. They had to reconcile themselves to being addressed as in this note which he wrote in 1850:

> DEAR SLADE—I forgot to say last night that you must breakfast here to-morrow, Sunday, at 10 *pas plus tôt*, because John Blackett is coming, who wishes to meet you. Ridiculous as such a desire is, it is too unimportant for me to refuse to gratify it.—Your faithful servant, M. ARNOLD. *Le Samedi matin.*

The gaiety, impudence, and aloofness of this are all characteristic. But Clough, despite Arnold's fear of becoming infected with certain of his mental habits, was an altogether dearer and more intimate friend than the rest. When he was thinking of resigning his fellowship, Arnold was in his confidence; when he was about to leave for America, Arnold, having already helped him, made a warm offer of further financial assistance; and on receiving the news of his death Arnold wrote to his mother that it was 'a loss which I shall feel more and more as time goes on, for he is one of the few people who ever made a deep impression upon me'.

Naturally, Arnold kept Clough well informed during the eighteen-forties and the earlier eighteen-fifties regarding his own poetic hopes and aims. He protested to him against the view, too much fostered by the examples of Keats, Shelley, and Tennyson, and, before them, of 'those d——d Elizabethan poets generally', that the object of poetry was 'to produce exquisite bits and images'. On the contrary, said Arnold in 1852, modern poetry can only subsist by its *contents*: by becoming a complete magister vitae as the poetry of the ancients did: by including, as theirs did, religion with poetry, instead of existing as poetry only, and leaving religious wants to be supplied by the Christian religion, as a power existing independent of the poetical power. But the language, style and general proceedings of a poetry which has such an immense task to perform, must be very plain direct and severe: and it must not lose itself in parts and episodes and ornamental work, but must press forwards to the whole.

Not that he wished to elevate content at the expense of style. 'For the style is the expression of the nobility of the poet's character, as the matter is the expression of the richness of his mind: but on men character produces as great an effect as mind.'

His first volume, *The Strayed Reveller, and Other Poems*, was published at the beginning of 1849. Its contents surprised his sister Mary. They seemed like a new introduction to him. She found much more 'practical questioning' in the book than she had expected: 'in fact it showed a knowledge of life and conflict which was *strangely like experience* if it was not the thing itself; and this with all Matt's great power I should not have looked for.' In another letter she traced her surprise to the '*moral consciousness*' manifest in the poems, 'something which such a man as Clough has, for instance, which I did not expect to find in Matt; but it is there.'

This must have been a fairly representative reaction to the volume on the part of those acquaintances who had not had Clough's or Jane's opportunities of knowing what lay behind the eyeglass and the careless elegance of Lord Lansdowne's private secretary. But those who read it carefully must have found it an excellent preparation for Arnold's second volume, *Empedocles on Etna, and Other Poems*, which appeared in the autumn of 1852.

On 29 September 1848, Arnold wrote to Clough from Switzerland, which he was visiting for perhaps the first time. 'Tomorrow I repass the Gemmi and get to Thun: linger one day at the Hotel Bellevue for the sake of the blue eyes of one of its inmates: and then proceed by slow stages down the Rhine to Cologne, thence to Amiens and Boulogne and England.' It may be that he had first met the possessor of these blue eyes during his previous Continental holiday in 1846-7. But there is no record of her at this earlier date. What his poems and letters make clear is that he saw her not only in 1848 but also when he revisited Thun almost exactly twelve months later; and that after 1849 there was no further reunion.

The lady's identity is unknown. The register of the Hotel Bellevue for the period in question has been destroyed; that of Thun Castle is also missing. The only available information about her is that contained in Arnold's poems and in the sentence already quoted from his holiday letter of 1848 to Clough. Both this letter and that which he wrote to Clough from Thun a year later are expressive of unusual emotional states. The former is almost exuberant, the latter sadly resolved.

In his volume of 1849, which was published during the interval between these two holidays, the lyric 'To my Friends, who ridiculed a tender Leave-taking' (later renamed 'A Memory-Picture') gave the lady the name, Marguerite, by which Arnold's readers were henceforward to know her and went on to describe her physical appearance. Combining this description with those given in the lyrical sequence 'Switzerland', of which certain items first appeared in the volume of 1852, it is possible to some extent to picture Marguerite. She had blue eyes; soft ash-coloured hair; a pale complexion; rounded cheeks; and a mouth which readily assumed an arch and mocking smile. She often wore a kerchief tied around her head. She moved with a 'pliant grace' and spoke in a clear, buoyant, and musical voice. She was French.

The setting for the love-affair is given with some fidelity in these poems. In one of them, the poet rides along the edge of the lake of Thun by moonlight, passes the poplar avenue and 'the roof'd bridge that spans the stream', the Aar, and hurries up the steep street towards Marguerite's light. The Hotel Bellevue does in fact stand in such a street as that to which these lines allude. In other poems, Arnold refers to the great mountains of the Oberland, which lie to the south, across the lake from the old town.

These are the facts of the case, as far as they are known. The temptation to supplement them with imaginings has proved too strong for some biographers. One of these believes that Marguerite was a governess, lady companion, or teacher; another guesses that she was an aristocrat; a third represents her as a Bohemian from the Parisian theatre. Such conjectures destroy one another.

Arnold's poems may not define Marguerite's social and economic status; but they do make it possible to some extent to trace the emotional graph of the relationship. Is it not reasonable, for example, to guess that Marguerite's 'unconquer'd joy' was one of the things which first attracted to her the young dandy who was striving so hard not to succumb to the doubts and discouragements which were infecting his friends? What is more certain is that from the start Arnold was obsessed with the notion that there was some insuperable obstacle in the way of his continued acquaintance with Marguerite. Even in the lyric which he published a half-year before their last meeting, he admitted that

> Time's current strong
> Leaves us fixt to nothing long. ('A Memory-Picture.')

In those which he published after 1849, the power which had finally separated him from her manifests itself as 'a God's tremendous voice', as a sea which rolls between them, and as 'the darting river of Life' which bears him away from her. It is impossible to say with complete confidence what real or supposed impediment to their union these metaphors hint at. But the poems themselves do suggest a partial explanation. The 'sea' which 'rolls between us' is said in 'Parting', the second of the 'Switzerland' series, to be 'Our different past'. The poem continues:

> To the lips, ah! of others
> Those lips have been prest,
> And others, ere I was,
> Were strain'd to that breast;
> Far, far from each other
> Our spirits have grown.

In 'The Terrace at Berne', the last of the 'Switzerland' poems to be written, this reference to Marguerite's past life is echoed in Arnold's conjectures regarding her existence since their parting ten years earlier. In fact, Arnold seems to have believed that Marguerite was sexually more experienced than himself; and that the great difference between their past lives would quickly force them apart.

On her side, Marguerite may well have been attracted by the elegance and apparent self-possession of her English admirer. She may even have seen him as a young Milton on his travels! But before long his mournful conviction that there was some insuperable barrier between them must, whether he expressed it openly to her or not, have made him appear wavering and half-hearted.

> And women—things that live and move
> Mined by the fever of the soul—
> They seek to find in those they love
> Stern strength, and promise of control.
> ('A Farewell.')

So Marguerite broke with him. 'Absence' suggests that he regained his emotional independence only slowly and with difficulty.

This account is based exclusively upon those poems in which there is explicit reference to Marguerite: 'A Memory-Picture', 'A Dream', and the 'Switzerland' series. It is possible that another eight or nine had their emotional source in the love-affair. In the case of 'The Forsaken Merman', this possibility becomes surely a probability: the lady's name is Margaret, and the lovers are separated by the uncompromising fact that they are most at home in different physical elements. But it would be foolhardy to build biography upon these doubtful instances.

Within nine or ten months of his last meeting with Marguerite, Arnold was in the thick of another courtship. In a letter to Wyndham Slade, the recipient during the previous year of the high-spirited invitation to breakfast already quoted, he wrote:

> Last night for the 5th time the deities interposed: I was asked specially to meet the young lady—my wheels burned the pavement—I mounted the stairs like a wounded quaggha, the pulsations of my heart shook all Park Crescent—my eyes devoured every countenance in the room in a moment of time: she was at the opera, and could not come. At the last

> moment her mother had had tickets sent her, and sent a note of excuse.
>
> I suffer from great dejection and lassitude this morning-having shown a Spartan fortitude on hearing the news last evening.

On 23 July 1850, Clough mentioned this elusive young lady to Tom Arnold: 'Matt comes to Switzerland in a month; after your sister's [i.e., Jane's] wedding. He is deep in a flirtation with Miss Wightman, daughter of the Judge. It is thought it will come to something, for he has actually been to Church to meet her.' Despite Arnold's pertinacity, it seemed subsequently that the affair might come to nothing; for Sir William Wightman, a somewhat testy Scot, forbade the lovers to meet. Since Arnold's income as private secretary to Lord Lansdowne was not large, and since the Oriel fellowship was his only as long as he remained single, Wightman's objection to the match is comprehensible; and Arnold eventually did what he could to meet it.

Meanwhile, Frances Lucy Wightman and her father were setting off on a Continental holiday. Arnold's 'Calais Sands', the first draft of which was apparently posted to the lady, tells how, 'Mixt with the idlers on the pier', he gave himself the pleasure of witnessing her arrival in France, without, however, presuming to show himself; and it concludes with his determination to spend that night in the same hotel as the Wightmans. On the following day, he left. 'On the Rhine', the fourth of the five lyrics composing the sequence 'Faded Leaves', was evidently written during the next stage of a tour which was taking him once again to 'the high Alps'. 'Faded Leaves' is concerned throughout with his love for Frances Wightman.

Soon after his return to England, Arnold began to look about him for a more stable and remunerative form of employment, such as would permit him to renew his courtship. On the advice of William Ralph Lingen, who had been his tutor at Balliol and who was by this time Secretary to the Committee of the Council on Education, he turned his thoughts to an Inspectorship of Schools. Lord Lansdowne, as President of the Council, was the nominal head of the Department of Education, and on 14 April 1851 he made Arnold an Inspector. Wightman's consent to the marriage had been obtained a fortnight earlier, presumably in anticipation of this appointment. The wedding took place on 10 June 1851, and the honeymoon was spent in France, Switzerland, and Italy.

'You'll like my Lucy; she has all my sweetness and none of my airs!' said Arnold, with characteristic impudence, to one of his old Oxford friends. Fanny Lucy, or Flu, was, indeed, very generally liked. The Arnold family took to her. Old Crabb Robinson, who met the couple at Fox How during the autumn of the year following the marriage, was favourably impressed. Clough wrote to his fiancee, 'I like the wife very well,—more, the more I see of her'. In 'Faded Leaves' there are a few references to her physical appearance as a young woman. The poet speaks of her brown hair and her grey eyes, or, rather, her

> Eyes too expressive to be blue,
> Too lovely to be grey. ('On the Rhine.')

In the first poem of the sequence, her 'mocking mouth' reminds the reader of Marguerite's. Did both ladies find that their suitor's affectations invited teasing?

Matthew and his wife had six children, four boys and two girls. One boy, Richard, and the two girls, Lucy and Eleanor, reached adult life. Of the other three boys, Basil died in infancy, Thomas and Trevenen ('Budge') in their teens. Despite these bereavements, it was a remarkably happy marriage. Both husband and wife were extremely sociable and kept in touch with a wide circle of friends.

Fanny Lucy also shared Matthew's love of travel; and he found that her company was essential to his fullest enjoyment of it. Tom had indeed been mistaken when, during his brother's engagement, he had described him as one of the very last men in the world to be happy in matrimony.

Arnold spent the greater part of his active life in an occupation, school-inspection, which seemed to have little connection with his serious literary endeavours. His wish to marry, and that alone, induced him to enter it; he approached it without enthusiasm, and to the end he disliked the routine work which it entailed. At first he dreamed of an early retirement to Italy or of a diplomatic appointment in Switzerland. Knowing that foreign life was thoroughly congenial to him 'and liberating in the highest degree', he longed to withdraw with his wife and children and to devote himself, probably among the Alps, to writing. But by the opening months of 1859 he was convinced that this longing was simply irresponsible. 'I shall work best in the long-run by living in the country which is my own.'

Living there did not necessarily mean grinding away as a school-inspector, however. In 1866, in 1867, and yet again in 1869, he had hopes of obtaining more agreeable employment. On each occasion he was disappointed. After his promotion to a Senior Inspectorship in 1870, he seems to have given up all thought of a change. In 1884, two years before his retirement, he became a Chief Inspector.

During the nineteenth century, the state accepted no responsibility for secondary education. So Arnold, for the thirty-five years of his service, was concerned in the ordinary course of his duty solely with primary, or elementary, schools and with training colleges for primary-school teachers. Until 1871, moreover, only inspectors in Anglican orders were appointed for Church of England schools. So Arnold, during the first twenty years of his career, was restricted to establishments under mainly Nonconformist control. In his dealings with these and with their managers, he acquired the familiarity with British middle-class life in some of its most characteristic manifestations, which helped to make him eventually so formidable a critic of it.

At first, his inspectorial district was very large. It stretched from the North Sea to Cardigan Bay and included the English midlands and practically the whole of Wales. For some years, in consequence, his life was one of almost incessant travelling; and he made it even more nomadic by acting as Marshal when his father-in-law went on official tours as a Judge. Arnold could enjoy travelling. But this was travelling at its worst and in association with work which he found tedious and depressing. A bad carriage on a filthy line; a bun snatched hastily in a railway station; thirty pupil teachers to examine in an inconvenient room, and nothing to eat except a biscuit given by a charitable lady; eighty training-college candidates to supervise for seven hours a day, with the gas burning most of the time 'either to give light or to help warm the room'—these were the conditions of which Arnold spoke in his letters and in which he had to seize what time he could for his poetry. 'I did not arrive here till just two, as the train was late; went to the school, and found there were three of them. About four o'clock I found myself so exhausted, having eaten nothing since breakfast, that I sent out for a bun, and ate it before the astonished school.' So he wrote of a visit made a few months before his *Poems* of 1853 appeared. On this particular occasion, things improved. 'Since then I have had a very good extempore dinner on mutton chops and bread pudding, all the Quaker household having dined early, and now'—an unwelcome prospect after the warm hospitality—'I am in for the pupil teachers till ten o'clock.' There can have been little poetry on this day, unless he made use of that morning train-journey. And how remote both the rue de Rivoli and the Alps must have seemed!

So restless was his life that it was not until 1858 that he was able to give his wife a settled home away from her parents. He wrote to a friend: 'We have taken a house in Chester Square. It is a very small one, but it will be something to unpack one's portmanteau for the first time since I was married, now nearly seven years ago.' Fortunately, his district had not remained as large as at first. Already, by 1858, it had been reduced to a more compact group of counties, most of them in the south-east; and it was eventually narrowed to the neighbourhood of London itself.

Although he now spent less of his life on the railway, Arnold still disliked the routine of inspecting and examining. But he never doubted the importance of educational work. He was himself the son of a great schoolmaster. He saw clearly that it was upon the teachers in the stateaided primary schools that the task would devolve of 'civilising the next generation of the lower classes, who, as things are going, will have most of the political power of the country in their hands'. He wrote these words in 1851, shortly after taking up his appointment. Later, he defined 'civilisation' as 'the humanisation of man in society'. This, and not mere instruction, was, he believed, the true aim of all education, the aim by reference to which alone the success of teachers, curricula, and administrative schemes could be estimated. Accordingly, he wrote again and again in his notes after visiting schools of which he approved: 'the children human'.

Arnold was not afraid to make education, so conceived, a responsibility of the state. In this he was following his own father and Coleridge and Burke in their insistence that the state had the positive duty of humanizing and civilizing its members. By the same token, he was defying the revered principle of *laissez-faire*. In the very year in which he became an inspector, the *Economist* denounced grants of public money in aid of schools as 'bounties on a species of production [an educated populace!] not at the moment in demand'. Ruskin's mockery of 'the divine principle of demand and supply' was assuredly called for and must in due course have been read with some sympathy by Arnold. Certainly, he advocated an extension of state influence. He wished to see good schools of various grades and types established throughout the country; and he wished these schools to be the constituent parts of a coherent national system of education. While adhering to the principle of feepaying, he maintained that attendance should be made compulsory at the primary grade.

In any primary school which was sincerely dedicated to the humanization of man in society, religious instruction would, he thought, be an integral part of the work. English, too, would be central if the school aspired to be genuinely 'formative and *humanising*'. French, in addition to its commercial utility, possessed a great cultural value; and Latin might profitably be taught to a few picked, older pupils. On the other side, Arnold went so far as to advocate the introduction of natural science as a compulsory subject in primary schools; but he insisted upon its subordination to the humanities.

To have the power of using . . . [the] data of natural science, a man must, in general, have first been in some measure *moralised*; and for moralising him it will be found not easy, I think, to dispense with those old agents, letters, poetry, religion. So let not our teachers be led to imagine, whatever they may hear and see of the call for natural science, that their literary cultivation is unimportant. The fruitful use of natural science itself depends, in a very great degree, on having effected in the whole man, by means of letters, a rise in what the political economists call *the standard of life*. ('*General Report* for 1876.')

To one who held such views as these, the Revised Code of 1862 was sadly retrogressive. According to this, two-thirds of the grant payable to a primary school was to depend upon the individual examination of its children in reading, writing, and arithmetic, and only one-third upon the number of them attending satisfactorily. This system of payment mainly according to the results obtained in the teaching of the three R's seemed to Arnold to couple a lowering of educational standards with what he derisively labelled 'a *prize scheme*'. He held that a grant ought to be 'given to a school not as a mere machine for teaching reading, writing, and arithmetic, but as a living whole with complex functions, religious, moral, and intellectual'.

By his pen, Arnold contributed notably to the defeat of the initial intention that grants should be entirely dependent upon the performances of the pupils in the three prescribed subjects. But his continued opposition did not prevent the system of 'payment by results' in its modified form from surviving him. At first he wondered whether his writing against the Revised Code might jeopardize his position in the Department of Education. 'I don't think, however, they can eject me,' he wrote to his wife, 'though they can, and perhaps will, make my place uncomfortable. If thrown on the world I daresay we should be on our legs again before very long. Any way, I think I owed as much as this to a cause in which I have now a deep interest, and always shall have, even if I cease to serve it officially.' But his brother-in-law, William Forster, was rightly of opinion that the authorities could not touch him and would bring a storm on their heads if they tried; and, after the Code had been modified, Lingen, the Secretary, and his wife attended a dinnerparty at the Arnolds' and were very amiable.

Arnold felt, and said, that the new regulations inevitably gave both to teaching and to inspection a mechanical turn which could only tend to stultify the intellectual life of the schools. He evidently strove in his own official visits to be as little as possible a mere registering clerk, as was required by the new system, and as much as possible a sympathetic supervisor, as had been required by the old. In consequence, a more orthodox colleague could cast doubt on his efficiency as an instrument of the Revised Code and could tell a no doubt exaggerated story about his method of inspection. According to this, a London school manager had said, 'Mr. Arnold inspects our school in Westminster . . . Of course we are much honoured, and the managers make a point of attending to meet him. He arrives in the course of the morning; shakes hands with the managers and teachers; and talks very pleasantly for a few minutes; then he walks through the classes between the desks, looking over the children's shoulders at some exercises, and so makes his way to the door, and we see him no more.' Evidently the elegant insouciance of Lord Lansdowne's private secretary mellowed into this urbane casualness of the middle-aged inspector. Though he could no longer be thought idle, he could at least assert, 'No one shall say that I am a punctual Inspector.' He still carried an eyeglass. And he was still capable of the old playful impertinence. When inspecting schools in Edmonton, he preferred not to remain overnight in that town but to travel there daily from his home. A heavy claim for expenses resulted, in response to which he received an official note: 'Mr. M. Arnold, H.M.I. Why not stay at Edmonton?''How can you expect me to stay at Edmonton,' he retorted, 'when John Gilpin couldn't?' His claim was allowed.

Despite his nonchalance, and despite his dislike of routine work, his inspecting was effective in precisely those ways which he himself rightly considered most important. According to a contemporary, 'He became the teachers' and children's friend, and though many a droll anecdote of his casual methods of marking and taking stock of his schools still goes the rounds, . . . none of his colleagues had a shrewder sense of what was wanting in each school he visited, or could reckon it up more readily. For the general body of elementary teachers he thus acquired an honest respect and liking.' His assistant inspector described him as having inspired many young teachers to the study of literature and to the undertaking of London degrees for their own improvement, and the eventual benefit of their pupils. Another younger colleague held that, 'indirectly, his fine taste, his gracious and kindly manner, his honest and generous recognition of any new form of excellence which he observed, all tended to raise the aims and tone of the teachers with whom he came in contact, and to encourage in them self-respect and respect for their work'. He had little to do with arranging the minutiae of educational administration, but, 'when questions of principle were involved, he was frequently consulted, and we who were his colleagues received from him at times very weighty and practical suggestions'. Even a teacher who was writing to defend his school against a severe report of Arnold's felt obliged to add, in a letter which Arnold was not meant to see, that he had not a word against the inspector, whom he would rather have than any other he had ever come in contact with, 'as he was always gentle and patient with the children'. The letter came to Arnold's notice, and he was naturally very gratified. Writing to his mother, he commented, 'The great thing is *humanity*, after all.'

Three times he was sent on special missions to the Continent. In 1859, he toured France, Holland, and Switzerland inspecting primary schools for the Newcastle Commission; in 1865, he went to France, Italy, Germany Austria, and Switzerland to report on secondary schools and universities for a Schools Inquiry Commission; and in 1885-6, immediately before his retirement, he investigated the German, Swiss, and French systems of free schools on behalf of his office. Much as he disliked any prolonged separation from his family, he rejoiced in these opportunities for extensive travel. In the autumn of 1865 he wrote, after spending six months on the Continent, 'I feel as if I should never want again to come abroad for those little six-week rushes which the English are so fond of, and which I once used to think the height of felicity.'

The six months in question constituted the only period during which he was officially concerned with secondary education. Nevertheless, he attached the greatest importance to the organization and improvement of those institutions to which, in the existing circumstances, the middle class, and that alone, owed such education as it received. This class was for the moment supreme. But its schooling in dismal academies like the tyrannical Mr. Creakle's Salem House, where David Copperfield suffered, could not be said to have fitted it for its responsibilities. If the middle class was worthily to discharge the functions which it had inherited from an aristocracy whose day was over, it was essential that it should be truly civilized in schools which had been brought into an effective connection with the state. Arnold therefore repeatedly urged his contemporaries to organize their secondary education; and, since it was desirable that some sort of university training should be available to the middle class, he recommended them to organize their higher education, too. His purpose in this was, as always, the humanization of man in society—the humanization, in this instance, of the puritanical middle class. The thought of the bad civilization of this class was, he said, the master-thought by which his politics were governed.

Shortly after the publication of the *Poems* of 1853, an old Oxford friend wrote to Tom, who was out of the country, that Matt was 'greatly improved by his marriage —retaining all the genius and nobleness of mind which you remember, with all the lesser faults pruned and softened down'. Responsibilities, both domestic and professional, were certainly disciplining the exuberance which could so disconcert his acquaintances. Moreover, he was feeling keenly the loss of his youth.

Admittedly, he was only entering his thirties. But the early Victorian period was one in which it was possible for a now forgotten poetaster of twenty-seven, contributing to a popular annual, to describe himself as on the verge of middle age and to vow that henceforth his muse should be the bride of heaven! Arnold was relatively moderate. He was very nearly twenty-nine when he wrote to Clough: 'we are growing old, and advancing towards the deviceless darkness: it would be well not to reach it till we had at least tried *some* of the things men consider desirable'. Four months later, he exclaimed to the same friend, 'How life rushes away, and youth. One has dawdled and scrupled and fiddle faddled —and it is all over.' True, this is a theme on which any correspondent might have been tempted to dwell in letters to one who had dawdled and scrupled and fiddlefaddled as much as Clough. But Arnold touched on it also in letters to Jane, though with a significant shift of emphasis. Five months before his marriage, he lamented to her that a man's commitment of himself to his particular course in life involved the renunciation of many other courses which had lain invitingly open to him in youth. As a result, he said, one grew up 'shorn of so many beams'. Late in 1853, he remarked to her 'how the cares of life deepen about one' after thirty. His sense of constriction was such that in the same year he confessed to Clough, 'I am past thirty, and three parts iced over'.

'Ten years later, he had very largely adjusted himself to his responsibilities. At times, he could still feel that he was getting old amidst a press of occupations for which he had not been born. 'I must go back to my charming occupation of hearing students give lessons. Here is my programme for this afternoon: Avalanches -The Steam Engine — The Thames — India Rubber — Bricks — The

Battle of Poictiers — Subtraction — The Reindeer -The Gunpowder Plot — The Jordan. Alluring, is it not? Twenty minutes each, and the days of one's life are only threescore years and ten.' But no one outside his most intimate circle ever heard him complain of the drudgery of his life. For years he had been making an habitual war on depression and low spirits. Moreover, he could feel that he was still slowly ripening; and he could wonder whether he would continue to feel so to the end. Having written very little verse in recent years, he resolved in 1861 to discontinue his critical writing for the time being and to dedicate his forties to poetry. 'It is my last chance. It is not a bad ten years of one's life for poetry if one resolutely uses it, but it is a time in which, if one does not use it, one dries up and becomes prosaic altogether.'

Poetry, however, was to employ very little of his time. Most of the volume, *New Poems*, which he published in 1867 had been written many years earlier; and after 1867 he practically ceased to write verse. But he had not been mistaken when he had spoken of himself as still ripening and as possessing an increasingly strong sense of purpose. What he had not suspected was the extent to which this purpose would fulfil itself in prose.

His first critical essay had been the 'Preface' to his *Poems* of 1853. Only when he was elected to the Professorship of Poetry at Oxford four years later did he, in preparing his lectures, begin to write literary criticism regularly. This post, which he held for the full permitted period of ten years, entailed only light duties such as he could perform in addition to his school inspection. Principally, he had to deliver three lectures each year. He was the first layman to occupy the chair and the first Professor to speak from it in English instead of Latin. As a lecturer, he was not outstanding, though he achieved some successes; and he derived little stimulus from his 'wooden' Oxford audiences. In preparing his material, he had to think not of the 'dead bones' who would come to hear him but of the public which would subsequently read him. Otherwise, he said, his spirit would have failed. When he relinquished the Professorship in 1867, he continued to address this wider public in prose criticism.

His acknowledged master was the great French critic Charles Augustin Sainte-Beuve, whose work he had admired since the Lansdowne House period. He sent to Sainte-Beuve copies of many of his publications from the *Poems* of 1853 onwards; and Sainte-Beuve inserted a translation of the 'Stanzas in Memory of the Author of Obermann' into his *Chateaubriand et son Groupe Littéraire sous l'Empire* (1860) and both in that work and elsewhere made respectful mention of his disciple. The two men met in Paris during the hot August of 1859, while Arnold was on the first of his inspectorial visits to the Continent. They dined at the Restaurant Pinson, returned to Sainte-Beuve's house for tea, and talked until midnight. Arnold walked back to his hotel but slept badly. His excitement was still evident when he described the meeting to his wife two days later. Further meetings occurred during his second official tour in 1865.

To Arnold, Sainte-Beuve was 'the first of living critics', an estimate avowed not only in letters to his mother and to Sainte-Beuve himself but also in published utterances. The flexibility, the delicacy, and the disinterested curiosity of the French critic had earned him this position; and Arnold, as has been seen, was later to bracket him with Goethe, Wordsworth, and Newman as one of the four men from whom he had learned 'habits, methods, ruling ideas'.

Shortly after Sainte-Beuve's death in 1869, Arnold contributed an obituary notice to an English periodical. In this he alluded to the poetry and the single novel which Sainte-Beuve had written as a young man and recognized that, despite the shortcomings of this creative work, 'his preference, his dream, his ideal' had been there, and that for him criticism had been labour of an inferior kind. But, said Arnold, Sainte-Beuve was a first-rate critic; and 'first-rate criticism has a permanent value greater than that of any but first-rate works of poetry and art'. It seems likely that in writing these words Arnold was thinking not only of his friend's case but also of his own.

He had by this date published three volumes of literary criticism: *On Translating Homer* (1861), *Essays in Criticism* (1865), and *On the Study of Celtic Literature* (1867). These had been followed by *Culture and Anarchy* (1869), the first of a number of works exemplifying his belief that the disinterested intelligence of the literary critic had an essential task to perform in fields generally thought to require the application of specialist techniques. In *Culture and Anarchy* and in the lighter *Friendship's Garland* (1871), he handled social and political problems; in *St. Paul and Protestantism* (1870), *Literature and Dogma* (1873), *God and the Bible* (1875), and *Last Essays on Church and Religion* (1877), he grappled with the question of religious belief. The sixties and seventies saw also the publication of several of his works on education and concluded with the appearance of a collection of political and literary studies entitled *Mixed Essays* (1879).

These works provoked a good deal of opposition. But Arnold was able to feel, from about 1868 onwards, that what he wrote as a critic was beginning to tell and that it was the more effective for his determination to preserve always an easy, good-humoured, urbane tone. He was right when he claimed in 1871 that John Morley had learned something from him, and knew it; and Morley was by no means his only disciple among the younger men. Nevertheless, Arnold was still not a popular writer. He said as much, though in rather special circumstances, when late in 1870 he appealed to the Income Tax Commissioners against their assessment of his profits as a man of letters at £1,000 a year. (This was as much as he earned by his inspecting.) 'You see before you, gentlemen,' he said, 'what you have often heard of, *an unpopular author*.' When the assessment was cut down to £200 a year, he told them that he would have to write more articles in order to prevent his being a loser by submitting even to this. 'Then the public', said the chairman politely, 'will have reason to be much obliged to us.'

Literature and Dogma, which appeared nearly three years later, was his first best-seller. Arnold derived much satisfaction from this wider dissemination of his influence. His self-assured manner was no longer a protective disguise; it was now the natural manner of one whose '*Werther* period' was well behind him. This period, says Goethe, belongs 'to the career of every individual who, with an innate free natural instinct, must accommodate himself to the narrow limits of an antiquated world. Obstructed fortune, restrained activity, unfulfilled wishes, are the calamities . . . of every individual man; and it would be bad indeed if everybody had not, once in his life, known a time when *Werther* seemed as if it had been written for him alone.' Arnold's poetry had been largely the product of his *Werther* period; but his criticism came from a well-adjusted, and eventually well-established, man of letters.

He mixed freely in London society. Once at least, he accepted no fewer than five dinner-invitations for a single week. At his club, the Athenaeum, he knew 'something resembling beatitude'. Admittedly, this was due partly to the excellent library; but he valued the social amenities, too. His relative and friend, T.H. Huxley, the scientist and agnostic, was a member; so was his mother's friend, Crabb Robinson, who complimented him there early in 1867 on his great reputation and was stimulated by the ensuing conversation to take up *Essays in Criticism*, probably the last book the old man read. On one occasion members were amused to see their radical theologian engaged in talk with a brace of bishops; and on another it was Disraeli, the conservative Prime Minister, whom Arnold greeted as he entered. He knew most of the leading writers of the day. Tennyson enjoyed what he called 'Mat's sublime waggery'; and Arnold had a particularly warm regard for Robert Browning, whom he would gladly have seen as his successor in the Chair of Poetry at Oxford.

During these middle years, Arnold was welcomed to many of the country houses of the aristocracy, the great fortified posts of the Barbarians as he laughingly termed them. He frequently visited Aston Clinton in Buckinghamshire, where he had an intimate friend and an understanding reader in Louisa, the wife of Sir Anthony de Rothschild. A poor shot, he himself said that he participated in the sports of the Barbarians in vain. But he enjoyed fishing and walking and skating. For their physically bracing effect, he especially valued his drillnights with the Queen's Westminster Rifle Volunteers. As for games, he played some croquet, grew very fond of billiards, and occasionally watched cricket.

In 1868 he and his family moved to Harrow, where the three sons were to be educated. Byron House, their new home, was well-built and roomy and had a large and attractive garden. Here Prince Thomas of Savoy, the young Duke of Genoa, was their guest while in attendance at the school. At the conclusion of his stay, his father, the King of Italy, honoured Arnold by the award of a decoration. Here, too, Arnold lost the two sons who died in their teens. As a result of these bereavements, the family moved in 1873 into a smaller house, Pains Hill Cottage, at Cobham, Surrey, within a few miles of Laleham. This was Arnold's home for the rest of his life. The daughter of his brother Tom who eventually became well known as Mrs. Humphry Ward liked in her old age to look back upon her visits here:

> . . . our expeditions to Cobham where he lived, in the pretty cottage beside the Mole [the stream which runs by Cobham], are marked in memory with a very white stone. The only drawback to the Cobham visits were the 'dear, dear boys'! —i.e. the dachshunds, Max and Geist, who, however adorable in themselves, had no taste for visitors and no intention of letting such intruding creatures interfere with their possession of their master. One would go down to Cobham, eager to talk to 'Uncle Matt' about a book or an article-covetous at any rate of *some* talk with him undisturbed. And it would all end in a breathless chase after Max, through field after field where the little wretch was harrying either sheep or cows, with the dear poet, hoarse with shouting, at his heels. The dogs were always *in the party*, talked to, caressed, or scolded exactly like spoilt children; and the cat of the house was almost equally dear. Once, at Harrow, the then ruling cat—a tom—broke his leg, and the house was in lamentation. The vet. was called in, and hurt him horribly. Then Uncle Matt ran up to town, met Professor Huxley at the Athenaeum, and anxiously consulted him. 'I'll go down with you,' said Huxley. The two travelled back instanter to Harrow, and while Uncle Matt held the cat, Huxley—who had begun life, let it be remembered, as Surgeon to the *Rattlesnake*!—examined him, the two black heads together. There is a rumour that Charles Kingsley was included in the consultation. Finally the limb was put in splints, and left to nature. All went well. (*A Writer's Recollections*, pp. 241-2.)

Arnold was particularly happy in his family life. His letters contain many fond records of his children's words and deeds. Dick and Lucy shared their parents' love of travel, Dick[2] and his invalid brother Tom their mother's taste for music. (This taste was as deficient in Matthew, who could speak of going to *see* a Wagner opera, as in his favourite sister, Jane.) Like his father, Dick took readily to fishing. Again like his father, he caused anxiety at home by his idleness at Oxford. He was reading history; and Matthew formed the lowest opinion of the course: 'nothing but read, read, read, endless histories in English, many of them by quite second-rate men; nothing to form the mind as reading truly great authors forms it, or even to exercise it as learning a new language, or mathematics, or one of the natural sciences exercises it'. Heavy debts incurred by Dick at Oxford were the ultimate cause of his father's later needing to make a large profit from his lecture-tour in the United States.

With the gradual settlement of his thought during the eighteen-sixties, Arnold became more and more aware that in his social and religious criticism he was conspicuously his father's son, 'and his continuator'. This realization seems to have given him additional confidence as he strove to charm and to convert 'the wild beast of Philistinism'—in other words, persuasively to correct the 'self-assertion and narrowness' of the British middle class. His sense of this purpose, and of his opportunity to fulfil it, was strong enough to keep him eager and sanguine despite increasing years; and his letters and notebooks show how rigorously he tried to plan his time to the best advantage. He had, indeed, emerged from his *Werther* period.

A lady who met Arnold at a party in London about eight years before his death was impressed by his humorous vivacity and affectionate kindliness. He was taking an almost boyish delight in being with some of his old college friends again. His hair was thick and black, while theirs had become thin and grey; and suspecting that one of them was staring at him Arnold exclaimed, 'Ah, Sandars, you are jealous! You think it is a wig! But pull it, Sandars, pull it!' His hair was indeed a 'perpetual miracle'; the only grey hairs he could claim were 'internal'.

His kindliness, geniality, and courtesy were widely acknowledged. Years later, a friend in Anglican orders wrote: 'One of his pleasantest characteristics was his perfect readiness to discuss, with complete command of temper, views and opinions of his own, which he knew I did not share, and thought dangerous. Many and many a conversation have I had with him at the Athenaeum, and never did an unkindly or peevish word fall from him.' This was echoed by another friend who spoke of his great charm and his having been a delightful man to argue with, 'even though he could be very patronising. But there was in all he said a kind of understood though seldom expressed sadness, as if to say, "It will soon be all over, don't let us get angry; we are all very good fellows," etc.'

During his last years, Arnold continued to lead an active social life. In 1880 he accepted an invitation from the Duchess of Norfolk to meet Newman; the two men had corresponded some years earlier, and Arnold had gracefully acknowledged that Newman was one of his masters. At this first and last meeting, the old man took Arnold's hand in both of his and said, 'I ventured to tell the Duchess I should like to see you.' At a party in London early in the following year, Arnold had a long talk with Disraeli, who at this last of a number of encounters scattered over several decades congratulated him on being 'the only living Englishman who had become a classic in his own lifetime'. Arnold understood this to refer to his successful launching of nicknames and catch-phrases such as 'Philistine' and 'sweetness and light'. Certainly these were widely current—so much so that as early as 1870 the Chancellor of the University of Oxford had said after conferring an honorary degree on Arnold that he ought perhaps to have addressed him as the sweetest and most lucid of men, *Vir dulcissime et lucidissime*!

During these last years, as always, Arnold travelled extensively in his own country and abroad both on duty and for pleasure. Whenever possible, he was accompanied by members of his family. His wife and his elder daughter Lucy were with him on his first visit to the United States, a lecture-tour, in 1883-4. Arnold's first glimpse of the New World showed him 'a beautiful *orné* landscape with spires, villas, hills, and woods'. 'Just like Richmond,' he remarked to someone on deck near him, 'and not a single Mohican running about!' This comment found its way into the American newspapers.

While it would be unfair to suggest that these were uniformly discourteous to the visitor, they certainly gave Arnold ample reason for disliking and eventually despising them. One of them published an impertinent description of him: 'He has harsh features, supercilious manners, parts his hair down the middle, wears a single eye-glass and ill-fitting clothes.' Shortly after his arrival, the *Chicago Tribune* attacked him violently for lecturing for 'filthy lucre'; after his departure, when a rival hoaxed it into ferociously denouncing him for an alleged severe criticism of Chicago and its people, the *Tribune* reported Arnold's denial of his authorship under the headlines: ' Arnold denies; Mr. Medill [the editor and supposedly Arnold's friend] refuses to accept Arnold's disclaimer; says Arnold is a cur.' Naturally enough, Arnold came to think the newspapers the worst feature of American life.

Occasionally they amused him. There was, for example, the comparison of himself, as he stooped now and then during a lecture to look at his manuscript, to 'an elderly bird pecking at grapes on a trellis'.

His first lecture, given in New York in a larger hall than he had ever used before, was unsuccessful. People were unable to hear him and left; among them was General Grant, the great military hero of the Civil War, who said,

'Well, wife, we have paid to see the British lion; we cannot hear him roar, so we had better go home.' Two brief periods of coaching by an Andover theological professor helped him to make himself more audible, and his tour, despite some resistance in the Mid-west, proved a very fair success. Everywhere, he was deeply gratified by the kindness of his hosts. One of these was the old showman, Phineas Barnum. He had sent an invitation: 'You, Mr. Arnold, are a celebrity, I am a notoriety; we ought to be acquainted.' Arnold had agreed and had become his guest. Barnum heard the lecture, 'Numbers', in which Arnold distinguished between the majority in any society and that 'remnant' which leavens the lump. He thought it 'grand' and resolved, he told Arnold, to belong to the remnant.

Before the tour was half over, Lucy detached herself from the '*Matthew Arnold troupe*' (as the party was called on the special theatrical railway tickets issued to it). She greatly enjoyed a long stay in New York and there became engaged to the American whom she later married. Her first daughter was the Arnolds' first grandchild and the immediate occasion of their second visit to America—this time with their younger daughter, the brown-haired Eleanor, or Nelly—in 1886. Following this visit, Arnold summarized his impressions in an essay entitled '*Civilization in the United States*'. He had found much to admire in American political institutions; his belief in the value of social equality had been confirmed by his experience of American life; but he had to insist that that life was grievously lacking in beauty and distinction.

The year 1886 was also his last year as an inspector of schools. In 1883 he had been greatly surprised when Gladstone, whom he had supposed hostile to him, had offered him a Civil list pension of £250 a year, 'as a public recognition of service to the poetry and literature of England'. At first it had seemed to Arnold that a man who was already drawing a substantial income from the public purse could not be justified in accepting such an offer; but his friends Morley and Lingen had urged him to take it. By persuading him to do so, they had greatly facilitated his retirement.

This was not to be the retirement to Italy of which he had once dreamed. Despite his lifelong attachment to Oxford, he thought Florence the most beautiful place he knew. But he could not uproot himself from his beloved cottage and garden at Cobham. There he spent most of his last eighteen months. During this time, he paid several visits: to his unmarried sister at Fox How, for example, and to the de Rothschilds at Aston Clinton. But in the main he lived quietly at home in Surrey.

Quiet was obligatory. In the spring of 1885 he had begun to suffer from a pain across his chest. 'I feel very unlike lawn tennis,' he had written to Dick, now married and living in Manchester, 'as going fast or going up hill gives me the sense of having a mountain on my chest; luckily, in fishing, one goes slow and stands still a good deal.' He had been mortified to find himself stopping half a dozen times in going up to Pains Hill. 'But so', he had reflected, 'one draws to one's end.' An optimistic diagnosis of indigestion had evidently left him sceptical.

By August, however, things had improved sufficiently for him to walk and to play lawn tennis as Lord Aberdare's guest while attending the Welsh national Eisteddfod. During the following winter, he had suffered little inconvenience on his last inspectorial visit to the Continent; and while spending Christmas at home he had skated. But the pain had returned more violently during his visit to America in the summer of 1886. He had found the climate trying; and a tumble while sea-bathing had introduced a week of particularly troublesome attacks. Lucy had been very good to him; but he could not seriously think of crossing the Atlantic on a third visit.

Back at Cobham, he soon felt restored. 'If I go too quick, I am stopped by a warning in my chest, but I can go about as much as I like if I go leisurely, and I have no attacks of sharp pain.' By this time he had certainly recognized the symptoms of *angina pectoris*, which had killed both his father and his grandfather. No doubt his busy and nomadic life had aggravated the condition. So he lived quietly, reading, writing, watching his garden, botanizing, playing tenderly with his domestic pets, and enjoying the company of his relatives and friends. During the winter of 1886-7 he skated once more; and there is surely disappointment in a remark of the following winter, 'the lake is all frozen, but the ice is rotten'.

The end came very suddenly. In 1888 Lucy and her daughter were expected in England. Arnold went from Cobham to Liverpool, where they were to land. On the afternoon of the next day, 15 April, overjoyed at the thought of soon meeting them, he leaped lightheartedly over a low fence while running for a tram and at once dropped dead. He was sixty-five years of age.

THE POET

Of the volumes of poetry which Arnold published before he was forty-five, six contain substantial quantities of new work; and there is very little of his verse which is not to be found in one or another of these six collections. The earliest of them have already been named: *The Strayed Reveller, and Other Poems* (1849) and *Empedocles on Etna, and Other Poems* (1852). These 'other poems' include many well-known works. "Resignation" "The Forsaken Merman", and the sonnet "Shakespeare" belong to the earlier volume, and "Memorial Verses", "A Summer Night", "Stanzas in Memory of the Author of Obermann", and most of the love poems to the later one. Both volumes were withdrawn as soon as Arnold had transferred to his Poems of 1853 as many of their contents as he wished at that date to preserve.

The new poems in this third collection include 'Sohrab and Rustum', 'Philomela', 'Requiescat', and "The Scholar-Gipsy"; *Poems: Second Series* (1855) opens with "Balder Dead"; otherwise, it contains only one short poem not salvaged from one or other of the two earliest volumes. *Merope*, a tragedy on the Greek model, followed in 1858, being calculated, as Arnold somewhat uninvitingly told a correspondent, 'rather to inaugurate my Professorship with dignity than to move deeply the present race of humans'. Finally, *New Poems* (1867) contained still further salvage from the volume of 1852—notably "*Empedocles on Etna*" itself—and, among its genuinely new poems, 'Thyrsis', "Dover Beach", "Palladium", "Growing Old", and "Obermann Once More". Of the new poems, several had certainly been written many years earlier; three had been printed in periodicals—only one of them recently—and a fourth in an anthology. It is clear that Arnold had not written a great deal of verse since 1855; and he was to produce only seven poems more, three of them elegies on household pets, during his remaining twenty years.

In the course of his many and sometimes radical rearrangements of his poems, Arnold revised his work very thoroughly. His revisions exemplify, among other things, his concern for 'literalness and sincerity', the qualities which he hoped in 1856 would always attract readers to his verse, though perhaps never in large numbers. Very rarely are his changes such as to lead a critical reader to hanker after the earlier, rejected versions. For this reason, the study of his poetry which follows is based upon the texts in that form in which he finally left them.

In a letter written in 1869, Arnold states that his poems 'represent, on the whole, the main movement of mind of the last quarter of a century'. There is some justification for this claim.

They represent, in the first place, the mid-nineteenthcentury reaction against the extravagant fervours and expectations and idealisms of the Romantic generation. Like the novels of George Eliot, who was to find in later life that of all contemporary poetry Arnold's was that which kept growing upon her, they are much concerned with the conflict between these romantic aspirations and the rigorous, impartial, and inescapable tyranny of circumstance and natural law. Thus Arnold several times alludes to Byron, who

> taught us little; but our soul
> Had.felt him like the thunder's roll.
> With shivering heart the strife we saw
> Of passion with eternal law;
> And yet with reverential awe
> We watch'd the fount of fiery life
> Which served for that Titanic strife.
> ('Memorial Verses.')

When he wrote this, Arnold clearly felt a spontaneous sympathy and admiration for Byron's revolt. But even then he knew that it was foredoomed to failure. Already, in 'Resignation', an early work which is manifestly assembled but in places equally manifestly felt, Arnold had preached the wisdom of submitting to 'time' and 'change', of learning 'to bear rather than rejoice'; and the protagonist of "*Empedocles on Etna*", similarly, urges Pausanias to 'Nurse no extravagant hope' and to 'moderate desire' in the face of a universe which is utterly indifferent to him, which will in any case proceed in accordance with its own laws, and to which he will obviously be well-advised to adjust himself.

This picture of the universe as no longer 'peopled by Gods' ("*Empedocles on Etna*", II) was the achievement of the scientists and philosophers of what Carlyle called the age of victorious Analysis, the eighteenth century. From

Blake onwards, the Romantics had rejected it. They could not destroy it, however. There was still for Clough the grim possibility that

> Earth goes by chemic forces; Heaven's
> A Mécanique Céleste;[3] ("The New Sinai.")

and for Arnold the neutrality of the universe, the sense that

> the circumambient gloom
> But hides, if Gods, Gods careless of our doom,
> ('Mycerinus.')

heightened his already painful awareness of the inevitable isolation of the individual human soul: 'We mortal millions live *alone*' ('To Marguerite—Continued'). This war between science and religion, reason and imagination, Bentham and Coleridge, is still being waged; it is the fundamental conflict of this, as it was of the last, century.

Arnold worked for a negotiated peace, a compromise. He held that reason, in the shape of physical science and German Biblical criticism, had already made belief in the supernatural impossible for many people and that it would quickly make it impossible for very many more. Instead of joining Tennyson and Browning in denying reason, Arnold characteristically accepted this growth of scepticism as inevitable and asked how the moral and other values traditionally associated with religion could best be preserved in the circumstances. It is with this question that he is preoccupied in 'Progress', which first appeared in the 1852 volume, and in several of the sonnets which he included in that of 1867.

His readiness to accept what he believed to be the inevitable and to work within the limits imposed by it is illustrated also by his dealings with 'the world'. Again and again in his verse, Arnold describes the distracting and bewildering and stupefying effect upon the individual of

> this strange disease of modern life,
> With its sick hurry, its divided aims,
> Its heads o'ertax'd, its palsied hearts.
>
> ('The Scholar-Gipsy.')

Seeking calm and self-possession, he withdraws from it to the Alps, to the Grande Chartreuse, to the countryside near Oxford which he had known in his youth, or merely to Kensington Gardens. But he can never forget that any but the briefest escape is impossible; he knows that he must return almost at once. So he leaves the Alps:

> I go, fate drives me; but I leave
> Half of my life with you.
> We, in some unknown Power's employ,
> Move on a rigorous line;
> Can neither, when we will, enjoy,
> Nor, when we will, resign.
>
> ('Stanzas in Memory of the Author of Obermann.')

The facetious comment which identifies the 'unknown Power' with the Department of Education serves at least to remind us that, unlike some of his immediate predecessors, Arnold was not protected by private income, personal gift, sinecure, or legacy from the obligation of working for a living in the ordinary Philistine sense of the phrase. Because he knew it in his own life, Arnold presents in his verse the dilemma of many who in the modern world are compelled to live their lives in circumstances which fail to satisfy their natures, which distract them indeed from learning what those natures are, and which they must for their own well-being periodically elude. If Arnold's landscapes are commonly those of a week-ender—and the Georgian poets are indeed his enfeebled successors—at least he also knew and gave utterance to that unease which drives the weekender to the countryside.

It is, then, in several respects a representative consciousness that is apparent in Arnold's verse. His poems describe simply and gravely his constant struggle to achieve stability, to make his romanticism submit to his realism, his unruly longings to his sense of things as they unalterably are. This is true whether his theme at the moment is his love for Marguerite or the decline of religious faith or 'this strange disease of modern life'. As a contemporary reviewer put it, 'Mr. Arnold's sentiment, his aspiration for life, is almost always in conflict with his critical perception of what life really is; . . . and hence he hits exactly many of the moods of an age which finds its desires for faith in strong contrast with what it deems the inadequate justification for those desires.'

But, while recognizing that Arnold does discuss in his verse many of the major interests which he shared with his more thoughtful and educated contemporaries, it still remains to ask whether he does so in such a way as to compel our imaginative participation—whether, in other words, he succeeds in making poetry out of them. My contention in the next section will be that he hardly ever does so.

In a letter to his sister Jane, written shortly after the publication of his 1849 volume, Arnold declares: 'At Oxford particularly many complain that the subjects treated do not interest them. But as I feel rather as a reformer in poetical matters, I am glad of this opposition. If I have health & opportunity to go on, I will shake the present methods until they go down, see if I don't. More and more I feel bent against the modern English habit (too much encouraged by Wordsworth) of using poetry as a channel for thinking aloud, instead of making anything.' To Clough, similarly, he wrote at about the same time that a certain friend 'urges me to speak more from myself: which I less and less have the inclination to do: or even the power'.

In keeping with these declarations, he speaks in his first volume through the mouth of a Strayed Reveller, of Mycerinus, of the Sick King in Bokhara; and in his second he tries to assume more elaborate dramatic disguises in '"*Empedocles on Etna*"' and in 'Tristram and Iseult'. But in none of these is his effort at 'making' something, at 'grouping objects', entirely satisfactory. His characters, in the situations in which he places them, illustrate themes and conflicts of urgent importance to him; but they lack the independent life without which it is impossible for them effectively to impose themselves, and thus to impose that which they are intended to embody, upon our imaginations. Sometimes, either in their own speeches or in his comments upon their situations, they seem to be mere excuses for their creator to indulge in that very 'thinking aloud' which he condemned; and elsewhere, more especially in the second volume in such poems as '"The Buried Life"', '"The Youth of Nature"', and '"The Youth of Man"', thinking aloud is offered without disguise.

> Murmur of living,
> Stir of existence,
> Soul of the world!
> Make, oh, make yourselves felt
> To the dying spirit of youth!
> Come, like the breath of the spring!
> Leave not a human soul
> To grow old in darkness and pain!
> Only the living can feel you,
> But leave us not while we live!

> . . . While the locks are yet brown on thy head,
> While the soul still looks through thine eyes,
> While the heart still pours
> The mantling blood to thy cheek,

Sink, O youth, in thy soul!
Yearn to the greatness of Nature;
Rally the good in the depths of thyself!
('The Youth of Man.')

These tired but faintly exclamatory ruminations are quite impotent as poetry.

Not that it is impossible to make poetry out of argumentation. In the finest passages of Pope *Essay on Man* the thought is organized and phrased with such elegance that it attains the status of an object created for our contemplation, instead of that merely of something exuded by the poet. The impotence of Arnold's ruminations is due to the fact that in them very little is thus shaped and presented. He is guilty of 'thinking aloud'. In a selection of the language then used by poets, he gives us a lucid recital of a series of ideas, about our reception of which he evidently feels a trifle uneasy-hence his attempts to soften-up our resistance by a barrage of italics, interjections, and marks of exclamation. We are interested—nearly always, outside Merope, Arnold can count on that—but we are not surprised, disturbed, stimulated, and actively involved. 'Obermann Once More' is a good instance. Though it contains the interesting ideas which critics have found in it, they are stated less precisely, with less supporting detail, and with a less evident sense of their full range of implication than in Arnold's prose works. And the only thing added by the verse form is a distractingly glib, jog-trot rhythm:

While we believed, on earth he went,
And open stood his grave.
Men call'd from chamber, church, and tent;
And Christ was by to save.

Arnold is more successful when, still consenting to speak from himself, he associates his ruminations closely with this or that particular landscape. To some extent he does so in both of the poems from which I have just quoted; but in each case the ruminations seem added to, rather than indissolubly bound up with, the particular landscape concerned. In his "'Rhapsody on a Windy Night'", Mr. T. S. Eliot is able to present a landscape and the memories which it evokes in such a way as to suggest, without ever describing, the observer's state of mind and criticism of life. I am not blaming Arnold for not going as far as this. But I think the contrast does show how Arnold is afraid to rely on his symbolic landscape, how he wishes to make everything fully explicit, and how, as a result, he tends to add much rumination to a little description and to call the total a poem.

This tendency is clearly visible in a small space in the opening lines of 'Consolation':

> Mist clogs the sunshine.
> Smoky dwarf houses
> Hem me round everywhere;
> A vague dejection
> Weighs down my soul.

In the first three lines, Arnold presents what Mr. Eliot might once have called an 'objective correlative' of his state of mind. He presents it sketchily enough; but even so it suffices to indicate his melancholy, his claustrophobia, his disgust at the meanness and ugliness of the life around him. Instead of going on from there, however, Arnold makes a fresh start with an explicit account in general terms of his dejection; and in these terms he can do no better than call it 'vague'. (A similar confession of failure occurs in *'The Buried Life'*: 'I feel a nameless sadness o'er me roll.') It may be replied that he called it vague because he really did find it impossible to pin it down and trace its outlines. But a reference to Edward Thomas should be enough to remind us of how the indefinableness of an indefinable feeling can be conveyed by poetic means. Arnold merely asserts it.

'"Consolation"', written at least in part in 1849, is an early poem. But the tendency can be traced even more clearly in the opening paragraphs of 'A Summer Night':

In the deserted, moon-blanch'd street,
How lonely rings the echo of my feet!
Those windows, which I gaze at, frown,
Silent and white, unopening down,
Repellent as the world;—but see,
A break between the housetops shows
The moon! and, lost behind her, fading dim
Into the dewy dark obscurity
Down at the far horizon's rim,
Doth a whole tract of heaven disclose!

And to my mind the thought
Is on a sudden brought
Of a past night, and a far different scene.
Headlands stood out into the moonlit deep
As clearly as at noon;
The spring-tide's brimming flow
Heaved dazzlingly between;
Houses, with long white sweep,
Girdled the glistening bay;
Behind, through the soft air,
The blue haze-cradled mountains spread away,
That night was far more fair—

But the same restless pacings to and fro,
And the same vainly throbbing heart was there,
And the same bright, calm moon.

And the calm moonlight seems to say:
Hast thou then still the old unquiet breast,
Which neither deadens into rest,

Nor ever feels the fiery glow
That whirls the spirit from itself away,
But fluctuates to and fro,
Never by passion quite possess'd
And never quite benumb'd by the world's sway?—
And I, I know not if to pray
Still to be what I am, or yield and be
Like all the other men I see.

Like Mr. Eliot's, Arnold's street is held in a lunar synthesis. Moonlight washes out the distracting multiplicity of detail and colour visible by day; the simplified and monochromatic world which it produces brings to mind that relief from the multiple distractions and demands of 'modern life' for which Arnold craves. This craving is implicit in the shift of his attention, essentially a movement of escape, from the repellent enclosing windows to the free space of the 'whole tract of heaven'. A recollected landscape follows; naturally, this, too, is moonlit. It is not Dover; no 'blue haze-cradled mountains spread away' from there. (Nor is it Thun, as sentimentalizers of the Marguerite affair sometimes like to suggest; the Swiss lakes are not tidal.) But the items of which it is composed are very largely those out of which Arnold, probably later, composed the landscape of his 'Dover Beach'. The moonlight, the soft or sweet air, the cliffs or headlands, the high tide, and even the metaphorical girdle are evidently details with a symbolic value for the poet who thus repeats himself. But the calm, stability, and poise for which they stand are denied to him; and from this thought the ruminations begin. Arnold tries to work them in unobtrusively by having the moonlight seem to address him, just as Mr. Eliot's street-lamps urge him to remark various objects of interest in their vicinity. But the moonlight is obviously Arnold talking to himself, warning himself of the alternative dangers of the expense of spirit in passion and the shrivelling of spirit in everyday life in the world, that is, of the alternative dangers of madness and slavery between which, in another poem, his Iseult of Brittany has steered. Inevitably it all seems too deliberate, too self-conscious; and the concluding lines of the third paragraph are even Pharisaical.

In the later paragraphs, the toilers in the brazen prison and the daring shipwrecked voyager are introduced to illustrate these opposing dangers of slavery and madness. But they are no more than illustrative. This is characteristic of Arnold. Broodingly, he states his thoughts; he introduces apt if sometimes bookish examples; but hardly ever does he create an aesthetically satisfying object which will adequately embody his thoughts and compel us, as we contemplate it, to relive them. After an opening in which it seems possible that something of the sort is going to emerge, *'A Summer Night'* slips into a series of lucid and despondent declarations which we believe because we happen to know that Arnold was a sincere man and not because they themselves force belief upon us.

'A Summer Night' is by no means unique. Most of *'Resignation'*, both of the *'Obermann'* elegies, the *'Stanzas from the Grande Chartreuse'*, *'Haworth Churchyard'*, *'Rugby Chapel'*, and *'Heine's Grave'*, all invite description in similar terms. So does much of Empedocles' soliloquy on Etna.

Even the love poems exemplify something of the kind. When Arnold attempts a direct statement of his feelings in them the usual result is a rather frigid self-pity; the best of the 'Marguerite' poems are those in which his feelings are conveyed by a remembered dream (*'A Dream'*) or a retold folk-tale (*'The Forsaken Merman'*) or the imagined situation of islands, once part of a single continent, which are now separated by the sea (*'To Marguerite—Continued'*). Yet none even of these lyrics is perfect. The last of them, that beginning 'Yes! in the sea of life enisled', closes with an impressive stanza in which Arnold's characteristic conflict is epitomized in the curt finality of the antithesis 'kindled, cool'd'; and which leaves the reader sadly contemplating an 'unplumb'd, salt, estranging sea'. But the second stanza, with its 'moon', its 'balms of spring', and its 'nightingales' which 'divinely sing' their 'lovely notes', remains a tame and therefore ineffective catalogue of nineteenthcentury poetic commonplaces.

'Dover Beach' is quite free from any trace of poeticality. It is a short poem, but in it Arnold relates the symbolic landscape which we have just glimpsed in *'A Summer Night'* to ideas which are also prominent elsewhere in his work. The general decline of faith and Arnold's own resultant bewilderment and melancholy constitute the theme of the *'Stanzas from the Grande Chartreuse'*; in *'The Buried Life'*, Arnold expresses the belief that in a successful love-relationship he may discover certain values which are not readily to be found in 'modern life'. Both of these ideas reappear in *'Dover Beach'*. It would be in keeping with all that we know of the psychology of artists to suppose that a poem which is thus a crystallization of ideas given separate and less definitive expression elsewhere must be later in date than the poems in which they receive that separate and less definitive expression. *'Stanzas from the Grande Chartreuse'*, the later of the two poems thus linked with *'Dover Beach'*, refers to a visit which Arnold made to the monastery in September 1851, during his honeymoon; he was apparently working on the poem during 1852; and it was printed in a periodical in 1855, twelve years before its inclusion in *New Poems*. The implication seems to be that *'Dover Beach'* must not be dated earlier than the middle years of this same decade. But no independent evidence is available to make this more than merely a critical intuition.

The 'moon-blanch'd' landscape described in the opening lines is composed of details which suggest the serenity, balance, and stability which Arnold desired for himself. This setting is evoked with considerable vividness.

> The sea is calm to-night.
> The tide is full, the moon lies fair
> Upon the straits;—on the French coast the light
> Gleams and is gone; the cliffs of England stand,
> Glimmering and vast, out in the tranquil bay.
> Come to the window, sweet is the night-air!
> Only, from the long line of spray
> Where the sea meets the moon-blanch'd land,
> Listen! you hear the grating roar
> Of pebbles which the waves draw back, and fling,
> At their return, up the high strand,
> Begin, and cease, and then again begin,
> With tremulous cadence slow, and bring
> The eternal note of sadness in.

We can point to the steady and weighty *rallentando* with which the first sentence completes its series of affirmations; to the contrasting tender appeal of the invitation which follows; and to the richness and fullness with which the sound and movement of the sea are rendered in the concluding eight lines. Examining these lines more closely, we can cite 'grating roar' as admirably conveying the two distinguishable but inseparable sounds made by waves breaking on shingle; we can acknowledge the almost physical stress given to the verbs 'draw back' and 'fling'; we can analyse up to a point the combination of syntactical and metrical means by which the ebbing and flowing motion of the waves is made actual; and we can admire the appropriateness of the Miltonic 'tremulous cadence slow' both as summarizing what has gone before and as permitting an easy and natural introduction of the 'eternal note of sadness'. But with all such comments we are in danger of substituting convenient but arbitrary rationalizations and simplifications for the rich complexity of our experience while reading the poem. The least inadequate criticism of any poem will always be that implicit in a reading of it aloud to an understanding hearer. Formal literary analysis can offer only a few crude indications of what one would be trying to do when giving such a reading.

The image which dominates this first paragraph of *'Dover Beach'* forms part of the 'full view' described by Mr. W.H. Auden in his poem beginning, 'Look, stranger, on this island now'. Like Arnold, Mr. Auden appears in his poetry as a tortured intellectual concerned with working out his own salvation. His inferior work, and his admirers' preference for it, gave him during the nineteen-thirties a reputation as a political poet. This was misleading. At his best, Mr. Auden is a highly subjective poet; and like Arnold he tends to relate his mental states to symbolic landscapes. But, whereas Arnold's more successful landscapes seem to be apprehended by direct sensory experience, Mr. Auden's consist largely of items culled from atlases, newsreels, the daily press, and political, psychological, and other reading. In short, his characteristic landscapes appear to be known to the intelligence rather than to the senses. This is exemplified at an extreme in *'Spain 1937'* and in the verse *'Commentary'* which concludes the sonnetsequence *'In Time of War'*. Admittedly, Mr. Auden's early favourite landscape of industrial decay is sometimes rendered in potently sensuous terms; but this is unusual.

In the poem beginning, 'Look, stranger, on this island now', Mr. Auden seems again to have made the unusual effort to impose the landscape he is describing upon the very senses of his readers. The result is a good poem; but it would have been a better poem if the effort had been less obtrusively visible. The second stanza is all that concerns us now:

Here at the small field's ending pause
When the chalk wall falls to the foam and its tall

ledges
Oppose the pluck
And knock of the tide,
And the shingle scrambles after the sucking surf
And the gull lodges
A moment on its sheer side.

The internal rhymes and successive emphatic beats in the second line, the aggressively tactile and kinaesthetic images introduced by 'pluck' and 'knock' in the third and fourth, and the onomatopoeic splitting of the word 'sucking' between the fifth and sixth are effective devices but too deliberate. It is precisely the effortlessness, the confident ease, of Arnold's description that is most remarkable when it is placed beside Mr. Auden's. Arnold is doing supremely well what comes naturally to him; Mr. Auden's description is, for him, *a tour de force.*

Having detected the 'eternal note of sadness', Arnold mentions a Sophoclean interpretation of it.

Sophocles long ago
Heard it on the Ægæan, and it brought
Into his mind the turbid ebb and flow
Of human misery; we
Find also in the sound a thought,
Hearing it by this distant northern sea.

The literary allusion serves not only to suggest that we have here to do with an archetypal image but also to introduce Arnold's own commentary.

This begins in a tone of straightforward exposition.

The Sea of Faith
Was once, too, at the full, and round earth's
shore
Lay like the folds of a bright girdle furl'd.

But instead of lapsing from this into rather flat rumination, which is what we have seen him do elsewhere, Arnold holds fast to the image of the sea. This has, so to speak, grown in his hands, so that it can now carry the whole weight of his feeling at the decline of religious faith. The symbol, so loaded, is presented in five haunting lines. The series of open vowels in the second of these, with the near-rhyme 'draw: roar', gives an eerie resonance which echoes down the remainder of the sentence with its 'falling' syntactical rhythm.

> But now I only hear
> Its melancholy, long, withdrawing roar,
> Retreating, to the breath
> Of the night-wind, down the vast edges drear
> And naked shingles of the world.

This is an early instance of the expressions of a horror of the utterly negative which occur from time to time in modern literature: in *A Passage to India* and *The Waste Land*, for example.

Critics acquainted with the extant manuscript of 'Dover Beach' sometimes complain that the last paragraph does not really belong with the remainder of the poem. In this draft, the last line is 'And naked shingles of the world. Ah love &c', which certainly suggests that the paragraph beginning 'Ah, love, let us be true' had already been written. But no amount of knowledge of its author's methods of composition can prove that a finished work is or is not a unified whole. With greater critical relevance, it may be argued that in this final paragraph Arnold has forgotten about the sea. But the sea has by this time served its purpose as a symbol; and that which it symbolized is still powerfully present in these last lines. Moreover, the darkness remains. Precisely because it is no longer possible to believe that the universe is in some degree adjusted to human needs, that it is informed by a divinity which sympathizes with men in their joys and sorrows and in their hopes and fears, the poet must seek in human love for those values which are undiscoverable elsewhere. Moreover—and this is the primary meaning of the last paragraph—the lovers must support each other if they are to live in the modern world without disaster.

> Ah, love, let us be true
> To one another! for the world, which seems
> To lie before us like a land of dreams,
> So various, so beautiful, so new,
> Hath really neither joy, nor love, nor light,
> Nor certitude, nor peace, nor help for pain;
> And we are here as on a darkling plain
> Swept with confused alarms of struggle and
> flight,
> Where ignorant armies clash by night.

As in the previous sentence, the main verb is introduced early; the result is what I have called a 'falling' syntactical rhythm, which contributes appreciably to the brooding melancholy of the whole paragraph. Metrically, this is the most regular section of the poem; after the initial short line, there are seven pentameters. The brief and therefore arresting last line carries the crucial phrase which discloses the full strangeness and horror of the concluding analogy. The

> darkling plain
> Swept with confused alarms of struggle and flight

is not remarkable; all the more powerful, therefore, is the harsh and surprising revelation, in the curtailed last line, of the nature of the battle: 'Where ignorant armies clash by night'. This image is Arnold's most impressive and most pregnant poetic utterance on 'modern life'.

'Dover Beach' is, I believe, his one great poem. As far as it is possible for a single short lyric to do so, it represents 'the main movement of mind of the last quarter of a century'; and it is the one work by Arnold which ought to appear in even the briefest anthology of great English poems. It may seem niggardly to limit such praise to a single work. But Arnold himself insists that excellence is rare; and a recognition of the uniqueness of *'Dover Beach'* need not inhibit a warm admiration for other poems. Two more lyrics, *'Growing Old'*, possibly a retort to Browning *'Rabbi ben Ezra'* (1864), and *'Palladium'*, must certainly be included among these. The former, a series of brief, bare sentences, discloses with bitter sincerity 'the gifts reserved for age' (*'Little Gidding'*); the latter, in which Arnold handles Homeric names with something of a Yeatsian evocativeness, expresses his aspiration not to lose sight of spiritual values even while in the thick of 'the battle in the plain'. Yet even in these, and despite his feeling 'rather as a reformer in poetical matters', his inability to free himself sufficiently from his age's preconceptions regarding what was truly poetical is responsible for such phrases as 'Is it for beauty to forego her wreath?' and

> Still doth the soul, from its lone fastness high,
> Upon our life a ruling effluence send.

A true reformer would have found it necessary to reform the very language of poetry, as Gerard Manley Hopkins was later to do.

Certain of Arnold's longer poems, too, call for particularly respectful attention—notably *'Empedocles on Etna'*, the Oxford elegies (*'The Scholar-Gipsy'* and *'Thyrsis'*), and *'Sohrab and Rustum'*. An examination of these should make it possible to define more closely the conditions in which Arnold achieves his most complete poetic successes.

At the head of a list of thirteen poems to be composed during 1849, Arnold placed 'Empedocles—refusal of limitation by the religious sentiment'. In the summer of the same year, one of his friends wrote to Clough: 'I saw the said Hero—Matt—the day I left London. He goes in Autumn to the Tyrol with Slade. He was working at an "Empedocles"—which seemed to be not much about the man who leapt in the crater—but his name & outward circumstances are used for the drapery of his own thoughts.' Arnold apparently went on working at *'Empedocles on Etna'* until it was published as the titlepoem of his volume of 1852.

Naturally, he acquainted himself as closely as possible with the life and thought of the pre-Socratic philosopherpoet who was to be his hero. But Clough's informant was right in believing that such data provided a mere framework for the drama. Moreover, Arnold did not restrict himself to these as his only literary sources. Above the list of thirteen poems already mentioned, he wrote the words *'Chew Lucretius'*. Lucretius was to some extent a disciple of Empedocles. Arnold had known his *De Natura Rerum*, a poem on the nature of the universe, since at least as early as 1845; and by 1849 he had certainly decided to make him the subject of a tragedy. He did much preparation for this play and probably never quite lost the hope of finishing it. That it nevertheless remained hardly begun even at his death was perhaps due to the fact that between 1849 and 1852 he gave expression in *'Empedocles on Etna'* to much that would otherwise have gone into it. Thus, the three stanzas of Empedocles' hymn which begin

> Is it so small a thing
> To have enjoy'd the sun

were originally written for the Roman tragedy. But Arnold was an admirer also of Epictetus, of Marcus Aurelius, of Spinoza, and of Senancour. Accordingly his Empedocles, while voicing many of the ideas of the epicurean Lucretius, is fundamentally a stoic.

The complexity of this character as imagined by the poet is well brought out in Arnold's own prose memorandum of what he planned to depict.

He is a philosopher. He has not the religious consolation of other men, facile because adapted to their weaknesses, or because shared by all around and changing the atmosphere they breathe.

He sees things as they are—the world as it is—God as he is: in their stern simplicity.

The sight is a severe and mind-tasking one: to know the mysteries which are communicated to others by fragments, in parables.

But he started towards it in hope: his first glimpses of it filled him with joy: he had friends who shared his hope & joy & communicated to him theirs: even now he does not deny that the sight is capable of affording rapture & the purest peace.

But his friends are dead: the world is all against him, & incredulous of the truth: his mind is overtasked by the effort to hold fast so great & severe a truth in solitude: the atmosphere he breathes not being modified by the presence of human life, is too rare for him. He perceives still the truth of the truth [*sic*], but cannot be transported and rapturously agitated by his grandeur: his spring and elasticity of mind are gone: he is clouded, oppressed, dispirited, without hope & energy.

Before he becomes the victim of depression & overtension of mind, to the utter deadness to joy, grandeur, spirit, and animated life, he desires to die; to be reunited with the universe, before by exaggerating his human side he has become utterly estranged from it.

Arnold's intention is further illuminated by a passage in his *'Preface'* of 1853 in which he explains why he has suppressed *'Empedocles on Etna'*.

I have done so, not because the subject of it was a Sicilian Greek born between two and three thousand years ago, although many persons would think this a sufficient reason. Neither have I done so because I had, in my own opinion, failed in the delineation which I intended to effect. I intended to delineate the feelings of one of the last of the Greek religious philosophers, one of the family of Orpheus and Musaeus, having survived his fellows, living on into a time when the habits of Greek thought and feeling had begun fast to change, character to dwindle, the influence of the Sophists to prevail. Into the feelings of a man so situated there entered much that we are accustomed to consider as exclusively modern; how much, the fragments of Empedocles himself which remain to us are sufficient at least to indicate. What those who are familiar only with the great monuments of early Greek genius suppose to be its exclusive characteristics, have disappeared; the calm, the cheerfulness, the disinterested objectivity have disappeared: the dialogue of the mind with itself has commenced; modern problems have presented themselves; we hear already the doubts, we witness the discouragement, of Hamlet and of Faust.

The representation of such a man's feelings must be interesting, if consistently drawn. We all naturally take pleasure, says Aristotle, in any imitation or representation whatever . . .; but, if the representation be a poetical one, more than this is demanded. It is demanded, not only that it shall interest, but also that it shall inspirit and rejoice the reader: that it shall convey a charm, and infuse delight . . .

What then are the situations, from the representation of which, though accurate, no poetical enjoyment can be derived? They are those in which the suffering finds no vent in action; in which a continuous state of mental distress is prolonged, unrelieved by incident, hope, or resistance; in which there is everything to be endured, nothing to be done. In such situations there is inevitably something morbid, in the description of them something monotonous. When they occur in actual life, they are painful, not tragic; the representation of them in poetry is painful also.

To this class of situations, poetically faulty as it appears to me, that of Empedocles, as I have endeavoured to represent him, belongs; and I have therefore excluded the Poem from the present collection.

During the fourteen years following this declaration, Arnold allowed only the five songs of Callicles and a short passage from Empedocles' soliloquy to be reprinted.

Then, in 1867, he reissued the whole work 'at the request of a man of genius, whom it had the honour and the good fortune to interest,—Mr. Robert Browning'.

'Empedocles on Etna' is virtually a monodrama. Apart from the protagonist, only two characters appear: Pausanias, a physician, a 'good, learned, friendly, quiet man', the confidant of Empedocles, the Horatio or Wagner to his Hamlet or Faust; and Callicles, a young harp-player, well loved by Empedocles and strangely drawn to him in his turn. The unhappy Empedocles is seeking solitude on Etna. Pausanias, accompanying him for part of the ascent, hopes to learn from him the secret of a miracle which he is said to have performed. Callicles, curious and anxious at their departure from the city, has followed them surreptitiously.

The poem opens with Callicles, who has outstripped the others, waiting shortly after dawn for them to come upon him as they continue their ascent. His opening soliloquy describes, in phrases sometimes reminiscent of Keats, the kind of setting which is common to both scenes of Act I:

> the sun
> Is shining on the brilliant mountain-crests,
> And on the highest pines; but farther down,
> Here in the valley, is in shade; the sward
> Is dark, and on the stream the mist still hangs;
> One sees one's footprints crush'd in the wet
> grass,
> One's breath curls in the air; and on these pines
> That climb from the stream's edge, the long grey
> tufts,
> Which the goats love, are jewell'd thick with dew.

Coolness and freshness are qualities which Arnold repeatedly opposes to those belonging to 'the broiling city'.

Pausanias discovers the young harp-player before Empedocles' arrival. He insists that Callicles keep out of the philosopher's sight—'One of his moods is on him that thou know'st'—but allows him to try the effect of his music from a distance upon the 'lonely man in triple gloom'. Pausanias is inclined to ascribe Empedocles' unhappiness to external causes such as his banishment from his own city and the alleged hostility of the sophists. But Callicles asserts that Empedocles' misery is due to factors within himself:

> 'Tis not the times, 'tis not the sophists vex him;
> There is some root of suffering in himself,
> Some secret and unfollow'd vein of woe,
> Which makes the time look black and sad to him.

This is confirmed by Empedocles' soliloquy, which occupies almost the whole of Act II and concludes with his suicide.

In 1867 Arnold denied that he had used Empedocles to express his own views. He pointed out that 'if Empedocles throws himself into Etna his creed can hardly be meant to be one to live by'. Nevertheless, it is impossible to disbelieve entirely the friend who, in 1849, said that Arnold was using Empedocles' name and outward circumstances 'for the drapery of his own thoughts'. The truth seems to be that while Arnold could quite honestly dissociate himself in 1867 from many of his protagonist's views, Empedocles' soliloquy had, in 1852, expressed for his creator a possible outcome of tendencies in himself of which he was only too well aware. When, moreover, we turn back from the soliloquy to the long hymn which occupies almost the whole of the previous scene, I. ii, we find Empedocles expressing views which are indistinguishable from those which Arnold either advanced elsewhere or may very reasonably be supposed to have entertained at the time of writing.

In this hymn Empedocles, accompanying himself for the last time on his harp, advises Pausanias on how so feeble a creature as man may best approach happiness in a universe which is totally indifferent to his welfare. In its metrical form the hymn is reminiscent of Shelley ode *'To a Skylark'*. The chief difference is that Arnold, wishing to unfold a consecutive argument, uses the rhyming syllables of the alexandrines to link the stanzas in pairs. His feeling is so far from the Shelleyan ecstasy that the hymn is quite prosaic. But its argument is interesting.

Empedocles begins by comparing man's fragmentary and disjointed vision of life with the series of images caught in a hanging mirror spinning in, and driving before, the winds. 'Is fate indeed so strong,' he asks, 'man's strength indeed so poor?' But his question is merely rhetorical. In what follows, he tacitly assumes an affirmative answer and substitutes for the metaphysical question an ethical one: How can man make the best of his precarious situation?

His advice to unhappy mankind is that of the stoics: 'Sink in thyself! there ask what ails thee, at that shrine!' Man is discontented, he struggles, raves, and is ill at ease, because he cherishes the delusive belief that the world exists for his benefit and that he has a natural right to happiness. (In making Empedocles repudiate the doctrine of natural rights, Arnold is following his father and Coleridge and Burke.) It is not wrong for man to seek happiness; but he is mistaken in supposing that he is entitled to it:

> Man errs not that he deems
> His welfare his true aim,
> He errs because he dreams
> The world does but exist that welfare to bestow.

The world goes on in its own, and not in our, way:

> In vain our pent wills fret,
> And would the world subdue.
> Limits we did not set
> Condition all we do;
> Born into life we are, and life must be our mould.

A wise man would seek happiness only within the limits imposed by circumstances. But most of us are unwise; and our immoderate expectations bring us to grief.

This ought to dispel our self-pleasing delusions. It does not, however. For we invent hostile gods upon whom to blame our misfortunes, 'With God and Fate to rail at, suffering easily.' Moreover, we invent kind gods who in some future state will satisfy those of our desires which are thwarted here and now. Empedocles is harshly scornful of such shifts:

Fools! That so often here
Happiness mock'd our prayer,
I think, might make us fear
A like event elsewhere;
Make us, not fly to dreams, but moderate desire.

These last two words, 'moderate desire', epitomize his advice to his credulous friend.

An attempt to present this doctrine in as cheerful a light as possible concludes the hymn:

Is it so small a thing
To have enjoy'd the sun,
To have lived light in the spring,
To have loved, to have thought, to have done;
To have advanced true friends, and beat down baffling
foes—

That we must feign a bliss
Of doubtful future date,
And, while we dream on this,
Lose all our present state,
And relegate to worlds yet distant our repose?

. . . But thou, because thou hear'st
Men scoff at Heaven and Fate,
Because the Gods thou fear'st
Fail to make blest thy state,
Tremblest, and wilt not dare to trust the joys there
are!

I say: Fear not! Life still
Leaves human effort scope.
But, since life teems with ill,
Nurse no extravagant hope;

> Because thou must not dream, thou need'st not
> then despair!

There is nothing blissful or rapturous about the life which Empedocles recommends to Pausanias. But to a poet as deeply infected by the sceptical spirit of his age as Arnold it must have seemed to offer the nearest approach to happiness compatible with the human situation.

It cannot, however, satisfy Empedocles himself. Dismissing Pausanias, he climbs beyond the last of 'all the woody, high, well-water'd dells' which have provided settings for the two scenes of the relatively genial Act I; and at the beginning of Act II he is, in his own words,

> Alone!—
> On this charr'd, blacken'd, melancholy waste,
> Crown'd by the awful peak, Etna's great mouth,
> Round which the sullen vapour rolls—alone!

This setting is entirely appropriate for a soliloquy expounding and exemplifying his deterioration into

> Nothing but a devouring flame of thought—
> But a naked, eternally restless mind!

Empedocles cannot deny that he has been a 'slave of thought'; and his bondage has resulted in the drying-up of his spirit's 'self-sufficing fount of joy'. His sickness resembles that which Arnold knew and feared in himself when he adopted a pose of dandyism in order to protect himself against the Rugby and Oxford depth-hunters of his acquaintance. But in Empedocles the disease is mortal. His suicide is a bold symbol of the ultimate destruction of the human person by the 'devouring flame' of and self-consciousness and restless speculation.

In the blank verse and occasional free verse of his soliloquy, he expresses himself with an ease and a naturalness which he rarely achieves in the short lines, constricting because demanding so rapid a succession of rhyming syllables, of his hymn. Much of the speech, nevertheless, remains uncreatively ruminative. Its content, very largely that of Arnold's prose memorandum already quoted, is interesting. Empedocles' complaint that in the uncongenial age into which he has survived

> Great qualities are trodden down,
> And littleness united
> Is become invincible

reminds us that his creator belonged to a generation keenly aware of the dangers which might arise from the growth of democracy; and his confession of dismay at the thought of the neutrality of a universe no longer 'peopled by Gods', a confession which Pausanias' presence has presumably inhibited until now, echoes what Arnold writes elsewhere. But it is only towards the end of the soliloquy that Empedocles' utterance gains urgency and life.

He has discarded the insignia both of his former 'unloved preëminence' among men and of the poetic office which kept him apart from them in solitude. Having come to ascribe to a failure of vitality in himself his feeling that the universe has lost its divinity, he longs for an end to be put to the restless thought and selfquestioning which have crippled him. He is content that his physical being should revert to the elements from which it was formed.

> But mind, but thought—
> If these have been the master part of us—
> Where will *they* find their parent element?
> What will receive *them*, who will call *them* home?
> But we shall still be in them, and they in us,
> And we shall be the strangers of the world,

And they will be our lords, as they are now;
And keep us prisoners of our consciousness,
And never let us clasp and feel the All
But through their forms, and modes, and stifling veils.
And we shall be unsatisfied as now;
And we shall feel the agony of thirst,
The ineffable longing for the life of life
Baffled for ever; and still thought and mind
Will hurry us with them on their homeless march,
Over the unallied unopening earth,
Over the unrecognising sea; while air
Will blow us fiercely back to sea and earth,
And fire repel us from its living waves.
And then we shall unwillingly return
Back to this meadow of calamity,
This uncongenial place, this human life;
And in our individual human state

Go through the sad probation all again,
To see if we will poise our life at last,
To see if we will now at last be true
To our own only true, deep-buried selves,
Being one with which we are one with the whole world;
Or whether we will once more fall away
Into some bondage of the flesh or mind,
Some slough of sense, or some fantastic maze
Forged by the imperious lonely thinking-power.
And each succeeding age in which we are born
Will have more peril for us than the last;
Will goad our senses with a sharper spur,
Will fret our minds to an intenser play,
Will make ourselves harder to be discern'd.
And we shall struggle awhile, gasp and rebel—
And we shall fly for refuge to past times,
Their soul of unworn youth, their breath of

greatness;
And the reality will pluck us back,
Knead us in its hot hand, and change our nature
And we shall feel our powers of effort flag,
And rally them for one last fight—and fail;
And we shall sink in the impossible strife,
And be astray for ever.

This is Arnold's finest passage of blank verse; and it is a genuinely dramatic speech. The repetitive sequences of harassed and despairing utterances, each one receiving very much the same degree of emphasis as its neighbours, convey insidiously the bewilderment of men driven hither and thither by 'thought and mind'; and the larger rhythm which unites the sequences carries us on, unrestingly and dizzily, to the desolate silence which follows the words 'And be astray for ever'.

While this speech describes and exemplifies what Arnold feared, and while Empedocles' hymn defines the utmost for which Arnold thought it prudent to hope, the five songs of Callicles express collectively a less realistic impulse. They are a product of Arnold's recurrent wistful yearning to escape from the 'darkling plain' to some place—early Greece, the countryside around Oxford, or the Alps—which is less inimical to the achievement of a joyful serenity. It was evidently his intention that they should exhibit the characteristics which, in his 'Preface' of 1853, he attributed to the early Greek genius, namely, calm, cheerfulness, and disinterested objectivity; and that Callicles, as the youthful exponent of these values, should stand in contrast with Empedocles, who represents the doubts and discouragement, 'the dialogue of the mind with itself', which are endemic on the 'darkling plain'. Callicles' qualities were to be those which Arnold, as a good Goethean, wished to realize in his poetry and for the sake of which he tried as a young man to hold himself a little aloof from his more Empedoclean friends. But in reading Callicles' songs we are less aware of a beautiful objectivity than of Arnold's plaintive longing to be 'Far, far from here', to be, perhaps,

> where Helicon breaks down
> In cliff to the sea.

These songs have great charm; but they have not the actuality and point of the lines I have quoted from Empedocles' soliloquy.

Nevertheless, they provide welcome relief from the sombre monologues of the introspective sage. It seems to have been Arnold's intention that each of them should have also a special relevance to the context in which it is placed. The first of them relates how Chiron, the aged centaur, imparted to the young Achilles an intimate understanding of natural things. His doctrine of nature contrasts with the harsher one preached by Empedocles in the hymn which immediately follows. After the hymn, Callicles sings of the placid and dumb contentment of Cadmus and Harmonia, metamorphosed in their old age and removed far from the scenes of 'their first sad life'. Again, a contrast seems to be implied. Empedocles,

> whose youth fell on a different world
> From that on which his exiled age is thrown,

can achieve no such peace of mind as theirs. It is interesting to note that *'Cadmus and Harmonia'* remained one of Arnold's favourites among his poems throughout his life.

Early in Act II, Callicles sings of Typho, the rebellious Titan whom Zeus subdued and buried beneath Etna. He ends with a picture of Zeus himself sitting with his fellow-Olympians. But Empedocles' sympathy goes out to Typho; he sees his fate as symbolizing the defeat everywhere of the 'brave, impetuous heart' by 'the subtle, contriving head';

and in his bitterness he strips himself of the insignia of his power. When Callicles interrupts him again with the story of Apollo's triumph over Marsyas, Empedocles' self-pity once more leads him to side with the victim, and the song celebrating the triumph of poetry becomes the immediate occasion of his forswearing poetry. Callicles' voice is not heard again until after Empedocles' death. He then concludes the poem with a joyful hymn to Apollo which switches the reader's attention from Etna to Helicon and Olympus.

As a dramatic poem, *'Empedocles on Etna'* is a failure. None of its three personages seems to speak or to act from an independent centre of vitality. Even if, changing our ground, we judge it as a body of subjective poetry, the verdict cannot be very much more favourable. Admittedly, the songs of Callicles have an authentic if conventionally poetical charm. But only once, in the passage quoted from the end of Empedocles' soliloquy, does the verse approach greatness. At the same time, both the general plan of the work and in many places the particular ideas which the characters express are genuinely interesting. It is, in fact, 'with more interest than rapture', as G. M. Hopkins wrote in 1873, that we read both this and most of Arnold's other poems.

Owing to its imperfections as a dramatic creation, the work is in practice less painful than Arnold feared when he suppressed it in 1853. It is worth noting, however, that the optimistic George Meredith was moved to a high-spirited protest:

> And this great Doctor, can it be,
> He left no saner recipe
> For men at issue with despair?
> Admiring, even his poet owns,
> While noting his fine lyric tones,
> The last of him was heels in air! ('Empedocles.')

It was in Joseph Glanvill *The Vanity of Dogmatizing* (1661) that Arnold found the story of an Oxford scholar who left his studies 'to joyn himself to a company of *Vagabond Gypsies*' and who hoped in time to learn from them the secret of their hypnotic powers. Arnold acquired his copy of this work in 1844 but left it unread at least until the autumn of the following year. Between then and 1849 he decided to write a poem about the scholar-gipsy. The twelfth item in his list, already mentioned, of thirteen poems to be composed during 1849 is *'The first mesmerist'*. Another list, drawn up about two years later, names this 'the wandering Mesmerist'.

The difference between the two titles is indicative of the direction in which the poem was developing. When it was published in 1853 there was little in it about the then fashionable science of mesmerism. But its hero was nothing if not a wanderer.

Arnold imagines him as still roaming through the countryside around Oxford, 'Seen by rare glimpses, pensive and tongue-tied'. In the stanzas describing how both rustics and Oxford men have had fleeting glimpses of him, these three characteristics are insisted upon and exemplified. He flies from the noisy company of 'smockfrock'd boors' and 'Oxford riders blithe'; he loves 'retired ground'; he haunts 'shy retreats' and 'shy fields and distant Wychwood bowers'; and at night he seeks his 'straw in some sequester'd grange'. Crossing a stream by punt, he leans backwards 'in a pensive dream'; housewives and children have known him 'hanging on a gate' —like the poet in *'Resignation'*— and giving up the entire day to contemplation of the life around him; others have been able to note his gipsy attire, 'hat of antique shape, and cloak of grey', and, more important, his 'soft abstracted air'. He speaks to nobody.

He is a lonely figure. He hopes to learn and to make known the gipsies' 'arts to rule . . . men's brains'; but, he says, 'it needs heaven-sent moments for this skill'. So we see him not so much consorting with the gipsies as waiting in solitude 'for the spark from heaven to fall'. Evidently more is in question than merely the technique of mesmerism. So much more that definition is impossible. All we can say is that some mysterious wisdom is the true object of his incessant wandering.

While his object can be described only in such general terms as these, the settings in which he is glimpsed are often most sharply and most vividly rendered. In conjunction with the setting in which the poet himself first appears, reading Glanvill's book and exhorting the 'shepherd' to renew the quest of the scholar, they constitute one of the finest of Arnold's symbolic landscapes, perfectly adapted to solitary, calm, and refreshing meditation. We see the scholar, for example,

> Crossing the stripling Thames at Bab-lock-hithe,
> Trailing in the cool stream thy fingers wet,
> As the punt's rope chops round.

The word 'stripling' has, over and above its immediate aptness, a wider relevancy in a poem so much concerned with its author's own youth. For 'The Scholar-Gipsy' embodies and expresses Arnold's intimate knowledge of and love for the countryside near Oxford which he had explored years earlier with Clough and Walrond and his own brother Tom. In a letter addressed to Tom in 1857 he writes that the poem 'was meant to fix the remembrance of those delightful wanderings of ours . . . before they were quite effaced'. This intention is clearly evident in such a stanza as the following:

> And, above Godstow Bridge, when hay-time's
> here
> In June, and many a scythe in sunshine flames,
> Men who through those wide fields of breezy

grass
Where black-wing'd swallows haunt the glittering Thames,

To bathe in the abandon'd lasher pass,
Have often pass'd thee near

Sitting upon the river bank o' ergrown;
Mark'd thine outlandish garb, thy figure spare,

Thy dark vague eyes, and soft abstracted air—
But, when they came from bathing, thou wast gone!

The opening lines of this stanza, with their sharp outlining of the 'black-wing'd swallows' against the dazzling landscape, are as Keatsian as those quoted earlier from Callicles. In its metrical structure, too, it is reminiscent of the stanzas of Keats' great odes. This influence pervades *'The Scholar-Gipsy'* but is particularly marked in the earlier, descriptive part with which we have so far been exclusively concerned. The last stanza of this part, in which Arnold tells himself that he is merely dreaming when he pictures the scholar as still roaming the countryside, provides another clear example:

thou from earth art gone
Long since, and in some quiet churchyard laid—
Some country-nook, where o'er thy unknown grave
Tall grasses and white flowering nettles wave,
Under a dark, red-fruited yew-tree's shade.

The transition to the second part of the work is effected by a turn which again recalls Keats. Having assured himself that the scholar is dead, the poet immediately rises in protest against the assertion. 'No, no,' he declares, 'thou hast not felt the lapse of hours!' and in the next stanza he goes on virtually to paraphrase the argument of the sixth and seventh stanzas of the *'Ode to a Nightingale'*:

> The generations of thy peers are fled,
> And we ourselves shall go;
> But thou possessest an immortal lot.

This immortality of the scholar is due to his having had 'one aim, one business, one desire'. He left the world early,

> with powers
> Fresh, undiverted to the world without,
> Firm to their mark, not spent on other things;
> Free from the sick fatigue, the languid doubt,
> Which much to have tried, in much been baffled, brings.
> O life unlike to ours!

He waits for the spark from heaven. So do we, 'Light half-believers of our casual creeds', but without his hope. Sadly the poet exhorts him,

> O born in days when wits were fresh and clear,
> And life ran gaily as the sparkling Thames;
> Before this strange disease of modern life,
> With its sick hurry, its divided aims,
> Its heads o'ertax'd, its palsied hearts, was rife—
> Fly hence, our contact fear!
> Still fly, plunge deeper in the bowering wood!
> Averse, as Dido did with gesture stern
> From her false friend's approach in Hades turn,
> Wave us away, and keep thy solitude!

> Still nursing the unconquerable hope,
> Still clutching the inviolable shade,
> With a free, onward impulse brushing through,
> By night, the silver'd branches of the glade—

Far on the forest-skirts, where none pursue,
On some mild pastoral slope
Emerge, and resting on the moonlit pales
Freshen thy flowers as in former years
With dew, or listen with enchanted ears,
From the dark dingles, to the nightingales!

But fly our paths, our feverish contact fly!
For strong the infection of our mental strife,
Which, though it gives no bliss, yet spoils for rest;
And we should win thee from thy own fair life,
Like us distracted, and like us unblest.
Soon, soon thy cheer would die,
Thy hopes grow timorous, and unfix'd thy powers,
And thy clear aims be cross and shifting made;
And then thy glad perennial youth would fade,
Fade, and grow old at last, and die like ours.

This is poetry of great charm. But it is poetry which belongs too completely to the world of poetry. It lacks the reality and urgency of the best of Arnold's Empedoclean verse. The first and third stanzas state clearly enough the predicament of those who dwell on the 'darkling plain'. But their predicament is not brought home to us as by the concluding image of 'Dover Beach' or the compelling rhythm of the last long paragraph of Empedocles' soliloquy. Instead, the statement is gracefully couched in conventionally poetical terms.

As for the second stanza, which movingly recalls the symbolic landscape presented earlier in the poem, what are we to make of 'the unconquerable hope', or, as it is named elsewhere, the 'mark', the 'one aim, one business, one desire', of the scholar? It is difficult to believe that Arnold had any very exact conception of what he meant by these terms. What does emerge is that the possession of 'one aim, one business, one desire' gives immortality to the scholar by protecting him against the 'strange disease' not only of 'modern life' but also of human life as such:

> For what wears out the life of mortal men?
> 'Tis that from change to change their being rolls;
> 'Tis that repeated shocks, again, again,
> Exhaust the energy of strongest souls
> And numb the elastic powers.

In fact, the scholar personifies an impulse of pure evasion. If the predicament from which Arnold wishes to escape is given little or no poetic substance, the secret for which he craves is almost as vague as the objective proposed in Longfellow *'Excelsior'*. What the poem really offers is a very delightful pastoral week-end. Arnold's indebtedness in it to the Keats who presided over the nineteenth-century poetry of the dream-world ought not to surprise us.

The poem ends with a coda which transports us to the early Greek world of which Callicles elsewhere is a belated representative. In this, a 'grave Tyrian trader' discovers that a 'merry Grecian coaster',

> Freighted with amber grapes, and Chian wine,
> Green, bursting figs, and tunnies steep'd in brine,

has put in at one of the Ægæan isles which he had been accustomed to regard as his own territory. He recognizes in these 'intruders on his ancient home' the 'young lighthearted masters of the waves'. He immediately turns from them, sails 'indignantly' to the western Mediterranean and out into the Atlantic, and begins to trade with those 'Shy traffickers, the dark Iberians', undoing 'his corded bales' upon the beach for this purpose.

In itself, this is a pleasing episode. But the thread which attaches it to the main body of the poem is very tenuous. Arnold introduces the Tyrian trader ostensibly in order to illustrate his advice to the scholar to 'fly our greetings, fly our speech and smiles!' But surely the scholar, with his 'unclouded joy' and his 'glad perennial youth' has more in common with the 'young lighthearted masters of the waves' than with the 'grave Tyrian' who flies 'indignantly' from them? Certainly the 'merry' Greeks could hardly offer a more complete contrast than they do with the palsied denizens of the 'darkling plain' with whom they are apparently equated. With rather more appropriateness, 'the dark Iberians' may be taken to correspond with the gipsies to whom the scholar has turned.

Several commentators have tried to demonstrate the relevance of this simile, usually by stressing the aloofness which the Tyrian shares with the scholar and by equating the Greeks with the 'smock-frock'd boors' and 'Oxford riders blithe' whom the scholar shuns. But there is nothing in the poetry to limit and direct our responses in this fashion. The interpretation is merely ingenious.

This is not the only poem of Arnold's to end with such a coda. On the contrary, the device was a favourite with him. It occurs, for example, in 'Tristram and Iseult', *'Sohrab and Rustum'*, and *'Stanzas from the Grande Chartreuse'*. His intention was evidently to round off each of these longer poems with a digression which would give some relief to the reader by taking his mind off the melancholy main theme of the work and which would at the same time redirect his attention to what was essential in that main theme by presenting a symbolic equivalent of it. Perhaps the final simile of *'The Scholar-Gipsy'* performs the first of these functions; it can hardly be said to perform the second.

Arnold was not altogether satisfied with the poem. In the year of its publication, he wrote to Clough: 'I am glad you like the Gipsy Scholar—but what does it do for you? Homer*animates*—Shakespeare animates—in its poor way

I think Sohrab and Rustum *animates*—the Gipsy Scholar at best awakens a pleasing melancholy. But this. is not what we want.

> The complaining millions of men
> Darken in labour and pain—[4]

what they want is something to animate and ennoble them. —not merely to add zest to their melancholy or grace to their dreams.' Others are unlikely to share Arnold's uneasiness at the mere melancholy of the poem. After all, a much more urgent, even desperate, pessimism characterizes his very finest work. But when he says that the poem 'at best awakens a pleasing melancholy', that it merely 'adds zest' to men's melancholy or 'grace to their dreams', he implies a criticism of it which is likely to gain much wider acceptance: he implies that there is something relaxing or enervating about it. This implication is so completely in line with the criticism of the poem which I have already made that I see no point in elaborating it now. All I wish to add is the suggestion that 'The Scholar-Gipsy' is the finest of the poems which may be taken to express the impulse which created Callicles.

The 'shepherd' addressed at the beginning of the poem was probably Clough; so it is not surprising that Arnold's elegy on him should have taken the form of a sequel to 'The Scholar-Gipsy'. 'Thyrsis' is set in the same surroundings and written in the same metrical form; and the wandering scholar appears three times in it.

'I shall some day', wrote Arnold within a week of receiving the news of Clough's death, 'in some way or other relieve myself of what I think about him.' He declined an invitation to contribute an obituary notice to a newspaper. But before the end of the same month, November 1861, he spoke warmly of his friend in the last of his Oxford lectures on translating Homer, praising him for the integrity of his literary life. Early in 1862 he was thinking of visiting the places near Oxford which they had known as young men; and by the spring of 1863 he had formed the plan of writing 'a new poem about the Cumner hillside, and Clough in connexion with it'. He seems not to have started this poem until 1864.

'Thyrsis' was first published in a periodical in 1866. Arnold said that the 'diction of the poem was modelled on that of Theocritus, whom I have been much reading during the two years this poem has been forming itself' and that he 'meant the diction to be so artless as to be almost heedless. In another letter he admitted that there was much in Clough, 'the whole *prophet* side, in fact', which could not be dealt with in the poem as he had conceived it and that 'one has the feeling, if one reads the poem as a memorial poem, that not enough is said about Clough in it . . . Still Clough*had* this idyllic side, too; to deal with this suited my desire to deal again with that Cumner country: anyway, only so could I treat the matter this time.'

Clough receives much more attention in *'Thyrsis'* than does either Edward King in *'Lycidas'* or Keats in *'Adonais'*. Nor does Arnold entirely neglect the 'prophet side' of him. Writing in the Theocritan pastoral convention, he explains Clough's departure from Oxford by saying that the shepherd Thyrsis could not contentedly accept the bucolic life he loved because

> Some life of men unblest
> He knew, which made him droop, and fill'd his
> head.
> He went; his piping took a troubled sound
> Of storms that rage outside our happy ground;
> He could not wait their passing, he is dead.

Towards the end of the poem he repeats this account of Clough's career:

> the music of thy rustic flute
> Kept not for long its happy, country tone;
> Lost it too soon, and learnt a stormy note
> Of men contention-tost, of men who groan,
> Which task'd thy pipe too sore, and tired thy throat—
> It fail'd, and thou wast mute!

Later in this same stanza, the phrase 'men of care' may well refer to the society which Clough entered as Principal of University Hall—'Doubting Castle', in Arnold's eyes-and which he soon left to resume his 'wandering way'.

Nevertheless, the poem is not primarily a portrait of Clough. It is an expression of Arnold's own persistent longing to relive those early days when he and Clough had rambled in the Cumnor hills together.

> I know these slopes; who knows them if not I?—
> But many a dingle on the loved hill-side,
> With thorns once studded, old, white-blossom'd trees,
> Where thick the cowslips grew, and far descried
> High tower'd the spikes of purple orchises,
> Hath since our day put by
> The coronals of that forgotten time;
> Down each green bank hath gone the ploughboy's team,
> And only in the hidden brookside gleam
> Primroses, orphans of the flowery prime.
>
> Where is the girl, who by the boatman's door,
> Above the locks, above the boating throng,
> Unmoor'd our skiff when through the Wytham flats,

Red loosestrife and blond meadow-sweet among
And darting swallows and light water-gnats,
We track'd the shy Thames shore?
Where are the mowers, who, as the tiny swell
Of our boat passing heaved the river-grass,
Stood with suspended scythe to see us pass?—
They are all gone, and thou art gone as well!

Arnold confessed to a special fondness for these two stanzas; 'but', he added, 'that is because they bring certain places and moments before me.'

It is worth noting that the 'darting swallows' and the epithet 'shy', here applied to the 'Thames shore', are among the many details which connect the symbolic landscape of this poem with that of 'The ScholarGipsy'. But an important feature is added to it in *'Thyrsis'*. This is the 'signal-elm' which crowns the 'hill behind whose ridge the sunset flames', the solitary tree which the two young Oxford men had prized, saying that, as long as it stood, their friend the Scholar-Gipsy would still be roaming the countryside. Revisiting the Cumnor hills after Thyrsis' death, the poet searches for it in vain until, flying from a 'troop of Oxford hunters' like the Scholar-Gipsy before him, he suddenly sees,

Back'd by the sunset, which doth glorify
The orange and pale violet evening-sky,
Bare on its lonely ridge, the Tree! the Tree!

At the end of the poem, he recognizes that he is now obliged to live amid 'city-noise'. But he hopes that 'through the great town's harsh, heart-wearying roar' Thyrsis' voice will come to him, driving away 'fatigue and fear':

Why faintest thou? I wander'd till I died.
Roam on! The light we sought is shining still.

> *Dost thou ask proof? Our tree yet crowns the hill,*
> *Our Scholar travels yet the loved hill-side.*

So the poem ends on a note of optimism. Just as Arnold in *'Obermann Once More'*, probably written in 1865-6, repudiates the defeatism of 'Stanzas in Memory of the Author of *Obermann*', written at least in part in 1849, so he clearly intended that *'Thyrsis'* should differ from 'The Scholar-Gipsy' in expressing a hopeful acceptance of the obligation to participate in 'modern life'. In his prose writings of this time can be found his reasons for feeling this temperate but genuine hopefulness. In his poetry its expression carries very much less weight. In *'Obermann Once More'* it is merely asserted. In 'Thyrsis' it is more skilfully suggested by means of the symbolism of the tree. But does not even this seem to be rather too deliberately introduced?

Much more persuasive is the expression of his melancholy longing for 'The years that are no more' ('Growing Old'). 'Thyrsis', like 'The Scholar-Gipsy', is memorable chiefly for its vivid, almost Keatsian recreation of the well-loved Cumnor landscape. This is so presented as potently to suggest by its details the coolness, freshness, and seclusion for which the poet yearned.

Containing this achievement, the Oxford elegies are poems of charm and distinction. But they are too far removed from the harsh exigencies of life for it to be easy to claim greatness for them. Arnold has himself supplied the criterion, 'Dover Beach', by reference to which this becomes apparent. Admittedly, the stresses and clashes of life are acknowledged in the poems; but they are much less concretely present there than is the idyllic landscape to which the poet flies from them. Nor is the 'quest' which inspires this revisiting of places long loved made any more real to us. What we are offered is a brief escape from the human predicament 'on the viewless wings of Poesy'. There are times when we are glad to make such an escape. But the fact remains that the greatest poetry is that which confronts and in some sense masters the predicament.

Several conclusions emerge from what has been said so far. The most important of these is that Arnold achieves poetic greatness only on one or two exceptional, Empedoclean occasions. When in early life he tried to protect himself by dandyism against those who might accentuate his tendency towards depth-hunting, he was probably doing what was most conducive to his own eventual personal happiness; but it would seem that he was denying himself the material best suited to his creative talent. In keeping with this programme, he tried to cultivate in his poetry the calm, cheerfulness, and disinterested objectivity which he ascribed to the early Greek genius; but the best of what I should call his Calliclean poems are what they are rather because they give moving expression to an essentially personal impulse of escape than because they embody with entire assurance the early Greek virtues he admired. There are three long works, however, in which he very deliberately attempted to realize these classical qualities without subjective adulteration. These are *'Sohrab and Rustum'*, *'Balder Dead'*, and *Merope*. *'Balder Dead'* is tame, and *Merope* is almost unreadable; but *'Sohrab and Rustum'* is a work of sufficient power to claim attention both for itself and for the critical theories associated with it.

These theories are expounded in the 'Preface' to his *Poems* of 1853. They clearly derive from views which we have already met in his letters to Clough. In the 'Preface', after explaining why he has suppressed 'Empedocles on Etna', he goes on to repeat that his condemnation of it was not due to its dealing with a subject belonging to a distant time and country. Critics are wrong, he says, to urge poets to forsake such subjects in favour of modern ones. An action which is excellent for poetic purposes may be either modern or ancient. In either case, however, it must be such as to appeal powerfully 'to the great primary human affections: to those elementary feelings which subsist permanently in the race, and which are independent of time.' Even so, poets should remember that the Greeks, 'with their exquisite sagacity of taste', felt that a modern action was 'too much mixed up with what was accidental and passing, to form a sufficiently grand, detached, and self-subsistent object for a tragic poem'; such an action, they felt, would be more appropriately treated in lighter verse.

So the poet must above all choose an excellent action for his poem, rejecting the advice of those who would, by encouraging him to make his poem a 'true allegory of the state' of his 'own mind', foster a romantic subjectivism in him. Arnold urges him to frequent the ancients, for they can teach him three indispensable things: 'the allimportance of the choice of a subject; the necessity of accurate construction; and the subordinate character of expression'. In practice, nineteenth-century critics deny the third of these and ignore the other two. 'They will permit the Poet to select any action he pleases, and to suffer that action to go as it will, provided he gratifies them with occasional bursts of fine writing, and with a shower of isolated thoughts and images.' The influence even of Shakespeare himself can help to seduce a poet into this heresy. So, too, can that of Keats, despite his exquisite genius'. While Arnold nowhere mentions any living English poet in this 'Preface', it seems likely that he had in mind, as a contemporary who had been so seduced, the *'Spasmodic'* Alexander Smith, the first of whose volumes of verse had appeared earlier in 1853.

In an 'Advertisement' to the second edition of his *Poems*, published in 1854, Arnold acknowledged that his doctrines were not directly applicable to lyric poetry. Of the three works which he attempted to write in accordance with them, two, *'Sohrab and Rustum'* and *'Balder Dead'*, are in the epic manner, and the third, *Merope*, is a tragedy.

'Sohrab and Rustum' appears as *'The Death of Sohrab'* in a list of projected poems which Arnold drew up probably in 1851. It is likely that he made slow progress with it at first. Then, in April 1853, he was able to tell Jane that he was writing 'a thing that gives me more pleasure than anything I have ever done yet, which is a good sign'. But school-inspection meant grievous interruptions; and 'whether I shall not ultimately spoil it by being obliged to strike it off in fragments, instead of at one heat, I cannot quite say'. He finished the poem by May 1 and wrote to Clough and to his mother saying that he thought it the best thing he had yet done.

He had originally met the 'very noble and excellent' story in an essay of Sainte-Beuve's. Sir John Malcolm *History of Persia* had then given him further information; Sir Alexander Burnes' *Travels into Bokhara* had helped him to orientalize the poem; and, as was consistent with the programme he was subsequently to draw up in his 'Preface', he had leaned heavily on Homer in attempting to give the work an epic quality.

It would not be grossly unjust to call *'Sohrab and Rustum'* a superbly accomplished piece of academic verse. Its dignity, genuine but rather self-conscious, is the product of a deliberate design to present an excellent action worthily in the Homeric style. Arnold himself suspected that his verse had not the rapidity, though he hoped that it had the fluidity, of Homer's; eventually, he came to think it too Miltonic. Moreover, twenty-two developed similes are rather more than Homer would easily have allowed himself in a passage of fewer than nine hundred lines; it may be that, in introducing so many, Arnold was succumbing to some extent to the very heresy which he denounced in his *'Preface'*. But in the main his poem is Homeric enough.

Twice at least it transcends mere literary virtuosity. The fight between the father and the son, like that on the 'darkling plain', is fought between 'ignorant' opponents—ignorant in this instance of the relationship which binds them.

> And you would say that sun and stars took part
> In that unnatural conflict; for a cloud
> Grew suddenly in Heaven, and dark'd the sun
> Over the fighters' heads; and a wind rose
> Under their feet, and moaning swept the plain,
> And in a sandy whirlwind wrapp'd the pair.
> In gloom they twain were wrapp'd, and they alone;
> For both the on-looking hosts on either hand
> Stood in broad daylight, and the sky was pure,
> And the sun sparkled on the Oxus stream.

During an interval, Sohrab proposes peace to his 'fierce' father. Rustum retorts:

> Girl! nimble with thy feet, not with thy hands!
> Curl'd minion, dancer, coiner of sweet words!

Is it fanciful to hear in these lines the voice of Dr. Arnold reproving the flippancy of young Matthew? Psychological criticism is often absurdly irrelevant, but in this instance a psychological explanation does seem to be called for. *'Sohrab and Rustum'* is, I suggest, from one point of view an imaginative projection of the conflict between Arnold and his formidable father who had died over ten years earlier. From this source, unrecognized presumably by Arnold himself, it derives much of the power which distinguishes it from the more completely objective *'Balder Dead'* and *Merope.*

As is natural, this power is most evident at the climax of the poem, in the description of the fight. In detail, this is Homeric. But Arnold has sharply visualized the whole affair, and he presents it directly, exactly, and vividly. Similes, elsewhere often very fully—and sometimes very charmingly—developed, are here forbidden to run beyond three or four lines each; and the language has an economy and a force frequently lacking in the long speeches which make up so much of the rest of the poem.

The reference to 'the Oxus stream', in the passage quoted, is one of many which, from the second line of '*Sohrab and Rustum*' onwards, prepare us for the fuller description of the river which forms a coda to the episode. In his letters, Arnold repeatedly voices the 'perfect passion for clear water' which he may well have caught from his father. In his poetic landscapes, not only mountains but also streams and the sea have important places. Again and again he writes of the river of life or time and of the sea of eternity; 'The Future' is a conspicuous instance. In '*Sohrab and Rustum*' the Oxus is never explicitly identified with the river of life. But no reader of the poem is likely to deny that it is so conceived in the concluding lines; and that its constant presence is largely responsible for the sense of fatality which broods over the whole work. In this last paragraph there is still much of literary virtuosity—the evocative use of resonant and exotic proper names, for example; nevertheless, the lines do constitute the second important region in which the poem transcends calculable achievement.

> But the majestic river floated on,
> Out of the mist and hum of that low land,
> Into the frosty starlight, and there moved,
> Rejoicing, through the hush'd Chorasmian waste,
> Under the solitary moon;—he flow'd
> Right for the polar star, past Orgunjè,
> Brimming, and bright, and large; then sands begin

To hem his watery march, and dam his streams,
And split his currents; that for many a league

The shorn and parcell'd Oxus strains along
Through beds of sand and matted rushy isles—
Oxus, forgetting the bright speed he had
In his high mountain-cradle in Pamere,
A foil'd circuitous wanderer—till at last
The long'd-for dash of waves is heard, and wide
His luminous home of waters opens, bright
And tranquil, from whose floor the new-bathed stars
Emerge, and shine upon the Aral Sea.

Describing how father and son were destined to engage each other in a single combat ending with the son's loss of 'youth, and bloom, and this delightful world', *'Sohrab and Rustum'* is unmistakably a work which at certain points engaged its author's deepest personal feelings. To this, I have suggested, it owes its superiority to *'Balder Dead'* and *Merope*. Arnold's attempts to select excellent actions such as would appeal 'to those elementary feelings which subsist permanently in the race, and which are independent of time', were quite misguided. It may well be a true critical observation that such actions excel those which appeal only to what is 'accidental and passing'. But is the criterion one which can be safely employed by the poet himself? If it induces him to prefer to a subject which interests him personally another which his critical intelligence tells him is superior but which interests him less, is the result not likely to be precisely the frigid academic versifying which we find in *'Balder Dead'* and *Merope*? From the fate of these *'Sohrab and Rustum'* was saved by the fact that in this instance the excellent action was also one which mattered a great deal more to the poet himself than he knew.

It is easy to sympathize with Arnold's wish to avoid the undisciplined subjectivism of certain of his contemporaries and immediate predecessors. But he attempted too entire an exclusion of subjective factors from the works with which we are now concerned. His artistic success, complete or partial, absolute or relative, in those poems in which he most relied upon symbolic landscapes—Dover, Berkshire, the Oxus—suggests that symbolism offered him the best possible opportunity of concentrating upon the presentation and grouping of objects while not denying himself the power which could only come from the full enlistment of his deepest personal feelings. But Arnold, though in many ways an excellent critic of his own work, did not admit this suggestion. As a result, too much of his work consists of uncreative ruminations and academic exercises. His good poems are regrettably few. Only once did he fully exploit a symbolic landscape in the service of his deeper, Empedoclean impulse; and on that occasion he wrote his one great poem, *'Dover Beach'*.

NOTES

1. A facing of piles and boarding along the bank of a river.
2. He was later the 'R.P.A.' of Sir Edward Elgar *Enigma Variations*.
3. The title of a work by Pierre Simon Laplace (1749-1827), the greatest theoretical astronomer since Newton.
4. Quoted from "'The Youth of Nature'".

2

Transformed Religion: Matthew Arnold and the Refining of Dissent

—David A. Ward

> I am persuaded that the transformation of religion, which is essential for its perpetuance, can be accomplished only by carrying the qualities of flexibility, perceptiveness, and judgment, which are the best fruits of letters, to whole classes of the community which now know next to nothing of them, and by procuring the application of those qualities to matters where they are never applied now.
>
> —Matthew Arnold
> (Preface to Last Essays on Church and Religion)

In chapter 52 of The Pickwick Papers the elderly Tony Weller exacts his revenge on the spindly Mr. Stiggins, "Shepherd" of Emanuel Chapel. Stiggins had led Weller's wife (now dead) into a life of gloomy piety. As Weller's goodhearted son Sam looks on in approval, the old man assaults the preacher savagely.

> [S]eizing the reverend gentleman firmly by the collar, he suddenly fell to kicking him most furiously, accompanying every application of his top-boot to Mr. Stiggins' person with sundry violent and incoherent anathemas upon his limbs, eyes, and body . . . It was a beautiful and exhilarating sight to see the red-nosed man in Mr. Weller's grasp, and his whole frame quivering with anguish as kick followed kick in rapid succession; it was a still more exciting spectacle to behold Mr. Weller, after a powerful struggle, immersing Mr. Stiggins' head in a horse-trough full of water, and holding it there, till he was all but suffocated. (662)

Valentine Cunningham notes that in popular imitations of Dickens' novel such as The Penny Pickwick (1838-42), the violence done to the Stiggins character (here named "Smirkins") is intensified: he is "degraded, pelted, bloodied, muddied, be-sooted and be-greased, horse-whipped, his eyes blackened, his nose dislocated" (227). In a later novel entitled Rosa Fielding (1876)—discussed in Stephen Marcus' Other Victorians (220-38)—he is tarred and feathered and carried into town in a wheelbarrow. No wonder that Anthony Trollope, in a comment on Dickens' scathing representations of religious hypocrisy, himself resorted to the imagery of public retribution; this novelist, he said, "gibbeted cant in the person of the Dissenters" (qtd. in Munson 209). Set against scenes like these, in which physical assault serves as a metaphor for removing the threat posed by religious Dissent to the Victorian body politic—by the simple means of force and exclusion—the calm and civility that Matthew Arnold exhibits in his famous comments on Dissenters in Culture and Anarchy (1869) present, to say the least, a sharp contrast. Culture, Arnold says, enables us to look at things "without hatred and without partiality, and with a disposition to see the good in everybody all around" (87). His celebrated work, as measured in its language as Pickwick is excessive, marks, one might say, a withdrawal from the pillory to the parlour. In it we move from the novelist's concentrated imagery of vengeance and reprisal to the careful tones and ironies of polite argumentation, from a highly visual ritual of abuse to abstractions and social analysis. If Dickens revivifies and circulates virulent eighteenth-century stereotypes of Dissent in order to legitimize the social ostracism he wished on them, Arnold, the self-styled "Liberal of the future," presents them in an entirely different light, in which they appear not as a dark menace to be purged from society but as misguided fellow citizens in need of instruction. This essay traces the emergence of this new mode of representation.

The Dickensian method, to borrow the words of James Wood (in an essay on Flaubert but entirely apt for his English contemporary), relies on "a pressure of detail; . . . of depiction rather than thought or commentary" (38); his is, first and last, a rich art of exteriors, the production of a man who, as George Orwell put it, "lives through his eyes and ears" (48). And since it was through their eyes and ears that Dickens claimed that his readers would be able to clearly recognize the Dissenters in their midst—and steer a wide berth around them—his vivid images of Dissent have, if not literal accuracy on their side, at least a certain measure of logic. What informs Arnold's representations of Dissent is not visible marks of physical difference and deformity but a long train of now-famous abstract formulations—"reason and the will of God," "Sweetness and Light," "the pursuit of perfection," "Hebraism and Hellenism," "our best selves"—all put to service in his case for culture "as the great help out of our present difficulties" (6) and all useful standards for measuring the shortcomings of Dissenters. True culture, he repeatedly tells us, is an inward operation, and the same can be said of his thorough-going appraisal of the nation's non-Anglicans, which is likewise resolutely internal in its focus. It is not a hideousness of appearance but of mental operation that is repugnant. Arnold bids his reader to consider the nation's Philistines (a class, in his thinking, largely synonymous with Dissent): "observe the literature they read, the things which give them pleasure, the words which come forth out of their mouths, the thoughts which make the furniture of their minds. Would any amount of wealth be worth having with the condition that one was to become just like these people by having it?" (52). Nowhere in Culture and Anarchy does one discover what a Dissenter looks like, while in Dickens, one might argue, one finds little else.

This shift in approach has less to do with genre—that is, with the disparate conventions of the novel and the expository essay—than with simply a change in tactics for dealing with Dissent. Arnold, ever the advocate for "seeing things as they are," recognized that the old ways for controlling those outside the Establishment, including the Dickensian desire to effect a kind of internal exile for them in Britain, were no longer tenable. Increasingly pluralistic, British culture in the mid-Victorian years was finding a new place in its workings for previously excluded members. Some went as far as suggesting that Dissenters should be admitted to the Church and that this was the only way in which a truly "national" establishment could be achieved. In a nation extraordinarily mindful of property rights and the sanctities of ownership, granting Dissenters full use of the country's numerous Anglican church buildings and grounds was unthinkable to many—a capitulation to groups with distorted, even fanatical, views of Christianity. One speaker in the House of Lords during debate on simply allowing Dissenters the right to perform their own burial services in parish graveyards proclaimed the idea "impracticable and unjust and offensive"; it was, he declared, a "more rude invasion of the sacred precincts of the churchyard" than he had ever been called upon to consider (Hansard 615, 611).

For others, however, embracing Dissenters was simply an embodiment of the idea that the Church is not an entity distinct from the State, but merely the State in its religious aspect. According to this line of reasoning, as Owen Chadwick puts it, "if citizen and churchman are still to be the same, the church must be extended and altered to include far more of the citizens than the contemporary members of the Church of England" (1: 45). Thomas Arnold, himself an ordained Anglican cleric, had proposed this sort of plan for Church-State unity as early as 1833 in a pamphlet entitled Principles of Church Reform, in which he suggested paring down the Articles of the Church to a few fundamental doctrines framed in non-dogmatic language and allowing worship services not grounded in the Anglican liturgy. A letter of his to the Reverend J. Hearn the following year makes clear the importance he placed upon uniting believers in a single ecclesiastical institution:

> I groan over the divisions of the Church, of all our evils. I think the greatest,—of Christ's Church I mean,—that men should call themselves Roman Catholics, Church of England men, Baptists, Quakers, all sorts of various appellations, forgetting that only glorious name of CHRISTIAN, which is common to all, and a true bond of union. (Stanley 1: 357)

Significantly, though, this apparent willingness to overlook the particulars of religious belief and practice that had separated these various groups for so long coexisted with a decidedly unfavorable assessment of the personality and intelligence of those outside the Church. Opening the doors of the parish to other Christians, therefore, did not necessarily mean putting Anglicanism and other forms of faith on an entirely equal footing. Non-Anglicans still had much to learn, and it was the Anglicans who would do the teaching. "Schism"—that is, willfully separating oneself from the central body of Christian believers—Arnold considered "a great evil," an action "inconsistent with the idea of the perfect Church, to which our aspirations should be continually directed." Anglicans were superior to sectarians in their moral understanding and, as a result, in their social efficacy: "what good is to be done, will be done . . . much sooner by numbers of the Church than by Dissenters" (Letter to the Reverend James Randall, September 20, 1841; qtd. in Stanley 2: 260-61). And in matters of intellect, there was simply no comparison between the two. Arnold declared himself "keenly alive to the mental defects of the Dissenters, to their "narrowness of view, and . . . want of learning and a sound critical spirit" (Letter to James Marshall, January 23, 1840; qtd. in Stanley 2: 184-85). Like his father, Matthew Arnold was willing to accept Dissenters in the Church, where he himself worshiped throughout his life, and was at the same time contemptuous of their ways of thinking and acting. Although his personal faith was much less fixed and dogmatic than that of many of his countrymen—indeed, he became a notorious free-thinker on matters of religion—his support of the State Church was unequivocal. As Stefan Collini notes, the words "national" and "public" always have positive connotations in his texts (72). It is significant that Arnold devoted so many years of his life to work as a civil servant, beginning in 1851 a thirty-five year career as an Inspector of Schools; his willingness to assume such a demanding position, which required long hours and much travel, was surely motivated, at least in part, by his commitment to the attitudes and values inherent in the Establishment and a desire to see them more widely diffused in the national community. Lionel Trilling describes his acceptance of the school inspectorship, which gave him, among other things, a thorough firsthand acquaintance with the culture of Nonconformity, as a "philosophical gesture" (160). And the same might be said of his considerable efforts, fairly late in his career, to produce a new version of the Old Testament book of Isaiah suitable for use in school curricula, the notes to which reveal his preference for a unifying, nondivisive approach to religious teaching (apRoberts 254).

Strong, centralized institutional authority was especially important, Arnold felt, in a time of social and religious factionalism, when an unchecked sectarian impulse threatened to splinter the Christian community into a welter of opposing camps, each mindlessly pursuing the great English enterprise of "doing as one likes," a phrase that echoes throughout Culture and Anarchy. Dissenters like John Angell James of Carr's Lane Chapel were proclaiming that "it is every man's indefensible right, and incumbent duty, to form and to follow his own opinion of the meaning of the word of God" (133). But Arnold believed that by enshrining individual freedom and personal choice without giving due attention to what is accomplished with that freedom and choice, the mid-Victorian nation was becoming mentally and spiritually impoverished, unable to discriminate between worthy goals and worthless claptrap. For many, all that was needed for propositions to be credible was that a person "says them decisively, and has a large following of some strong kind when he says them" (Culture and Anarchy 111). Complaints such as these on Arnold's part evidence not only his well-known anxiety about England's expanding democracy, in the wake of passage of the Second Reform Bill and the Hyde Park riots of 1867, but his uneasiness over phenomena like the Moody and Sankey revivals of the same year and Spurgeon's large Metropolitan Tabernacle (completed in 1861), which was then thriving in London.

And for every large tabernacle, there were many more inconspicuous chapels springing up, each largely unrooted in institutional tradition and unattached to any ecclesiastical hierarchy. Arnold bemoaned this "endless splitting into hole-and-corner churches," whose existence was defined by a stubborn separatist mentality and whose congregants were cut off from the main streams of national life (28); they went about their small worlds of sermons, tea meetings, and petty disputes, blind to any higher notions of beauty and wisdom and to "the variety and fullness of human existence" (14-15). Given Dissenters' increasing numbers, their ignorance and divisive temper of mind were, he believed, doing serious harm to the nation, putting human perfection "farther off out of our reach" and increasing "the confusion and perplexity in which our society now labours" (11). High on their list of specific offenses, in his thinking, was their furious opposition to educational reforms, such as those contained in Sir James Graham's factory bill of 1843, which foundered after debates arose over the nature of the religious instruction it would provide. Furthermore, Dissenters' seeming insensibility to the life of the mind, encouraged by sweeping pulpit pronouncements against fiction and literature, was obviously antithetical to his view of culture as the "great help" for the nation's problems. "Certainly we consider them to be in the main, at present, an obstacle to progress and to true civilization," Arnold declared definitively in St. Paul and Protestantism (74).

But England's historic Church, grounded in order, dignity, and tradition, could have a refining and instructive influence on them. Presumably, the prospect of a rise in social status and increased material prosperity would be sufficient motivation for many Dissenting ministers to join the Church, if it were true, as Arnold frequently asserted, that Nonconformity was shot through with jealousy of the Establishment. But worldly motives notwithstanding, such a union of believers was vitally important: by including Dissenters and by enforcing a certain measure of uniformity in ritual and ceremony—Arnold was less flexible than his father when it came to the external forms of religious worship—the Anglican Church could be a bulwark against the anarchic tendencies of Victorian life. State-sanctioned "unity and continuity in public religious worship" would counter the vulgarizing influence of the proliferation of "ignorant and fanatical little sects" (Last Essays 110, 97). In 1877 Arnold observed that there were over one hundred such groups in Britain, including "Ranters, Recreative Religionists, and Peculiar People" (Last Essays 96), who presented, among other things, an onslaught of bad music (Arnold hated popular Christian hymns) and ridiculous language and imagery. By contrast, the noble forms and time-honored traditions of Anglicanism nourished the mind and spirit in extraordinarily important ways. By participating in historic rituals not of his own making, the Dissenter would not only fulfill his desire for worship but enter a process of mental growth:

> Instead of battling for his own private forms for expressing the inexpressible and defining the indefinable, a man takes those which have commended themselves most to the religious life of his nation; and while he may be sure that within those forms the religious side of his own nature may find its satisfaction, he has leisure and composure to satisfy other sides of his nature as well. (Culture and Anarchy 15)

In his preface to the popular edition of Literature and Dogma (1883), he pronounced, "The Church is necessary, the clergy are necessary; the future of Christianity is hardly conceivable without them" (146). In democratic societies, strong national institutions were indispensable, therefore, not simply for political order but for the greater moral and intellectual good of the nation. Nineteenth-century America was the great monitory example of a people left to themselves—of the backwardness and chaos that result from the open and unregulated expression of ideas in a country without any authoritative arbiters of intelligence and values. It had no Establishment and "no effective centres of high culture" to counter its rampant individualism (Culture and Anarchy 36) and, consequently, it had become a byword for crass materialism and provinciality. Religious movements like Mormonism and Shakerism, which had gained sizeable followings, were prominent manifestations of the unhealthy mental attitudes that were developing, to Arnold's dismay, on both sides of the Atlantic. "America is just ourselves," he observed, "with the Barbarians quite left out, and the Populace nearly" (20); in other words, it was a nation of middle-class Philistines, whose cultural barrenness was matched only by its Puritan rigidity. "From Maine to Florida, and back again, all America Hebraises," he sweepingly pronounced (20), employing his now-familiar dichotomy between the narrow spirit of the Old Testament Jews (Hebraism) and the expansive consciousness of the Greeks (Hellenism), who strove to remove ignorance and to see all things "in their essence and beauty" (135).

But there were edifying examples for England as well. The people of France, unlike their American counterparts, had a keen sense of the national self and of the usefulness of asserting collective authority over the vagaries of individual opinion, as evidenced in their efficient lycee system of education, which Arnold lauded in A French Eton (1864), and their national academy of the arts, a type of institution England conspicuously lacked. France also had, of course, the example of the Roman Catholic Church, which exercised the kind of discipline over private judgment that Arnold found immensely appealing (Culler 110), to say nothing of the aesthetic richness of the French Catholic experience, which contrasted sharply with the drab worship of white-washed English chapels, a way of life "so unlovely, so unattractive, so incomplete, so narrow, so far removed from a true and satisfying ideal of human perfection" (58). Arnold's great fear was that British culture, largely because of the influence of Dissenters, was moving in an American rather than a Continental direction, toward ever-increasing parochialism and complacency rather than the large-mindedness and sophistication he associated with the highest ideals of human living. These latter goals were achievable only with the aid of State-sanctioned corporate entities, including the Church, which could resist the country's strong bent toward "vulgarity, hideousness, ignorance, [and] violence" (Culture and Anarchy 150).

Samuel Lipman is not alone in seeing in Culture and Anarchy "a kind of hymn to the State" (218). Arnold himself declares, with an air of reverence difficult to imagine in a present-day cultural critic, that "the very framework and exterior order of the State, whoever may administer the State, is sacred" (204). But he is careful not to align the centralized power he advocates with a particular class or party. Indeed, throughout the work, he is at pains to argue that the cultural program he advocates operates disinterestedly, outside the realm of party politics; this despite his own relentless exposure of the shortsighted comments and attitudes of numerous public figures, especially those associated with the middle class and religious Dissent, such as the radical politician John Bright, ultra-Protestant firebrands William Murphy and the Reverend W. Cattle, the popular Charles Haddon Spurgeon, and anti-State Church crusader Edward Miall, all of whose names come up repeatedly in Culture and Anarchy. (Tim Marshall refers to Arnold's strategy of "inverted name-dropping," a rhetorical tactic in which he "parades particular individuals, . . . inflecting their names with his meanings" [360].) In Arnold's explaining, the State is a kind of transcendent force, "entrusted with stringent power for the general advantage, and controlling individual wills in the name of an interest wider than individuals" (75); its authority is not centered in any particular class, for no one group—the Barbarians, the Philistines, or the Populace—is adequate to the task of national leadership, fixated as they are on their own narrow allegiances, and lacking as they are in sweetness and light. Arnold's careful sifting of these three classes and their representative figures (the most methodical aspect of a thoroughly unmethodical book) is largely an inventory of their shortcomings, and those positive remarks that do appear tend to be cut short by the kind of barbed generalization one comes to expect in his prose, such as when he follows a discussion of the admirable "manners and dignity" of the aristocracy with the observation that their serenity "appears to come from their never having had any ideas to trouble them" (83-84). For an author whose notion of culture was grounded in "reading, observing, and thinking" (89), not to have any ideas was a serious defect, but it was perhaps less of a hindrance to the cause of culture than that posed by the middle class, whose minds were cluttered with the wrong ideas, including a misguided faith in the value of various liberal reforms, the obsessive pursuit of which tended to crowd out all other concerns and to make public life in Britain an arena of endless strife. Men of culture, on the other hand, were not prisoners of the "ready-made judgments and watchwords" of partisan politics (70), and it is through their example of the intelligent and humane use of knowledge that the country could achieve a worthy government, one that was, as Trilling puts it in his seminal study of Arnold, "above all sects, above all classes, synthesizing their diversities, resolving their conflicts" (186).

The final chapter of Culture and Anarchy, "Our Liberal Practitioners," attempts to demonstrate what can be accomplished by approaching significant social and political issues in a nonpartisan way—by "letting our consciousness play freely and simply upon the facts before us" (195) rather than by deploying conventional party arguments and rhetoric. The issues Arnold discusses have largely faded from view in the twentieth-century; disestablishment of the Irish Church, the Real Estate Intestacy Bill, and marriage to a deceased wife's sister have long ceased to compel interest. But resolving complex public policy debates with "reason and justice" is obviously a continuing challenge for any democratic society, a fact that helps explain Arnold's enduring significance despite the enormous topicality of much of his cultural analysis. A reasoned outlook on the vexed question of the status of the Irish Church, Arnold asserts, would recognize that the best course of action would be to apportion State funds equitably among various Christian groups, given the fact that there were "large and radically divided religious communions in that country" (166-67). (Unlike in England, Anglicans in Ireland were only a small portion of the population.) But this would mean granting Church property to Catholics, something that Dissenters would hardly look kindly upon, because of both their strong aversion to Romanism and their "antipathy to Church establishments" as a matter of principle (167). In order to maintain good relations with Dissenters, whose "obstructive and oppositional activities and sheer noise-making capacities . . . were formidable" (Collini 79), Gladstone's Liberal party in Britain therefore proposed disendowing the Irish Church altogether, that is, removing all State support for religious activity. His policy was dictated not by reason and justice but by crass political opportunism; not by a searching, intelligent examination of the problem but by the stock maxims of Nonconformity: No Popery! No Church Establishments! By not going along with such ill-conceived plans, the man of Culture shows that far from being an effete, ineffectual bystander in the world of public affairs, he is actually involved in operations that are eminently practical in value.

Ostensibly, Arnold's primary goal in writing Culture and Anarchy was to encourage this kind of detached objectivity, the impartiality that was necessary—and that in his view an ideal State might provide—in order to make the nation's communal life more than just a contest of competing ideologies. Jean Gooder has put it succinctly:

> If Arnold has a design on the British public it is to free it from the effects of divisiveness and the exclusive domination by group interests. He wanted

> to enable people to live not from identities given them by circumstance, but from their "best selves"—selves that had acquired a perspective above the local. (8)

For Arnold, centralized authority, administered by enlightened, unbiased citizens of this sort, drawn from all classes, was the only way of establishing a "strict standard of excellence" (109) for the country. Their importance to his vision of a renewed and healthier Victorian society is suggested by the number of unmistakably "Arnoldian" phrases he presses into service when describing them:

> [I]n each class there are born a certain number of natures with a curiosity about their best self, with a bent for seeing things as they are, for disentangling themselves from machinery, for simply concerning themselves with reason and the will of God, and doing their best to make these prevail;—for the pursuit, in a word, of perfection. (108)

This conception of the cultured individual as above the partisan fray—as involved in operations that are not ideologically predisposed one way or another—was a useful one for Arnold's purposes, allowing him to pursue political ends while openly disavowing any such intention. "It is not culture's work or aim," he assured his readers, to enter directly into partisan disputes and "to give the victory to some rival fetish" (Culture and Anarchy 10). P. J. Keating is among those scholars who find such pronouncements on Arnold's part rather disingenuous; no matter how far removed Arnold may seem to be from the day-to-day rough and tumble of English government, Keating asserts, "it is foolish to deny that . . . the driving force behind much of his work is profoundly and deeply political" (229). It would be equally foolish to deny, however, that for the time in which he was writing, this pose of innocent nonpartisanship was a cunning strategy for dealing with Dissent. One suspects that Arnold was just as repulsed by Dissenters as Dickens was. There is certainly a disparity between his public statements about them, which articulate in careful language the concerns of a high-minded citizen, and his private observations to friends and family, in which he appears far less tolerant and kindly disposed toward them. For all their outward deference and humanity, his published representations of Dissent are fundamentally hostile in purpose, designed to thwart their political strength and defeat their worldview. Ruth apRoberts registers surprise that "for a secular and topical book, Culture and Anarchy has a great deal of religious talk" (151), but this seeming incongruity disappears when one recognizes that Arnold's religious objective is central to the text and that the secular ideals and topical references are there precisely because they serve that central objective.

"Certainly we are no enemies of the Nonconformists" (10), Arnold loftily declares in his preface to Culture and Anarchy as he lays out his plan for "develop[ing] their full humanity more perfectly" (11). But in a letter to his publisher he refers to this same preface, which does little besides comment on Nonconformity, as an opportunity "to chaff my enemies" (Letter to George Smith, January 6, 1869; Letters 3: 307), and he made sure that staunch Churchman Benjamin Disraeli was among the influential policymakers who received a copy of it (Letter to Louisa Lady de Rothschild, December 30, 1868; Letters 3: 306). Other comments in his letters confirm, in a remarkably direct way, that despite his talk of "see[ing] the good in everybody all around" and of approaching issues "without partiality" (87), that he had dedicated himself to curtailing the growing power of non-Anglican Christianity. In 1864 he told his mother, Mary Arnold, that he intended "to deliver the middle class out of the hands of the Dissenting ministers" (Letters 2: 282). Other personal remarks from his correspondence are even more sweeping, such as his assertion in 1869 that his feeling of the harm the Dissenting mentality was doing in the nation was "the source of all that I have written on religious, political, and social subjects" (qtd. in Collini 79). A letter to Charles Kingsley, who had praised Culture and Anarchy as "an exceeding wise and true book," makes clear how central Arnold's preoccupation with Dissent was in the genesis of that work:

> The being thrown so much for the last twenty years with Dissenters, and the observing their great strength and their great impenetrability—how they seemed to think that in their "gospel"—a mere caricature, in truth, of the real Gospel—they had a secret which enabled them to judge all literature and all art and to keep aloof from modern ideas—set me thinking how they might be got at . . . (Letters 3: 449)

A year earlier, this proponent of sweet reasonableness had observed, after noting his plans to complete St. Paul and Protestantism, that the "Dissenters will more and more feel that it is war between us, and that what I am doing strikes at the very root of their influence and power" (Letter to Mary Penrose Arnold, September 23, 1869; Letters 3: 366). Here, too, one can see an identity of purpose with Dickens, but if the aims of cultural critic and novelist coincided, their methods, as I have already suggested, were quite divergent. Arnold recognized that Dickens' venomous anti-Dissenting discourse, which is premised on the possibility of physically excluding them from polite Victorian society, was increasingly disconnected from the material facts of everyday life. There was simply no going back to pre-democratic England, when large segments of the population could be denied a role in government, barred from higher education, and compelled (through church rates) to support an Establishment they had no part in—when authority could lay hands on the bodies of Dissenters, quite literally, in order to maintain existing hierarchies of privilege. Novels like The Pickwick Papers and Bleak House, with their resolute attention to the external, physical abnormalities of Dissenters had attempted to replicate this constraining force of institutional authority, to create a population thoroughly convinced of the Otherness of Dissent and of the need to resist in a direct way its presence in Victorian society. By making the deviance of Dissenters a matter of outward display, Dickens not only strengthened the notion that theirs was an alien, un-English identity (in the same way that the physical traits of Jews were thought to be evidence of their foreignness) but he also gave credence to the idea that they could, as a practical matter, be readily distinguished in public and hence easily eliminated from polite circles. Arnold, too, hoped that the rising influence of Dissent might yet be contained, and he even seems quite sympathetic at times to the usefulness of racial categories (as evidenced, for example, in his book On the Study of Celtic Literature [1867]), but he knew that his ends would likely not be achieved by attempting to enforce a religious quarantine of the sort that had prevailed in previous generations; Dissenters were simply too numerous and, by the 1860s, too thoroughly represented in British politics and society for isolation to be a viable tactic. Another strategy had to be found. His best hope was to remake them in his own image, to encourage their broader participation in the universities and the Church—under the courteous guise of simple humanitarian concern—and let the modern, secularizing impulses of those institutions (as he conceived them) efface Dissenters' outworn rigidities and supernaturalism. His plans for Dissent, therefore, went hand in hand with his efforts to nurture an Anglicanism that was unattached to conventional orthodoxy. And thus the program of Culture and Anarchy, which appeared in 1869, led directly to his religious works of the following decade: St. Paul and Protestantism (1870), Literature and Dogma (1873), God and the Bible (1875), and Last Essays on Church and

Religion (1877), in which Culture largely assumes the role of religion, as T. S. Eliot and many other scholars have been quick to point out (351). In other words, Arnold could conceive of Dissenters having full standing as citizens and Churchmen in the Victorian nation—provided they stopped thinking and acting like Dissenters. His representation of them, thus, centers upon a paradox: welcoming them into society was a means of removing them from society. The price of acceptance was the loss of identity.

In short, in Arnold a new discursive strategy for confronting Dissent emerges, grounded not in a rhetoric of repression, like Dickens', but in a rhetoric of assimilation. The Dissenter is no longer an abhorrent and misshapen monstrosity to be forever exiled from English culture but rather a wayward citizen who must be re-educated and re-fitted for a role in national life; he is not a stranger to be repulsed but a patient to be restored. Dickensian banishment gives way to Arnoldian therapeutics: "ousted they will not be, but transformed" (37); their lives are blighted by narrowness, but we "wish to cure it" (23).

Accordingly, the temper of Arnold's texts concerning Dissent is altogether different from Dickens', most notably in their pose of charity and compassion. For beneath the comic and ironic elements in Arnold's prose (or what he called his "persiflage"), there is a bedrock of serious intent and earnest argument; what is most memorable is not the colloquialisms and deft humor (e.g., his recounting of "Mrs. Gooch's Golden Rule" and "Mr. Murphy's lectures") but the elevated ideals of his work, as suggested by his famous chapter titles ("Sweetness and Light"; "Doing As One Likes"; "Barbarians, Philistines, Populace"; "Hebraism and Hellenism"; "Porro Unum Est Necessarium"; "Our Liberal Practitioners"). For all his commentary on the sermonizing of Dissenters, Arnold can wax homiletic himself at times: the program of culture, he observes, "moves by the force, not merely . . . of the scientific passion for pure knowledge, but also of the moral and social passion for doing good" (45). It is grounded in "the love of our neighbour, the impulses towards action, help and beneficence, the desire for removing human error, clearing human confusion, and diminishing human misery, the noble aspiration to leave the world better and happier than we found it" (44). It is my argument that high-minded statements such as these by Arnold need to be taken at more than face value. They need to be read in the broader context of his hostility toward Dissent and with an awareness that his seeming benevolence actually furthered a malevolent intent, at least as it concerned that standing and influence of Dissenters in Victorian society.

These encouragements to altruism, it is important to note, were directed primarily at the influential members of society whom Arnold regarded as his main audience (Keating 212), rather than Dissenters themselves or the public at large. Dickens writes, invariably, for the common Englishman, whose revulsion at Dissent, he hoped, would block its advance in British culture, but Arnold sets for himself a quite different task: to persuade the national elite, with whom he was well acquainted—royalty, Parliamentarians, Churchmen, authors, and the like—that inclusion of Dissenters in a more broadly conceived Establishment was in the country's best interests—and the best way of dealing with the problem of Dissent. Hence, the complex tone and style of Culture and Anarchy—Geoffrey Tillotson speaks of its "opposed aesthetic constituents" (56) and Jean Gooder of its "posturings ranging from knock-about clowning to the solemnities of the sacerdotal" (6)—for in his scheme Arnold must demonstrate both the deficiencies of Dissent and its worthiness for reclamation; both the damage its absurd divisiveness inflicts and the benefits of national unity. These dual purposes perhaps help account for the appellation "elegant Jeremiah," which a contemporary critic had applied to him, which aptly suggests, says James A. Berlin, "that even as Arnold criticizes and questions, he is trying to charm" (35). Throughout the work, the idea of acting decisively upon Dissenters—to "extirpate" their provincialism (22)—must be made palatable to his readers through the language of "right reason" and Christian charity; the curtailing of their power must be seen as a byproduct not of crass worldly motives but the enlightened ideals of sweetness and light. If Culture and Anarchy is indeed "a skillfully improvised, virtuoso performance" (Marshall 360), nothing is more brilliantly handled in it than his highly calculated representation of religious Dissent.

One looks in vain for any grain of goodness in the religious outcasts that Dickens fashions. But Arnold's discourse, although thoroughly convinced of the defects of Dissenters, does not present them as paragons of corruption. In fact, he is at pains, at times, to remind his readers of their merit and potential. Dissenters make up, he says, "a large part of what is strongest and most serious in this nation, and therefore attract our respect and interest" (11); their convictions contain that which is "solid and respectable" (28). America, the great embodiment of the Dissenting mindset (particularly in its fetishism of individual opinion and its aversion to institutional authority), is nonetheless a land of "energy and fine gifts" (19). Spurgeon is a man capable of eloquence (168). Even Edward Miall, whose campaign to disestablish the Anglican Church was anathema to Arnold—and whose newspaper The Nonconformist represented, in his view, Nonconformity at its worst—receives a nod of courtesy as "a personage of deserved eminence among the political Dissenters" (87).

The positive remarks that Arnold makes are calculated to give his text an air of even-handedness, so that the strong criticism that he does offer appears as the judicious assessment of a dispassionate observer of the English scene—rather than a bald assertion of authority. Only by a "sinuous, easy, unpolemical mode of proceeding," he had noted in a letter a few years earlier, "could one hope to gain access in a country such as ours" (Letter to Mary Penrose Arnold, December 7, 1864; qtd in Letters 2: 354). The "access" he hoped to gain, of course, was not primarily to the country as a whole—large segments of which, he knew, would be deaf to his entreaties—but to those in a position to do something about the problems he describes. And his defining of those problems, as they related to the nature of Dissent, had to make clear that they were curable ones.

If Dickens had sought to manifest the malign power present in Dissent, its contaminating influence (figured visually in yellowed complexions and groaning, gyrating bodies), the burden of Culture and Anarchy is to demonstrate what is crucially absent in its character. Again and again in the essays that make up this work, Arnold calls attention to that which is lacking in Dissent, and, as a consequence, the nation as a whole. If Culture ("the best that has been thought and said in the world") is the great help out of England's present difficulties, promoting, as it does, "a stream of fresh and free thought upon our stock notions and habits" (6) and working inwardly to perfect our humanity, Dissenters are the signal examples of those without it. They have given so much attention to the religious side of human life that all other aspects have been neglected:

> But we have got fixed in our minds that a more full and harmonious development of their humanity is what the Nonconformists most want, that narrowness, one-sidedness, and incompleteness is what they most suffer from; in a word, that in what we call provinciality they abound, but in what we may call totality they fall short. (12)

Arnold sounds this note of absence repeatedly. Dissenters' demands for disestablishment, he says, "seem at first a little like that proposal of the fox, who had lost his own tail, to put all the other foxes in the same case by a general cutting off of tails" (16). Dissent's churches are marked by their "insufficiency" (148). They are "without great men, and without furtherance for the higher life of humanity" (29). America, steeped in Hebraism, falls short in "general intelligence." The language of Reverend Edward White (a Congregationalist minister) is "devoid of all real solidity" (23). Martin Luther, the great Philistine genius, had a "lack of spiritual delicacy" (30). These are all shortcomings, of course, that in Arnold's view, the Established Church was eminently capable of addressing. As a host of critics have pointed out, Arnold not only urges the adoption of a flexible, humane spirit as a remedy for these ills; he illustrates it in the sort of text he produces and the authorial persona he creates. As Stefan Collini observes, "he embodied, as well as recommended, the virtues of a certain cast of mind" (2); what he promotes is conveyed "by example rather than description" (Holloway 243); he is "himself the sweetness and light of which he speaks" (Gooder 15). John P. Farrell puts it most simply: Arnold "is what he advocates" (128). What these and other critics have largely neglected to point out, though, is that Culture and Anarchy not only enacts a certain way of reading and thinking; it enacts a certain way of reading and thinking about the Bible. That is, it trains its readers in the kind of perceptive, open-minded, and intelligent handling of texts that Arnold believed was essential for a right (i.e., liberal) interpretation of Scripture. Thus, even the rhetorical techniques of Culture and Anarchy—e.g., its topicality and contemporary idiom, its shifting, unsystematic organization, and its use of repeated phrasings ("our best selves," "sweetness and light," "the study of perfection," etc.)—are intimately linked to Arnold's desire to curtail the growing influence of Nonconformity. Culture and Anarchy is topical, unsystematic, and indefinite largely because the Bible, he believed, demonstrated these qualities as well. By inculcating habits of mind in his audience attuned to these complexities of language, he hoped to create an Establishment that was inhospitable to the narrow literalism of Dissenters. In short, Arnold's undermining of Nonconformity is accomplished not simply through direct statements about them, but, obliquely, through language intended to replicate the elusive, indefinite qualities of the Bible. This is not to say that Arnold was somehow placing his achievement on an equal plane with Holy Writ, but simply that his text calls for the same sort of educated understanding and mental agility in its audience. Culture and Anarchy resists a Dissenting reading.

For this point to register fully, more needs to be said than has been thus far in this essay about Arnold s view of Christianity and Anglicanism. For Arnold the value of the Establishment—and the faith it embodied—was eminently practical:

> I regard the Church of England as, in fact, a great national society for the promotion of what is commonly called goodness, and for promoting it through the most effectual means possible, the only means which are really and truly effectual for the object: through the means of the Christian religion and of the Bible. (Last Essays on Church and Religion 65)

Implicit in this statement is what is perhaps the central idea of Arnold's voluminous religious writings, namely, that the essence of Christianity is experience, not doctrine: right religion consists of righteous living, or "goodness," after the example of Jesus Christ rather than the embracing of a certain set of abstract, narrowly defined propositions about deity and the condition of mankind. Scripture is to be read, in other words, not as a register of theoretical statements about the Godhead—a textbook divulging a complex theology and metaphysics—but as lofty poetry, earnest but imprecise attempts by Jews in ancient and later days to come to terms with "that vast not ourselves which transcends us" (Literature and Dogma 409). To understand the Bible correctly, Arnold asserted, in a frequently quoted passage of Literature and Dogma, one must recognize that its language is "fluid, passing, and literary, not rigid, fixed, and scientific" (152). In its striving for God, Israel "had but poetry and eloquence and no system" (188); Scripture is the emotive, inexact expression of a Semitic people, and it is only an Anglo-Saxon man of business who could have turned its rhetorical figures into technical jargon, its beautiful spirituality into a repelling "machinery of covenants, conditions, bargains, and parties-contractors" (St. Paul 14). This "heavy-handed Protestant Philistine," says Arnold, is "the interpreter in whose slowly relaxing grasp we still lie." "Sincere, gross of perception, prosaic, he saw in Paul's mystical idea of man's investiture with the righteousness of God nothing but a strict legal transaction, and reserved all his imagination for Hell and the New Jerusalem" (Literature and Dogma 70). The "scientific," anthropomorphizing approach to the Bible, which informs orthodox theology and which finds in the Scriptural narrative, grounds for believing in a literal heaven and hell and a divine scheme of redemption and eternal salvation, is a colossal blunder, an "immense misunderstanding of the Bible" (279), an "artificial religion" (195). Interpreting Scripture as an authentic record of external events is a doomed enterprise, for miracles do not happen, and Bible prophecy is simply an illusion. In time, they will go the way of other exploded myths; supernatural occurrences "will drop out, like fairies or witchcraft, from among the matters which serious people believe" (324). Fantastic events, such as the anticipated Second Coming of Christ and the setting up of a glorious New Kingdom for believers, he termed Aberglaube, or "extra belief" (212), i.e., unfounded teachings attributable to misinformed followers of Christ, not Christ himself, who, Arnold assures us, never dealt in eschatology or "speculative theory" of any sort (297).

True spirituality is this-worldly in its focus, and it is as much emotional in its content as intellectual and logical, notwithstanding the vast tracts of scholarship and commentary that have accumulated around Christianity over the centuries in abstruse debates over church government, the nature of the eucharist, baptism, and countless other topics. As Arnold declared in St. Paul and Protestantism, "the Church exists, not for the sake of opinions, but for the sake of moral practice" (97), and his famous definition of religion as "morality touched by emotion" echoes this view. It is the natural truth of the Bible that is all important, what it tells us about human nature and the obligations of our social existence in the here and now. In the text of Scripture one can discern one's ethical responsibilities and the pattern for achieving a "higher self." For all their differences, Calvinism and Methodism both go awry, in Arnold's view, by failing to recognize this emphasis. They make divinity rather than humanity their all-consuming focus, placing all their weight "on the assertion of certain minutely described proceedings on God's part, independent of us, our experience, and our will" (St. Paul and Protestantism 18-19).

Arnold does say many things that conservative Christians, including Calvinists and Methodists, would agree with. He asserts, for example, that we achieve peace and happiness as human beings only when we subdue our selfish impulses—when we severely discipline our bodily appetites and govern our passions. And he presents Jesus Christ as the great exemplar of this kind of productive self-denial; by "identifying ourselves" with Christ, sympathizing with him fully in heart and mind, and striving after righteousness, we can realize a transformed life. In this process no mortal weakness is beyond control, as

Arnold explains in an exhortatory passage that would be at home in even the most orthodox of Christian devotionals: "Never mind how various and multitudinous the impulses are; impulses to intemperance, concupiscence, covetousness, pride, sloth, envy, malignity, anger, clamour, bitterness, harshness, unmercifulness. Die to them all, and to each as it comes! Christ did" (St. Paul and Protestantism 48).

When Arnold speaks of the value of the death of Christ, however, he is invariably attaching a rhetorical signification to that term rather than a literal one. And the same can be said of his use and understanding of other central Christian concepts, such as "Adam's Fall," "resurrection" and "eternal life," which in their original use among the Jewish people were figurative in their signification. Christ's "death," as it is important for believers, is not a physical event but a spiritual one, a restraining of "every self-willed impulse blindly trying to assert itself," a complete governing of the "motions of unrighteousness" (St. Paul and Protestantism 47). Likewise, his "resurrection" is not a magical, supernatural occurrence resulting in an empty tomb but rather a rebirth into righteousness by mortifying the deeds of the flesh; if we cultivate the spirit of Christ in our own lives, then "eternal life begins for us" (53). We ascend not to an everlasting home in the skies but to an existence so qualitatively different from our previous one that it is a heaven for us here on earth.

Culture and Anarchy, which, as already noted, led directly to Arnold's religious writings of the 1870s, seems to duplicate some of the qualities of mind and language that he associates with the Bible. To confront his work is to confront some of the same quandaries of reading and questions of interpretation that Scripture presents. If it is true, for example, that the language of the Gospels is "not all of the speaker's own, and invented by him for the first time, but . . . full of reminiscence and quotation" (qtd. in Riede 20), the same might be said of Arnold's work, which makes frequent use of the words of others and roots itself, like Scripture, in the images and idioms of its own culture. The topicality of Culture and Anarchy, which led F.R. Leavis to dismiss Arnold's work as essentially "pamphleteering," is, in other words, part and parcel of its religious design. His colloquial turns of phrase and sarcastic banter, citation of popular journalism and public figures, and immersion in mid-Victorian controversies make for a text that is idiosyncratic and culturally embedded to a remarkable degree, despite the high seriousness of its stated purpose to advocate Culture as a means of societal redemption. Arnold complains in Literature and Dogma of the tone-deaf, uninformed reading habits of modern dogmatists, who "are not conversant enough with the many different ways in which men think and speak" (316). Part of the task of the educated reader, he felt, was to be sensitive to the ways in which all texts, including the Bible, are shaped by contemporary pressures at the time of their writing. Culture and Anarchy foregrounds this process by resorting, at virtually every turn in its argument, to items close at hand for an English audience in 1869, its popular quips and politicians' gaffes, the inanities of the press, and, above all, the wooden-headedness of Dissent.

Another lesson to be learned, of course, is that language is not always exacting and precise—or subsumable into a coherent system of some sort. The Western, Puritan mind does violence to the Bible when it presses its tentative, emotional words, which were "thrown out at an object of consciousness not fully grasped" (Literature and Dogma 189), for logical and intellectual consistency. Poetry must be read as poetry, not made to serve an artificial ideological agenda that turns the language of "approximate figure" into "scientific definition." Culture and Anarchy forces its reader into the former mode of apprehension, refusing to articulate clear definitions of its central terms and to present its thought in a rigorously organized form. T. S.

Eliot famously complained of its vagueness and "circular flights" of reasoning (as did many of Arnold's contemporaries). "Nothing in his prose work . . . will stand very close analysis," he observed, "and we may well feel that the positive content of many words is very small" (346). Anthony Lane is a bit more blunt: "no one, least of all the author himself, has ever been able to decide what [Arnold] means by the word `culture'" (75). For Arnold, however, this seeming obtuseness was far from unintentional; for his work is quite powerful without sharp definitions, and its slippery, unsystematic form would, he hoped, lead his many readers away from the overly rigid approach to Scripture characteristic of Dissenters. In Literature and Dogma he reminds his readers that the "rules of criticism" that apply to other books apply to the Bible as well. For our understanding of Arnold and his attitude toward Dissent, we might remember an inverted form of this principle: the rules of criticism that apply to the Bible apply to Culture and Anarchy as well.

REFERENCES

apRoberts, Ruth. *Arnold and God.* Berkeley: U of California P, 1983.

Arnold, Matthew. *Culture and Anarchy.* 1869. Ed. J. Dover Wilson. Cambridge: Cambridge UP, 1932.

——.*Last Essays on Church and Religion.* 1877. In *Essays Religious and Mixed.* Vol. 8 of *The Complete Prose Works of Matthew Arnold.* Ed. R. H. Super. Ann Arbor: U of Michigan P, 1972. 9-162.

——.*The Letters of Matthew Arnold.* Ed. Cecil Y. Lang. 4 vols. Charlottesville: UP of Virginia, 1997.

Baines, Edward. *Education Best Promoted By Perfect Freedom.* Victorian Nonconformity. London: Edward Arnold, 1973. 131-34.

Berlin, James A. "Matthew Arnold's Rhetoric: The Method of an Elegant Jeremiah." *Rhetoric Society Quarterly.* 13.1 (1983): 29-40.

Chadwick, Owen. *The Victorian Church.* 2 Parts. London: Adams and Charles Black, 1966.

Collini, Stefan. *Matthew Arnold: A Critical Portrait.* Oxford: Clarendon Press, 1988.

Cunningham, Valentine. *Everywhere Spoken Against: Dissent in the Victorian Novel.* Oxford: Clarendon Press, 1975.

Eliot, T.S. "Arnold and Pater." *Selected Essays: 1917-1932.* New York: Harcourt, 1932. 346-57.

Farrell, John P. "`What I Want the Reader to See': Action and Performance in Arnold's Prose." *Matthew Arnold in His Times and Ours: Centenary Essays.* Eds. Clinton Machann and Forrest D. Burt. Charlottesville: UP of Virginia, 1988. 123-34.

Gooder, Jean. "Matthew Arnold and the Idea of the Modern." *Cambridge Quarterly.* 24.1 (1995): 1-16.

Hansard Parliamentary Debates. Third Series. 15 May, 1876.

Keating, P.J. "Arnold's Social and Political Thought." *Writers and Their Background: Matthew Arnold.* Ed. Kenneth Allott. London: G. Bell and Sons, 1975. 207-35.

Lane, Anthony. "Poetry and Principle: Why Did the Muse Leave Matthew Arnold?" *The New Yorker.* 1 February 1999: 74-79.

Leavis, F.R. "Revaluations (XI): Arnold as Critic." *Scrutiny.* 7 (December 1938): 319-32.

Lipman, Samuel. "Why Should We Read Culture and Anarchy?" *Culture and Anarchy by Matthew Arnold.* Ed. Samuel Lipman. New Haven: Yale UP, 1994. 213-27.

Marshall, Tim. "Culture and Matthew Arnold's `Condition of England' Discourse in Culture and Anarchy." *QWERTY: Arts, Literatures & Civilisations du Monde Anglophone.* 5 (October 1995): 359-66.

Munson, James. *The Nonconformists: In Search of a Lost Culture.* London: SPCK, 1991.

Orwell, George. *Dickens, Dali, and Others: Studies in Popular Culture.* New York: Reynal and Hitchcock, 1946.

Riede, David. *Matthew Arnold and the Betrayal of Language.* Charlottesville: UP of Virginia, 1988.

Stanley, Arthur Penrhyn. *The Life and Correspondence of Thomas Arnold,* D.D. 2 vols. London: B. Fellowes, 1844.

Trilling, Lionel. *Matthew Arnold.* 2nd ed. New York: Columbia UP, 1949.

Trollope, Anthony. *Clergymen of the Church of England. 1866.* Leicester UP, 1974.

Wilson, J. Dover. Introduction. *Culture and Anarchy by Matthew Arnold.* Cambridge: Cambridge UP, 1932. vii-xl.

Winston, Diane. *Red-Hot and Righteous: The Urban Religion of the Salvation Army.* Cambridge, MA: Harvard UP, 1999.

Wood, James. "Half-Against Flaubert." Rev. ed. Gustave Flaubert: *Selected Letters.* Trans. Geoffrey Wall. *New Yorker* 18 Jan. 1999: 37-42.

3

Arnold Among the Neoconservatives

—Eugene Goodheart

In 1994 Yale University published a new edition of Matthew Arnold's Culture and Anarchy edited by Samuel Lipman, the late publisher of the neoconservative periodical The New Criterion. The edition includes essays that are not of a neoconservative cast (for instance, those of Steven Marcus and Gerald Graff), but Lipman's essay suggests a special affinity between Arnold and the neoconservatives.

It is not hard to see why Matthew Arnold has become the intellectual property of the neoconservatives: he stands or seems to stand for all the values denigrated by the cultural left: disinterestedness, aesthetic autonomy, authority (the original title of Culture and Anarchy was Authority and Anarchy). Arnold is a good source for those who wish to combat leftwing cant, surpassed only by George Orwell. And he provides support for conservative vigilance about social unrest. One might expect a neoconservative to view the underclass of the contemporary inner city in much the same way as Arnold saw the working class of nineteenth-century England: "raw and half-developed . . .

long lain half-hidden amidst its poverty and squalor . . . now issuing forth from its hiding place to assert an Englishman's heaven-born privilege of doing as he likes, meeting where it likes, bawling what it likes, [and] breaking what it likes" (Culture, 71). This is the Arnold of law and order, concerned only with the effect of anarchy upon society, who could quote with approval his father's words: "As for rioting, the old Roman way of dealing with that is always the right one, flog the rank and file, and fling the leaders from the Tarpeian Rock" (Culture, 135).

There is, of course, another Arnold, whose compassion for the poor moved him to indignation. In "The Function of Criticism at the Present Time," Arnold answers the triumphalists of the Industrial Revolution (avatars of our own neoconservatives) with a murmuring refrain "Wragg is in custody." Against the trumpeting of "our unrivaled happiness" by the eulogists of the Industrial Revolution, Arnold evokes a scene of "grimness, bareness, and hideousness . . . the workhouse, the dismal Mapperly Hills, — how dismal those who have seen them will remember; — the gloom, the smoke, the strangled illegitimate child!" (Selected Essays, ed. Noel Annan [Oxford UP, 1964], 31).

The illegitimate child is still with us and in great numbers. The neoconservative refrain is louder than a murmur, and the target of its wrath is the welfare state. Of course, it is not the welfare state that created Wragg, but a version of the unregulated industrial system that the neoconservatives promote. The neoconservatives speak of moral responsibility and exhort us to, read and practice The Book of Virtues. So did the Victorian critics. But the object of their moral passion was quite different from that of our conservatives. Arnold found moral irresponsibility in all the classes: aristocratic, middle, and working. The cardinal sin of the upwardly mobile middle class (Arnold's principal audience) was and still is its passion for accumulating wealth. The neoconservative ethic revives the Calvinist gospel mercilessly exposed by George Eliot in her characterization of Bulstrode in Middlemarch, a gospel glorifying the virtues of capital accumulation. The Victorian social critics viewed the spirit of laissez-faire (what Arnold disparagingly called "doing as one likes" and what modern conservatives approvingly call "the free market") as destructive of the moral fabric of society.

In matters of politics, it may be more accurate to speak of an opposition between the neoconservatives and the Victorian critics. Arnold affirms the state as an expression of the best self, and Samuel Lipman, from his conservative perspective, is quick to note a failure in Arnold "to see that the state bore within itself a monstrous tyranny" ("Why Should We Read Culture and Anarchy?" in Culture, 225). Lipman has in mind modern totalitarianism in its Nazi and Stalinist incarnations. Of course, the threat in Arnold's time was not totalitarianism, but the misery of the masses. The captains of industry did not offer a solution to the social problem and neither did civil society, the intermediate institutions like the church that stand between the person and the state.

In turning to the State, Arnold, Carlyle, and Ruskin left an ambiguous legacy: on the one hand, a law and order rhetoric that liberals and radicals find repressive and on the other, a justification for necessary political reforms like the regulation of child labor, social security (all the components of the welfare society that constitute the safety net). Staunch supporters of law and order, the conservatives have as their real target the tyranny that might result from revolutionary or even reformist passion. "The conservative revolution," the mantra of Newt Gingrich and his cohort, is an unremarked oxymoron. Conservative arguments against state intervention to create social reform tend to abuse the metaphor of the slippery slope. It is not true that the logic of social welfare is tyranny or, worse, totalitarianism. The Environmental Protection Agency is not the Gestapo, potentially or actually, as a Republican member of the Congress recently asserted.

In their attack on the travestics of the cultural left (its ways of politicizing all discourse), the neoconservatives have adopted the stance of disinterestedness. Lipman cites with approval Arnold's caveat to the cultured individual: "Neither . . . is public life and direct political action permitted to him. For it is his business . . . to get the present believers in action, and lovers of political talking and doing, to make a return upon their own minds, scrutinize their stock actions and habits much more, value their present talking and doing much less; in order that, by learning to think more clearly, they may come at last to act less confusedly" (Culture, 164-65). Lipman then goes on to chastise Arnold for compromising this admirable ideal by uncritically affirming the state. But shouldn't the same strictures apply to the neoconservatives who have uncritically adopted the stock habits of thought associated with free market capitalism?

One doesn't have to agree with the cultural left that the claim to disinterestedness is always a case of ideological mystification to suspect the neoconservative defense of it. The tendentiousness of neoconservatism reveals itself in the way that it defends the Western literary canon. It is not enough, for instance, that Harold Bloom defends it; for a neoconservative like Peter Shaw its defense must also mean, as it does not for Bloom, a defense of the West and its tradition of what he calls rational thought (see "Pseudo-Reform in the Academy," Partisan Review 1 [1996]:94-106). But the canon is not a homogeneity of rational" thinking. (Does Shaw mean rationalist thinking?) It accommodates quarrels between the rationalist Plato and the immoralist Nietzsche, between Enlightenment liberalism and Burkean conservatism, between the Augustan affirmation of Reason and the Romantic celebration of the imagination. The energies of art are often subversive and not easily contained within a canon, which is a term of theological orthodoxy. In "The Function of Criticism at the Present Time," Arnold acknowledges and values what might even be dangerous in the intellectual and imaginative life. "It must be apt to study and praise elements that for the fullness of spiritual perfection are wanted, even though they belong to a power which in the practical sphere may be maleficent" (Selected Essays, 39). The fact that liberalism and radicalism have developed their own pieties does not justify an opposing set of pieties.

If we accept Arnold's characterization of the essential activity of the cultured mind as thinking against oneself, an activity imperfectly realized in Arnold's own thought (and one suspects in anyone's thought), we can begin to appreciate how both our cultural left and our cultural right mirror each other in their tendentiousness. Neoconservatives are no more disinterested as social or cultural critics than the ideology critics on the left. They have given themselves over to a ruthless politics which promotes a doctrinaire antistatist view in the interests of an unregulated free market, a view anathema to the Victorian social critics, whom they claim to admire. It is impossible and undesirable always to resist the temptations of politics. Arnold himself is proof of the impossibility. But the life of the mind depends upon its refusal to sacrifice itself to the cause of party or ideology.

4

Matthew Arnold's "Tristram and Iseult": Greater Significance than Love and Death

—Laura Lambdin

"Tristram and Iseult" (1852) is Matthew Arnold's only Arthurian work, and Arnold employed the ancient narrative as a veneer for social criticism in much the same manner as did his contemporaries Alfred Tennyson, William Morris, and Algernon Swinburne. These nineteenth-century poets did not attempt to reproduce accurately medieval civilization so much as to express particular moral stances. The inherent emphasis upon extinction caused by ecstasy, or love leading to death, cannot be eradicated from any version of the Camelot tragedy; however, the theme of guilty, fated love can vary in its significance. Certainly the exotic atmosphere is particularly entertaining, but Arthurian Legends, even in the medieval period, have been consistantly used to inspire rather than to amuse.

Arnold, although his approach is more understated, echoes Tennyson's concern with moderation. Still, "Tristram and Iseult" reflects less the Christian didacticism of The

Idylls of the King and displays more simple family concerns. Arnold had little sympathy for the lovers and did not, as did Swinburne in Tristram of Lyonesse, excuse their passion as fated or drug induced. His emphasis upon Iseult of Brittany as an abandoned wife and his invention of her two small children appear intended to reflect the problems that an immoral love creates in the domestic sphere, a love driven by foolish obsessions that gradually consume spirituality. The solution proposed seems to be a retreat into imagination and calming aesthetic pleasures. If individuals learn to distinguish universal themes in art, Arnold's theory may be that their own concerns will be deflected and thereby lessened in importance. As does the hectic pace of life, passion and melancholy both cloud understanding of the value of real familial love. Further, the loss of creativity destroys spirituality, increasing a sense of confinement on earth and decreasing expectations of the afterlife. With a few small alterations, the long unused tale of Tristram and Iseult was resurrected as the ideal conveyor of Arnold's message.

The Tristram legends probably originated in the late eighth-century Pictish kingdom in Scotland. The original Tristram was most likely Drust, son of the Pictish King Talorc, who ruled in Scotland around the year 780.[1] From here, Tristram legends can be traced through Welsh, Cornish, and Breton sources. In one of her lays, Marie de France mentioned Tristram as an ideal lover, and Chretien de Troyes also claimed to have written about the hero, although this work is no longer extant. The earliest surviving long poem about Tristram is a version by Thomas, who wrote at the Plantagenet Court in England after 1150. Thomas was followed by Eilhart von Oberge around 1170, and also by another Norman poet, Beroul, about 1190. Further, from Thomas' Tristan, a condensed version, Sir Tristrem, was composed in Middle English approximately a century later; this is the only other treatment of the subject in Middle English, except for Malory's reworking that comprises about one-third of the Morte Darthur. Over many years, the Tristram romances became very complex, "with comic and tragic, savage and civilized, cynical and idealistic parts."[2]

When Matthew Arnold published "Tristram and Iseult," in Empedocles on Etna, and Other Poems (1852), it was the first English retelling of the story in nearly 400 years. Arnold's poem was followed by Richard Wagner's opera Tristan und Isolde (1865), Tennyson's poem "The Last Tournament" (1872), and Swinburne's poem "Tristram of Lyonesse" (1882). Arnold wrote a letter to Herbert Hill, dated 5 November 1852, in which he explains that his source for the poem was an article in a French journal:

> I read the story of Tristram and Iseult some years ago at Thun in an article in a French Review on the Romance Literature: I had never met with it before, and it fastened upon me: when I got back to England I looked at the Morte d'Arthur and took what I could, but the poem was in the main formed, and I could not well disturb it. If I had read the story first in the Morte d'Arthur I should have managed it differently.[3]

Arnold wrote here that his "poem was in the main formed," but not necessarily that it was even on paper yet. As we shall see, there are many similarities between Arnold's work and Malory's specific version, including several passages that are almost direct quotes; thus, the poet must have been somewhat more influenced by the Morte than his letter would lead one to believe.

Arnold's primary source has been traced to Theodore de la Villemarque's "Les Poems gallois et les Romans de la Table-Ronde," from the Revue de Paris, the third edition of 1841.[4] La Villemarque's outline, which discusses only a small portion of the extant material about Tristram, was mostly followed by Arnold for his poem's plot: Tristram wins the hand of the beautiful Iseult of Ireland for his uncle, King Marc of Cornwall. While Tristram and Iseult are en route to the wedding, they accidentally drink a magic potion created by Iseult's mother for the bride and groom. This powerful drink was intended to ensure an enchanted and eternal love between the married couple. However, since Tristram drinks the potion instead of Marc, he constantly desires Iseult. The Irish princess continues to return Tristram's lust — even after she has married King Marc. When the lovers' liaisons are discovered by the king, Tristram flees to Brittany, where he marries Iseult of the White Hands, yet constantly pines for Iseult of Ireland. He seeks forgetfulness in knightly adventures and is mortally wounded. His wife tends his wounds, but Tristram sends for Iseult of Ireland and he dies in his paramour's arms. Iseult of Ireland falls over the corpse, immediately dying of grief. The lovers are buried together, leaving behind Iseult of the White Hands with her two young children.

Arnold's conclusion is very different from any other treatment of the tale. In La Villemarque's summary, when Iseult of Ireland is told that Tristram is dead, she runs madly through the streets, finds her dead lover, and dies upon Tristram's corpse. Malory, as almost an afterthought following the Grail Quest, significantly after his conclusion to the Trystrame section, eventually related Trystrame's death at the hands of Mark, and La Bealle Isode's subsequent death. Neither of these authors mentioned Iseult of Brittany's existence after her husband's death, nor that the couple produced any offspring. Malory made it clear that the marriage of Trystrame and Isode le Blaunche Maynys was never consummated:

> And soo whanne they were abedde bothe, Sire Tristram remembryd hym of his old lady La Beale Isoud. And thenne he toke suche a thought sodenly

> that he was alle desmayed, and other chere maade he none, but with clyppynge and kyssynge; as for other flesshly lustes, Sire Trystram neuer thoughte nor hadde adoo with her.[5]

Tristram and Iseult's children were Arnold's invention. The poem reflects Arnold as "simultaneously a traditionalist and a radical innovator."[6]

Particularly because Arnold left Iseult of Brittany in this quiet domestic situation, many critics have found the poem to be typical of the author's period. Commentators, who attack the poem as being too Victorian, and lacking sufficient medieval atmosphere or attitudes, find that because Arnold did not understand the real meaning of the story, the poet wrote a domestic tragedy, rather than the high tragedy that he should have written:

> It is obvious that Arnold missed the essential tragic import of the Tristram and Iseult story as we now see it: the tragedy of an overmastering passion . . . in which love transcends all other human relations and in which the lovers are innocent victims of a well-intentioned but accidentally misappropriated magic philtre.[7]

Arnold, like Tennyson, was not a medieval scholar and used his poetic imagination to speak to his own age. However, because much of the original charm of the Tristram legends is absent from the poem, those among Arnold's contemporary critics who knew the older material did not praise the work.[8] Even those Victorian readers who knew little of medieval writing — and were, thus, unlikely to be bothered by modern elements — disliked the work because of its fragmented style of narration.[9]

In addition to frequent mode shifts, from dramatic dialogue to third person narrative to first person reverie, there are also many temporal juxtapositions. Inasmuch as Arnold wrote the first modern version, the love story of Tristram and Iseult was not well known in nineteenth-century England. Readers were likely to become frustrated when they attempted to understand the plot of "Tristram and Iseult," because it is not presented in a linear fashion. Arnold seems to have been purposefully obscure, because he may have been unsure of the details himself. Perhaps, however, the constant sequential disruption was intended to make the actual story less important than the codas at the end of each section, in which the narrator discusses small situational concerns in such a way that they become of universal importance.

Part 1, "Tristram," is 373 lines of mostly trochaic tetrameter written in a ballad manner. Here the injured and delirious hero recalls the highlights of his love affair with Iseult of Ireland. His wife, who has been tenderly nursing his wound, watches and listens nearby. Part 2, "Iseult of Ireland," is 193 lines of dramatic duet in quatrains of alternating trochaic and iambic pentameter, beginning as the lovers are reunited. Their stichomythic conversation ends with their deaths. Part 3, "Iseult of Brittany," is 224 lines of quiet, mature heroic couplets that describe the life, one year after the lovers have died, of the widowed Iseult and her children.[10] This innovative style makes the poem often confusing, "but, even so, its poetical accomplishments are real, and it leaves little doubt but that Arnold could have been one of the major poetic craftsmen in the modern tradition."[11]

Arnold's poem shows little sympathy for Tristram's predicament. The poet's purpose is reflected in the narrator's coda about "how this fool passion gulls men potently" (3.134). Like Swinburne, Arnold could "perceive in the Tristram myth a profound vision of the power of passion in the world";[12] however, unlike the later writer, Arnold did not consider this surrender to love to be ennobling. Further, the poem examines the conditions of life that deaden the human soul. The following sections will discuss these themes as they are demonstrated in each character's speech and actions, particularly as they are seen in each figure's responses to love and death.

TRISTRAM

Iseult of Brittany's quiet life in seclusion was mentioned earlier as an ending that is unique to Arnold's version; even more startlingly different is Arnold's point of entry into the narrative. "Tristram and Iseult" opens with its hero weak, feverish, and ranting on his deathbed. All of the important, courageous, and gallant events of Tristram's early career are subordinated, while the poem concentrates on Tristram in middle age, a pathetic, "fever wasted," knight. A reader is immediately aware that this is not the same character who was glorified in the medieval romances. Speaking excitedly, while in delirium, Tristram recounts four important episodes of his past life. These flashbacks, intermittently explicated by the narrator, serve to emphasize Tristram's degeneration through passion. The first two of these vividly recalled incidents concern his experiences with Iseult of Ireland, while the last two illustrate his haunting memories of the earlier love affair, after his marriage to Iseult of Brittany.

Arnold subordinated these segments of Tristram's early life to expose the effects of his overwhelming passion:

> [T]he first two segments of Tristram's life seem to imply not only the present and past in his life but the present and past of Europe — its past vital, heroic, and unified; its present disintegrating and deriving its only vital power from the spirit of the past. The poem is the work of a man conscious of living in an age of transition.[13]

Arnold's work frequently reflects this unease concerning his era, but nowhere did the poet make this feeling so clear as he did in "The Grand Chartreuse" (1855):

> Wandering between two worlds, one dead, The other powerless to be born, With nowhere yet to rest my head, Like these, on earth I wait forlorn. (85-88)[14]

Arnold sometimes seemed to have had the desire to stand back from reality, watching and waiting for change without facing challenges.[15] This may explain why "Tristram and Iseult" begins in such a detached manner, and why the poem retains this feeling of distance, even through the seemingly unresolved conclusion.

Arnold concentrated on the knight's "waning time," rather than "his resplendent prime" (1.70, 71), to show that the brief joy of the Irish Iseult's love was not worth the price of a lifetime of banishment from Cornwall. Tristram, weak and pale, is unable to use his green hunter's dress and his golden harp, the two items that generally characterize this knight when he appears in medieval romances; these items lie untouched on Tristram's bed, relinquished with his youth. His wife stands by the dying fire, watching and pitying Tristram, as the knight suffers the effects of a tyrannous and obsessive passion. Tristram does not realize that the Iseult he married is even in the room, and he compulsively recounts aspects of his earlier life: Iseult of Ireland asking Tristram to pledge her for courtesy with the drugged wine; the lovers discovered during a winter garden walk, and Tristram fleeing after one last kiss; the brave knight seeking to overcome his passion through challenges and, thereby, being wounded in King Arthur's war against Rome; and Tristram seeking refuge and solace in a forest, only to see Iseult of Ireland's face, when the moonlight shines upon the water of a spring. The narrator's enlargement upon Tristram's ranting is the bulk of Arnold's exposition in "Tristram and Iseult."

Obviously, Arnold's omissions were intended to simplify the material and to focus attention upon Tristram in his last days, but a reader unfamiliar with the story would be likely to misunderstand exactly what is occurring.

Following his fevered recollections, Tristram notices that his wife is in the chamber, and he speaks a few words to her that are much kinder than the heartless ones he spoke to her at the poem's beginning: "Ah! not the Iseult I desire" (1.8). Odd though it seems, Tristram speaks harshly to his lover Iseult when she arrives, weary from her sea voyage:

> Thou art come at last, then, haughty Queen! Long I've waited, long I've fought my fever; Late thou comest, cruel thou hast been. (2. 2-4)

This chilly welcome is no celebration, but proves even more the suffering and agitation caused by an adulterous union. The passion of Tristram and Iseult has long since passed, and there is in the poem no outpouring of ecstasy caused by romantic love. Tristram finally accepts his Queen's arrival, but with a weary questioning of her faithfulness to him.

Iseult of Ireland quickly explains her loyalty to Tristram, but once he is satisfied and relaxed, his death immediately follows. Thus, less than halfway through the poem, the hero departs to his eternal rest, and the remainder of the verses are devoted to the other characters' lives without him. Before Tristram dies, he explains that his doleful life and quick passing were to be expected:

> This is what my mother said should be, When the fierce pains took her in the forest, The deep drafts of death, in bearing me. "Son," she said, "thy name shall be of sorrow; Tristram art thou called for my death's sake." (2. 82-86)

This section distinctly echoes Caxton's Morte in which Trystram's mother, Elyzabeth, says as she is dying after giving birth·

> A, my lytel sone, thou hast murthered thy moder, and therfore I suppose thou that arte a murtherer soo yong, thou arte ful lykely to be a manly man in thyn age. And bycause I shal dye of the byrthe of the, I charge the, gentylwoman, that thou pray my lord Kynge Melyodas that whan he is crystned, lete calle hym Trystram,[16] that is as moch to saye, as a sorouful byrthe.[17]

Although Arnold includes a passage very much like the one in the Morte, his poem does not reinforce Malory's belief that the sorrowful life of Trystram was fated or predestined. The poet also did not particularly stress, as earlier writers did, the idea of Tristram and Iseult's passion being simply the result of their ingestion of the enchanted drink. Indeed, Arnold's narrator yet again, in his maddening way, comments on anything else rather than discuss the exact causes of Tristram's problems. It can easily seem that "Tristram and Iseult" has as many ambiguities as the whole of Tennyson's Idylls. To discover what message Arnold may have intended to portray through the character of Tristram - beyond the idea that passion is deadly - one must examine the other characters.

ISEULT OF IRELAND

Arnold devotes the second part of "Tristram and Iseult" to Iseult of Ireland, "the most passionate heroine he ever conceived."[18] Just as Arnold invented Tristram's brown hair, he assigned raven locks and dark eyes to the Irish princess; this makes her a more perfect foil for Arnold's golden-haired Iseult of Brittany, and therefore, "in the opposition of the two Iseults there is a hint of the classic Victorian concern about the Eve/Mary contrast."[19] The first

Iseult is haughty, beautiful, and full of movement, while the second Iseult is sweet, pale, and static.

Arnold did not overtly judge Iseult of Ireland,[20] but simply showed the effects of the violent sexual passion that "consumed her beauty like a flame, / And dimmed it like the desert-blast" (2.134-35). Marc's Queen arrives at Tristram's bedside full of anguish as well as excuses for her late arrival. She announces that she has been detained in "royal state with Marc, my deep-wronged husband" (2.45). Tristram questions her fidelity since she has been with "silken courtiers whispering honeyed nothings" (2.47). Iseult claims that she has been true to Tristram and equally miserable:

> Ah, on which, if both our lots were balanced, Was indeed the heaviest burden thrown — Thee, a pining exile in thy forest, Me, a smiling queen upon my throne? Vain and strange debate, where both have suffered, Both have passed a youth consumed and sad, Both have brought their anxious day to evening, And now have short space for being glad! (II 49-56)

Both lovers have been wretched while apart, and the reader remains uncertain about how much of their passion stems from natural feelings of love, and how much is the effect of the magic potion. La Villemarque blames their lust entirely on enchantment, and Malory, in his much longer explanation, does the same. Malory, however, constantly refers to the relationship in glorified or exalted terms as a connection bringing enormous bliss to the lovers:

> And to telle the ioyes that were betwixe La Beale Isoud and Sire Tristram, there is no tonge can telle it, nor herte thynke hit, nor penne wryte hit.[21]

Clearly, Arnold's position is the opposte of Malory's.

The lovers do indeed "have now short space for being glad" (2.56); immediately after Iseult has comforted Tristram, he realizes that he is dying. Iseult, despite the immorality of their entire relationship or her pagan association with sorcery, demands that Tristram ask heaven for help: "Call on God and on the holy angels!" (2.79). In the next line, Iseult, more characteristically, for one so lacking in Christian spirituality, utters an oath: "Christ! he is so pale" (2.86). Tristram pleads with Iseult, asking that she not go far from his grave; with this for encouragement, Iseult kisses Tristram and dies with him.

The long-separated, middle-aged lovers have been wasted by passion, but are granted a final tranquil moment in death. The proud, petulant, and imperious Irish Iseult is relieved of the stale court life in which she has been unable to hide her secret:

> And the dames whispered scoffingly: "Her moods, good lack, they pass like showers! But yesternight and she would be As pale and still as withered flowers, And now tonight she laughs and speaks And has a color in her cheeks; Christ keep us from such fantasy!" (2.124-30)

A great change comes over Cornwall's Queen when she is relieved of the tormented passion that has consumed her life and looks. The narrator describes how this release returns her former beauty:

> And though the bedclothes hide her face, Yet were it lifted to the light, The sweet expression of her brow Would charm the gazer, till his thought Erased the ravages of time, Filled up the hollow cheek, and brought A freshness back as of her prime — So healing is her quiet now. (2.136-43)

Iseult of Ireland becomes, with death, more like her former rival, Iseult of Brittany.

It has been noted that the narrator's first line, "What knight is this so weak and pale" (1.9), unmistakably echoes Keats' "La Belle Dame sans Merci."[22] This connection is ended when Iseult of Ireland is destroyed along with her exhausted knight. Part 2 is the most dramatic part of "Tristram and Iseult," and this section is not as good as the others:

> It is the least successful part of the poem, and I think one may say that it is intended to be . . . It presents the fact of a violent sexual passion, and the meaning of the poem consists in the attitude taken up by the poem as a whole toward this fact. As Empedocles spoke and then leaped into the volcano, so the lovers do the only thing left to them to do — die and leave the field to Iseult of Brittany.[25]

Their bodies are taken by ship to Cornwall where they are buried in state by King Marc, who now regrets his having separated the lovers. The final section of the poem barely mentions the lovers, but focuses upon the lonely life of Iseult of Brittany.

ISEULT OF BRITTANY

Arnold treated Iseult of Brittany with unprecedented expansiveness by devoting all of Part 3 of "Tristram and Iseult" to her life without her husband. The reader only once before saw her interact with Tristram, when he awakened from delirium to find that she had been in the chamber, listening to his excited talk about Iseult of Ireland. To her credit, Iseult of Brittany reacts as the perfect Patient Griselda by sympathetically regarding her husband:

> Not with a look of wounded pride, A look as if the heart complained — Her look was like a sad embrace; The gaze of one who can divine A grief, and sympathize. (2.320-24)

Iseult of the white hands is much kinder to her husband in "Tristram and Iseult" than she is in most earlier sources, where we find the incident of the white and black sails: Tristram, dying of a wound from a poisoned lance, sends a messenger to notify Iseult of Ireland that her lover requires that she come to him. So that Tristram can assess the result of his plea from a distance, the messenger is instructed to display a white sail on his return voyage if the Irish Iseult is accompanying him, black if she is not. Iseult of Brittany, finally furious about her husband's long-term affair, overhears the plan; when Tristram asks his wife what color the sails are, she lies in reporting that the sails are black. Tristram dies immediately of a broken heart, and Iseult of Ireland, arriving soon after, expires on his corpse.[24]

This "pitiful malice" felt and acted upon by Iseult of Brittany is not in the Morte;[25] however, it is mentioned, without being fully developed, by La Villemarque. By ignoring this portion of the Tristram legend, Arnold created an Iseult of Brittany devoid of treacherous intentions and one able to arouse the reader to sympathetic feeling. We pity the wife who loved and nursed her husband, bore his children, and yet had to endure his constant obsession with another woman. Iseult of Brittany is presented in the poem before her rival Iseult, and this wife is described by the narrator in words that would particularly appeal to a Victorian audience:

> Who is this snowdrop by the sea? — I know her by her mildness rare, Her snow-white hands, her golden hair; I know her by her rich silk dress, And her fragile loveliness — The sweetest Christian soul alive, Iseult of Brittany. (1.49-55)

Tristram's parting words concerning Iseult of Brittany also reinforce this idea of her as an understanding Christian wife; he tells his lover Iseult to find his wife and "speak her fair, she is of royal blood! / Say, I willed so, that thou stay beside me - / She will grant it; she is kind and good" (1.94-96). This passage echoes Malory's explanation of why Trystrame married the second Isode, despite the enchantment that kept him eternally tied to the Irish Isode:

> Thenne by the grete meanes of Kynge Howel and Kehydyus, hys sone, by grete profers there grewe grete loue betwixe Isoud and Sire Trystram, for that lady was bothe good and fayre, and a woman of noble blood and fame. And for bycause Sir Trystram had suche chere and rychesse and alle other plesaunce that he hadde, allmoost he hadde forsaken La Beale Isould.[26]

In the Morte, Isode le Blaunche Maynys is encouraged to marry Sir Trystrame by her father, King Howell of Bretayne, and by her brother. La Villemarque mentions Iseult's father, but omits her brother, while Arnold calls her "the lovely orphan child" (1.92). The poet's change of this character's family situation might be intended to increase the pathos of her lonely existence. A reader's pity for the wife would also be heightened by the presence of her two children, who are not noted in any other source of the Tristram story.

Arnold's description of the Irish Iseult as proud and petulant is unlikely to encourage an audience's affection. Further, the focus upon the long suffering wife, whose children are not of much importance to their father, ensures a reader's distaste for Tristram. Apparently Arnold, like Tennyson, did not intend for adulterous love to be viewed as attractive. Swinburne is the only other poet to expand the wife's role, but his intent was to further glorify the lovers: "Thus Love reigns supreme in the universe and those who submit to it unconditionally achieve heroism and fame."[27] In the third section, Iseult of Brittany becomes the central figure of Arnold's poem, and it is this character who is likely to remain in a reader's memory and to be recalled as the most likable. Through the addition of details about her domestic life and activities with her children, Arnold made Iseult of Brittany much more substantial than her rival queen. In Arnold's poem, "the two Iseults represent the contrast between passion and devoted serviceable love; between a strained world of violent action and tranquil retreat."[28] Neither woman is perfect, but Iseult of Brittany is treated more sympathetically.

One year after the lovers' deaths, left with only her children and servants in the seaside castle, Iseult is lonely and languid. The narrator asks the obvious questions, without answering them:

> And is she happy? Does she see unmoved The days in which she might have lived and loved Slip without bringing bliss slowly away, One after one, tomorrow like today? Joy has not found her yet, nor ever will — Is it this thought which makes her mien so still, Her features so fatigued, her eyes, though sweet, So sunk, so rarely lifted save to meet Her children? (3.64-72)

Iseult's only joy is playing on the heath with her children. The poem ends with the three walking among the hollies on a winter's day as Iseult tells her children "an old-world Breton history" (3.37), the tale of Merlin and Vivian.[29]

This interpolated tale is puzzling because it is out of place, distracting, and a very strange conclusion to the poem. It has been noted that Arnold included the story as a diversion, because the poet wished to end with a flourish; and because "such a story, adorned with much descriptive detail but divested of its sinister elements, might very well amuse little children."[30] Further, it has been found that if the story does relieve sadness, it is through terror.[31]

The story of Merlin's horrible fate does not seem a particularly appropriate topic to relate to small children, but entertaining youngsters was not Arnold's intention; the storytelling session is more a type of therapy for Iseult of Brittany.

If we view such stories as assuming "the function of medieval exempla,"[32] we are left with the feeling that passion creates a state of death-in-life. Applied to Arnold's characters, Merlin is Tristram and the fay Vivian seems, at first, to correspond with the enchanting Iseult of Ireland. However, because Arnold included few of Vivian's physical characteristics, the specific mention of her "white right hand" (3.174) intentionally connects the character with Iseult of Brittany. This connection is strengthened when we remember that the wife Iseult did, in effect, imprison Tristram through marriage and, thus, hasten his death by parting him from his lover; his raison d'etre.

Iseult's judgements on her marriage are "emotions recollected in bitter tranquility,"[33] and her sorrow may well be transmuted into the aesthetic experience of storytelling. Arnold used Malory's darker view of Merlin's story and omitted La Villemarque's more softened version,[34] in which Vivian is eternally remorseful for the damage that she does to Merlin. Malory explained Nenyve's enchantment of Merlin by having his narrator report that "she was euer passynge wery of hym."[35] Arnold again distinctly echoed Malory in the last line of "Tristram and Iseult," with Iseult's explanation of Vivian's treachery: "For she was weary of his love" (3.224). After having a year to recall Tristram's limitations as a spouse, Arnold's Iseult may believe that she is well rid of a husband who was not of much use to her children. Iseult's passive life with Tristram gradually eroded any spirit she may have had before her marriage — leaving her trapped in a state like that of Merlin. Perhaps Iseult's telling of this particular tale indicates her understanding of her own confined state, and suggests her possible future renewal, as well as the idea that she is now content to have lost Tristram.

Arnold leaves Iseult of Brittany's feelings ambiguous. All that is certain is that her feelings of weary melancholy, bordering on ennui, are the result of Tristram's passion for another woman and his death. Grief would be acceptable, but Iseult's lack of vibrance, attitude of emptiness, and telling of the story of Merlin and Vivien are disconcerting.

THE NARRATOR

If it is true that "Arnold's poetry almost invariably implies the solution to the problems which it poses,"[36] then the solutions in "Tristram and Iseult" are to be found in the narrator's commentary. The narrator is forceful and involved, but always obscure and ambivalent — even when he seems most vehement.[37] His formal, archaic, minstrel-like tone frames many of the conversational speeches with undramatic, explicit exposition. This character presents the poem's conflict in his opening segment:

> There were two Iseults who did sway Each her hour of Tristram's day; But one possessed his waning time, The other his resplendent time. (1.68-71)

What makes Arnold's narrator of such interest, and creates such controversy among critics, are the codas at the end of each of the poem's three main sections. These codas widen the poem's range by making a moral application somewhat clearer and more universal. Arnold used the narrator's position in numerous other ways as well:

> It kept the poet wholly effaced; it cast in the narrator role, implanted in the text, a qualified commentator

> who could be expected to see vividly, tell crisply, ruminate relevently, speculate on the significance of the total action with appropriate circumspection and depth, interpret worthily but not infallibly; and it brought the poet and the reader into analogous roles - watching a fascinating watcher watch.[38]

Arnold's commentator speaks with a detachment that borders on dramatic irony when, at the end of each section, he "emphasizes the contrast between transient suffering and permanent art."[39]

In the first coda, the narrator moves from watching the children sleep to the visions their imaginations could create, if they viewed the night landscape from a window. Ultimately, however, the commentator notes that these inspiring observations are unnecessary, because the children are able to see more stimulating prospects in their dreams. In the second coda, the narrator looks at a tapestry wherein the timeless figure of a huntsman apparently comes to life and looks down at the dead lovers (reminding one of the narrator in "The Grande Chartreuse," and showing that this same problem of immobility can exist in another period). The hunter, on a chase with his dogs, pauses to wonder at the sight of what he thinks is a sleeping knight with his lady next to him, kneeling in prayer by the bed. The huntsman does not realize that death has overtaken the couple, and the narrator says to the figure trapped in the tapestry:

> O hunter! and without a fear Thy golden-tasseled bugle blow, And through the glades thy pastime take — For thou will rouse no sleepers here! For these thou seest are unmoved; Cold, cold as those who lived and loved A thousand years ago. (2.187-93)

This fusion of artistic forms creates an aesthetic effect of harmony between immediacy and distance, especially compared to the last two lines which give the poem's present a millenial rhythm that fuses especially well with the huntsman's perspective.

The narrator's third coda contains the heart or essential meaning of "Tristram and Iseult." Although further action is denied the characters of Arnold's ancient story, those of the modern world must still face a similar situation. It is not suffering that stunts our ability to see, feel, and grow:

> No, 'tis the gradual furnace of the world, In whose hot air our spirits are upcurled Until they crumble, or else grow like steel — Which kills in us the bloom, the youth, the spring — Which leaves the fierce necessity to feel, But takes away the power — this can avail, By drying up our joy in everything, To make our former pleasures all seem stale. (3.119-26)

This appears to represent Arnold's version of Carlyle's "Centre of Indifference":

> He [Arnold] is one of the first in English to take into himself the assertion of the 'Everlasting No,' that modern inference from the breakdown of classical metaphysics, to the effect that life lacks moral purpose and that the universe is not merely mechanical or neutral, but finally, hostile.[40]

The solution that Arnold may be suggesting is an embracement of storytelling and other expressions of imagination. In this way, "the poem is a reaction against the 'unpoetrylessness' of Arnold's age and is a positive statement — even if it begins and ends with melancholy poignancy."[41]

Further, it is in this third section that Arnold's narrator partially unveils his views about the adulterous relationship between Tristram and Iseult — or, at least, his feelings about those who respond only to "some tyrannous single thought":

> Call it ambition, or remorse, or love — This too can change us wholly, and make seem All which we did before, shadow and dream. And yet, I swear, it angers me to see How this fool passion gulls men potently; Being in truth, but a diseased unrest, And an unnatural overheat at best. (3.130-36)

The narrator's commentary suggests that both the "gradual furnace" of the world and the "single thought" are equally undesirable and destructive. Iseult of Brittany is an example of the former, Iseult of Ireland of the latter. Tristram has been destroyed by the worst possible combination of the two.

Arnold used the power of artifice in an ancient tale to yield new meanings by enhancing his readers' understanding of contemporary life. The slow destructive power of the world is just as debilitating as the consumptive force of passion. The poem's balanced opposition, shown in the contrast between two kinds of women and two kinds of love, is disturbing. Arnold revealed that this dichotomy can be neutralized through imaginative power combined with the serenity that this power can create. The poet's message may be that moderation and an understanding of the larger issues treated in the universal themes of art are the essential aspects of a fulfilling life. Love should not be a debilitating obsession or a force that gradually burns away all spirit, leaving only melancholy.

NOTES

1. Richard Barber, ed., *The Arthurian Legend* (London: Dorset, 1979), 74.

2. Roger Sherman Loomis, *The Development of Arthurian Romance* (New York: Norton, 1963), 82.

3. Paull F. Baum, *Ten Studies in the Poetry of Matthew Arnold* (Duke U. Press, 1958), 36.

4. James P. Carley, Introduction, *Matthew Arnold and William Morris* (Rochester: Boydell, 1990), 2.

5. William Caxton, bk. 8, chap 36, lines 31-34 in James W. Spisak and William Matthews, eds., of Caxton's Malory (U. of California Press, 1983), 235. All subsequent Malory quotations are from this edition.

6. Anthony H. Harrison, *Swinburne's Medievalism* (Louisiana U. Press, 1988), 2.

7. Baum, 36. This is perhaps the most frequently cited reference in this regard. G. Robert Stange, in *Matthew Arnold: The Poet as Humanist* (Princeton U. Press, 1967), 271, responds to Baum's argument by suggesting that Arnold's more sentimental version is an attempt to give an old work a new interpretation suitable for his audience.

8. J. Phillip Eggers, *King Arthur's Laureate* (New York U. Press, 1971), 131.

9. William E. Buckler, *On the Poetry of Matthew Arnold* (New York U. Press, 1982), 124.

10. A. Dwight Culler, in *Imaginative Reason: The Poetry of Matthew Arnold* (Yale U. Press, 1966), 144-45, argues that these varied poetic forms are intended to comment upon the contents of each section. Further, he finds the first section to be written like Coleridge's Christabel, the. second like many of Byron's lyrics, and the third like the more polished works by Keats or by Cowper.

11. Buckler, 124.

12. Harrison, 81.

13. Eggers, 133.

14. Arnold, "The Grand Chartreuse," in *The Works of Matthew Arnold*. 15 vols. (London: Macmillan, 1903-4). All references to "Tristram and Iseult" are from this text.

15. Alan H. Roper, "The Moral Landscape of Arnold's Poetry," *PMLA* 87 (1962): 289.

16. As mentioned by Jerome Hamilton Buckley and George Benjamin Woods, eds., *Poetry of the Victorian Period* (Atlanta: Scott, 1965) 43n, the name Tristram is derived from the Latin word tristitia, meaning "sorrow."

17. Caxton's Morte, Book 8, chapter 1, page 200, lines 12-16.

18. Stange, 220.

19. Carley, 3.

20. Arnold does not include Iseult's treachery to her maid Brangion, who, in earlier legends, was forced to take Iseult's place in King Mark's bed and was then given by Iseult to two murderers to ensure her silence. This incident is omitted by Malory and La Villemarque, so Arnold may not have known about it.

21. Caxton's Morte, Book 9, Chapter 17, page 259-60, lines 40-41.

22. Carley, 2.

23. Culler, 145.

24. The episode of the sails as a signal of success or failure seems to have been derived from the Theseus legend of Classical Greek mythology. Also involved in early Tristram legends is a half-bestial adversary who demands tribute every seven years, and is very similar to the Minotaur slain by Theseus as Barber notes, 74.

25. John Colin Dunlop, *History of Prose Fiction* (1814; rpt. New York: Burt Franklin, 1970), 206.

26. Caxton's Morte, Book 8, Chapter 36, page 235, lines 25-29.

27. Rebecca Cochran, "An Assessment of Swinburne's Arthuriana," in *King Arthur through the Ages*, ed. Valerie M. Lagorio and Mildred Leake Day (New York: Garland, 1990), 70.

28. Stange, 257.

29. Critics have not previously noted that the description of the tale of Merlin and Vivien as an "old-world Breton history" is anachronistic, Merlin is always associated with the court of King Arthur, as are Tristram and his two Iseults. (Tristram is known as a fine competitor in Arthur's jousts and as a close friend of Lancelot.) Therefore, it is odd that Iseult tells a story "she gleaned from the Breton grandames, when a child" (3.108), because Merlin and Vivien are her contemporaries. Arnold may have been confused about this point, since he was not an Arthurian scholar. Perhaps, however, Arnold was simply general, and reviewing the implications of the Merlin and Vivien story in particular, to resist including this specific tale as one passed down through several generations.

30. Baum, 51.

31. Buckler, 125.

32. Stange, 276.

33. Barber, 121.

34. It is possible that Arnold read La Villemarque's article about Merlin and Vivien called "Viste au tombeau de Merlin" at the same time that he discovered the one concerning Tristram and Iseult that so influenced him.

35. Caxton's Morte, Book 4, Chapter 1, page 94, line 10.

36. Roper, 289.

37. Masao Miyoshi, "Narrative Sequence and the Moral System: Three Tristram Poems," *Victorian Newsletter* 35 (1969): 9.

38. Buckler, 123.

39. Stange, 266.

40. David J. DeLaura, "Matthew Arnold and the Nightmare of History," *Victorian Papers* (London: Edward Arnold, 1972), 41.

41. Carley, 6.

5

Arnoldian Ethnology

—Vincent P. Pecora

> What the French call the science des origines, the science of origins, — a science which is at the bottom of all real knowledge of the actual world, and which is every day growing in interest and importance...
>
> —Matthew Arnold, *On the Study of Celtic Literature* (3: 299)

In the light shed by current trends in "cultural studies," Matthew Arnold's version of culture would seem to be precisely that which must be contested: a grand edifice housing only those Europeans responsible for what *Culture and Anarchy* (1869) calls "the best that has been thought and known in the world" (Arnold 5:113), dead white males whose "desire after the things of the mind simply for their own sakes and for the pleasure of seeing them as they are" (5: 91) provides an elite heritage of disinterested reflection to guide the rest of us. And to a large extent, this view of Arnold is correct, albeit terribly reductive. In demonizing Arnold, however, we may overlook the degree to which an element of his work that has always been something of an embarrassment for his interpreters—

Arnold's confusing and inconsistent approach to the relation between race (or nation) and culture — continues to be an embarrassing problem for us today. Arnold was clearly egalitarian when it came to the dissemination of "sweetness and light" (5: 99), and he was hardly a purist when the issue was race, emphasizing instead the hybrid vigor of the English. He strongly disliked the dominant, bourgeois mentality of his time, limited as it was to "the concern for making money, and the concern for saving our souls" (5: 186), and showed a distinct affection for lost, oppressed, or simply non-English cultural traditions. He was also thoroughly interdisciplinary and transnational in his methods, eschewing any systematic codification of knowledge that might hinder the interpretive play of the mind. In all of this, Arnold is more our contemporary than many would now care to admit. Arnold's difficulties in exploring the relations between race, nation, and culture thus should have a peculiar claim on our sympathies, for they are not as far removed from our own complicated obsessions with such terms as they might seem. Like the Celtic sensibility Arnold found buried within the English soul, Arnold's ethnology represents a conceptual knot that has refused to go away in spite of all sincere attempts to ignore it.

The opposition between Hellene and Hebrew in Matthew Arnold's writing is a remarkably persistent trope in post-Enlightenment thought. Arnold's rhetoric both echoes prominent strains in Romantic (especially German) literature and philosophy, and is in turn reproduced by a large segment of the Modernism to follow. Such rhetoric depends on the belief that ancient Greece represented a condition of natural harmony, grace, spontaneity, vitality, and freedom, a condition that needed to be recovered (if only on a higher plane) in a modernity plagued by excessive spiritual strivings and an ascetic narrowness of mind. It is a perspective essential to Winckelmann's art history, apotheosized so famously a century later by Pater. As

Lionel Gossman describes it, this "philhellenism or neohumanism" (4) was widespread in German writing, from Wolf and the Humboldts to Goethe, Schiller, Hölderlin, Hegel, and Heine (the widely credited source of Arnold's views on the topic), for many of whom the worship of Hellas paralleled an even more ubiquitous desire to rediscover the innocence and wholeness lost in the Mosaic legend of the fall of man. It lay behind Byron's (and many other educated Europeans') support for Greek independence from the Ottoman Empire, and was elaborated in another, more estranging key by Nietzsche toward the end of the century. Moreover, as Gossman observes, this affection for Greece was often both anti-Semitic (or at least opposed to Judaism as a religion, that is, anti-Judaic) and anti-Christian in character.

But the distinction between a higher, disinterested curiosity linked to the pagan Greeks and the Philistine (or Evangelical) pragmatism of England's merchant classes is also fundamental to English Romanticism in the poetry of Wordsworth and Shelley and Byron, and it is reproduced in the neo-romantic modernism of Pater, Wilde, Hardy, and Forster (see Gottfried and De Laura). Joyce playfully manipulated the Hellene-Hebrew dichotomy as the basis of his great mock-epic-"Jewgreek is greekjew. Extremes meet," we read in *Ulysses* ([1922] 15: 2097-98) — but only because, like many others around him, he accepted on some deep level the ethnological assumptions it embodied (see Ellmann 395). D. H. Lawrence turned the distinction into something palpable in the bodies of his characters and in their relation to an instinctual life repressed by modernity as a whole. In *Lord Jim* (1900), Conrad specifically labels Cornelius, who is among the most abject examples of pathological *ressentiment* in all of his work, "the Nazarene" (173). The word echoes Heine's use of the term to describe the "natural disposition" ("Ludwig Börne: Eine Denkshrift", trans. and qtd. in Gossman17) of ascetic Jews and Christians alike in their difference from life-affirming Hellenes — though Conrad strangely puts the epithet in the mouth of Jim's faithful and obedient Malay servant, Tamb' Itam, who gives no indication of having read Heine.

Gossman more or less absolves Matthew Arnold of any overt complicity in the (racially based) anti-Semitism or (religiously based) anti-Judaic tendencies of his time — rightly, I think, at least on the whole. In this, Matthew would prove to be quite different from his father Thomas, who had profoundly influenced him in so many other ways, and whose rather strong anti-Semitic opinions were voiced publicly. Moreover, for Gossman, even the distinction between Hellenism and Hebraism in Arnold is less a dialectic of opposites (as in Heine's thinking) than a flexible and pragmatic search for synthesis (which Heine's "want of moral balance," in Arnold's words, prevented him from achieving ["Heinrich Heine" (1863) 3: 132]), a "spiritual balance" (Arnold 5: 173) that appears all the more plausible because of Arnold's characteristic lack of conceptual rigor. Arnold may indicate at times that Hellenism is itself the essence of true "culture" while Hebraism tends toward narrow enthusiasm and unthinking action, but for Gossman it is really the awkward accommodation of playful intelligence and righteous morality that Arnold is after, an "inclusive, pluralistic vision of 'culture'" (Gossman 36) that parallels an English parliamentary tradition dedicated less to organic unity than to imperfect consensus amid difference.

Gossman's approach also persuasively detaches Arnold's thinking from the more fully elaborated notions of racial identity and racial consciousness available at this time — if only by default of Arnold's fuzzy concepts — and emphasizes instead what might be called the intellectual, emotional, or ideological "impulse" (Arnold 5: 178), "bent" (5: 179), "force" (5: 179), or "tendency" (5: 180) that would urge the. behavior marked either as Hellenism or Hebraism.

For example, Arnold's Hebraism would seem to depend less on any notion of innate racial composition — it makes no reference to the anatomy or mental capacity of Jews — than on a moral imagination, supposedly traceable back to Jewish law, and powerfully sustained in the modern period by Christian Evangelical fervor. Hebraism thus appears to be a learned perspective rather than a racial inheritance, a perspective that in its unhealthy or extreme forms turns moral rectitude and practical efficacy into ends in themselves. It is also a perspective that can be moderated by other learned perspectives, such as Hellenism. In this view, culture as Arnold imagines it does not demand the modification of any particular "natural disposition," racial or individual, but only the surrender of the ideology of religious certainty, or "strictness of conscience" (5: 176) — which can of course take many forms — in order that an alternative tendency toward disinterested inquiry, or "spontaneity of consciousness" (5: 176), can flourish unconstrained by moral and political imperatives.

This way of reading *Culture and Anarchy* has been a fairly dominant one, even among those, like Lionel (in *Matthew Arnold*) and Raymond Williams (in *Culture and Society*), who criticize the shortcomings of Arnold's logic and political sentiments. Who could object to Arnold's ambiguous terminology, once it is understood as simply demanding a practical (parliamentary) balance between pluralism and righteousness, between free inquiry and ethical concern? (For a usefully skeptical view of what this practical balance represents, however, see Graff.) Indeed, George Stocking provides an anthropological historian's support for the view that Arnold's sense of the word "culture" is actually much closer to the usage of modern, relativist anthropology, which at least strives to detach itself from racism and ethnocentrism, than was that of Arnold's contemporary E.B. Tylor, who is often cited as the source of anthropology's culture concept., Tylor, a Nonconformist, positivist, and utilitarian who would have been a perfect example of Arnold's Philistine, elaborated an evolutionary, developmental notion of culture (or civilization) in the singular. Along a universal (though obviously not uniform) progression toward the material and moral condition of Tylor's own time and place, different peoples and races could be normatively ranked. Arnold, with his neo-Romantic alienation from modern Western society and its rationalist machinery, instead develops what for Stocking is a sense of culture as "an integrative, organic, holistic, inner manifestation" (Stocking 796), a view that was supposedly more likely than Tylor's to imply modern anthropology's relativism. Indeed, Stocking does not mention race at all in his discussion of Arnold.

Gossman's recent account of the German Romantic roots of Arnold's thinking, certainly among the most thorough yet provided, may emphasize more than have most Arnold's "pragmatic" (if "conservative") view of the State and his affection for Hebraism. But Gossman is in good company when he finds little in *Culture and Anarchy* that suggests biological race as a cultural determinant and much that prefigures later efforts at pluralism, whether humanist or anthropological. Previous and equally comprehensive accounts of Arnold sources for *Culture and Anarchy*, like that of David J. DeLaura, likewise do little to explore the race-culture link in Arnold's work itself.

Writing more than half a century earlier, Lionel Trilling could not have been more opposed to certain of Gossman's interpretations. For Trilling, Arnold's State is an "essentially mystic conception" (Trilling 255), a "liberal" myth that ignores the realities of power; and Arnold's Hellenism is clearly the implicitly favored impulse, a proper human end to which Hebraism should serve only as a (modestly pursued) means. Like Gossman, however, Trilling's reading of *Culture and Anarchy* suggests neither a specifically "racial" content (242) nor any anti-Semitism; Trilling even notes in a footnote how far Heine's GreekJew distinction was accepted by many Jewish intellectuals of Heine's era, such as Moses Hess (256n). Trilling's book, however, has room to discuss a work by Arnold that neither Gossman nor Stocking mentions at all — *On the Study of Celtic Literature* (1867) — and here the problem of race in Arnold is squarely faced. "Science," writes Trilling, "the anthropology of his day, told him that the spirit of a nation — what we might call its national *style* — is determined by 'blood' or 'race' and that these are constants, asserting themselves against all other determinants such as class, existing social forms, and geographical and economic environment" (232-33). As Trilling's brief survey of the essay demonstrates, the evidence for Arnold's belief in inherited racial characteristics is very strong. Still, Trilling's rightly critical focus on the Victorian assumptions about race in *Celtic Literature* does not go very far in exploring its significance for the reading of *Culture and Anarchy.*

Just over a decade after Trilling's discussion, Frederic Faverty published *Matthew Arnold, the Ethnologist*, a study that takes the racial assumptions so evident in *Celtic Literature* as keys to Arnold work, *Culture and Anarchy* included. While, for Faverty, "it must be admitted at the start that Arnold was no systematic racialist" (1), it is also clear that 'like his contemporary, Taine, he sought always for the dominant trait (pensée maîtresse) in the race or nation under discussion" (186). Faverty accepts much of what animates Gossman's approach — that Arnold rejected the anatomical absurdities propagated in books like Emile Burnouf *La Science des Religions* (1888), with its grotesque caricature of Semitic anatomy; that Arnold actually displays "a profound admiration" (174) for Hebraism and found it a necessary component of a balanced human perfection; and that, whether discussing Indo-Europeans or Semites, Arnold generally pointed out virtues and defects alike. But for Faverty, these virtues and defects were still racial dispositions, at least in their origins, and his conclusion is as harsh as criticism of Arnold gets: "To the unfounded assumptions of the racial hypothesis Arnold lent the weight of a distinguished name. His pronouncements upon the Celt, the Saxon, and Jew have not gone unheard; they have told upon the world's practice" (191-92). Faverty's penetrating work has been too often ignored in major Arnold studies, even though, as Ruth apRoberts noted a few years back, his "rich study . . . is by no means dated" (97; see also Graff 191, and Lloyd 145n11). Faverty's own currency aside, how should we address today the very real problem of Arnold's relationship to the ethnological assumptions of his day, a problem raised more obviously by a work like *Celtic Literature* than by any of Arnold other writings? And to what extent should Arnold sentiments in *Culture and Anarchy* be assimilated to those in *Celtic Literature*, published serially in *The Cornhill Magazine* in 1866, only one year before the earliest elements of *Culture and Anarchy* began appealing there? As recent work on culture and race has begun to demonstrate, these are questions with continuing relevance for current criticism (see Young 55-89 for a wide-ranging, if flawed, effort to address such issues).

The difficulty facing any attempt to reconcile the ethnological assumptions in *Celtic Literature* with those implied by *Culture and Anarchy* is not hard to see. Stocking is quite impressed, for example, when Arnold admits that he could easily have been an aristocratic Barbarian:

> Place me in one of his great fortified posts, . . . with all pleasures at my command, with most whom I met deferring to me, everyone I met smiling on me, and with every appearance of permanence and security before and behind me, — then I too might have grown, I feel, into a very passable child of the established fact, of commendable spirit and politeness, and . . . a little inaccessible to ideas and light. . . ." (Arnold 5: 144; as qtd. in Stocking 795-96)

Though Stocking oddly does not state it bluntly, what he really seems to admire here is simply Arnold's sense that a different environment, a different "way of life" or set of customs, would have produced a different person, a notion supposedly both more in tune with modern anthropology and quite different from Tylor's emphasis on a fixed evolutionary sequence. That Arnold is talking more about *class* within a nation than about races or nations, and that a recognition of environmental influence in this narrow context need not necessarily contradict more broadly based assumptions about racial inheritance — all this goes by unobserved in Stocking's essay. Yet Stocking's point is still a good one: Arnold's humanism implies in such passages that "human beings shared a capacity for various types of development" (Stocking 795), including development of either Hebraistic or Hellenistic tendencies, a capacity that much of the anthropology of his time seemed to be repressing.

By contrast, what Trilling addresses in *Celtic Literature* would seem directly to refute all that Stocking claims about Arnold. Arnold argues that

> [m]odes of life, institutions, government, climate, and so forth, — let me say it once for all, — will further or hinder the development of an aptitude, but they will not by themselves create the aptitude or explain it. On the other hand, a people's habit and complexion of nature go far to determine its modes of life, institutions, and government, and even to prescribe the limits within which the influences of climate shall tell upon it. (3: 353)

It is a refutation especially pertinent to Stocking's argument in that, as Trilling points out, Arnold's target here seems to be Henry Thomas Buckle, whose emphasis on "the non-racial determinants of culture" (Trilling 235) implies something far closer to a shared "capacity for various types of development" than is suggested by Arnold's rather frankly biological "complexion of nature." In rejecting Buckle, of course, Arnold is surely not implying the evolutionism that inspired Tylor, but he is clearly rejecting the essential elements of Stocking's "modern" anthropological perspective.

One possible impediment to comparing *Culture and Anarchy* with *Celtic Literature* in this way is that Arnold was never much bothered by inconsistency. Like 1Emerson across the Atlantic, Arnold's mind was perhaps too deliberately free of the hobgoblins of systematic thought to concern itself with the ethnological niceties described by Stocking. In the "Introduction" to *Celtic Literature*, Arnold admits the "provisional character" (3: 387) of his remarks quite openly, and goes so far in the published version of his lectures as to include footnotes by Lord Strangford that time and again point out the errors (or worse) propagated by Arnold's superficial knowledge of philology, Celtic and otherwise. Oddly, Arnold apparently felt no need either to correct his text for publication or to refute Strangford-the contradictions and mistakes remain unresolved.

If the text of *Celtic Literature* itself can be so riddled with contradictions, all the more reason to think that the gap between *Culture and Anarchy* and Arnold study of the Celts mattered little to him. While *Culture and Anarchy* develops a liberal and inclusive view of culture as "a harmonious expansion of all the powers which make the beauty and worth of human nature" (5: 94), *Celtic Literature*'s pseudo-scientific ethnological categories are at times not that far from those of Joseph Arthur de Gobineau: "As there are for physiology physical marks, such as the square head of the German, the round head of the Gael, the oval head of the Cymri, which determine the type of a people, so for criticism there are spiritual marks which determine the type, and make us speak of the Greek genius, the Teutonic genius, the Celtic genius, and so on" (Arnold 3: 340). *Culture and Anarchy* focuses in large part on a sense of culture as "cultivation," on what the German Romantics had called *Bildung*, both as a search for inward perfection and as an egalitarian drive "to make the best that has been thought and known in the world current everywhere, to make all men live in an atmosphere of sweetness and light" (Arnold 5: 113) — a principle that has seemed to a great many to be still unsurpassed as a humanist ideal. By contrast, *Celtic Literature* is dedicated to an account of culture as a set of identifiable physical, linguistic, and spiritual characteristics that seem to derive more from a medieval theory of the humors than from any positivist or evolutionary Victorian ethnology.

Arnold uses and italicizes the word "humour" both in *Culture and Anarchy*, where he describes the English nation as "eminently Indo-European by its *humour*" (5: 174), and in *Celtic Literature*, where the unique *"humour"* of the English appears to be Germanism awkwardly leavened by "hauntings of Celtism" (3:360). The phlegmatic Germans (Arnold actually refers at one point to "the Saxon's phlegm" [3: 348]) are dull, steady, and "humdrum," even "ignoble," yet methodical in their "patient fidelity to Nature, — in a word, *science*" (3: 341). The sanguine Celts are sentimental and lively (3: 343), yet lacking in patience or self-control (that is, "feminine" — hence their chivalry); they are close to "natural magic," prone to "extravagance and exaggeration" (3: 347), "ineffectual in politics" (3: 346), and *"always ready to read against the despotism of fact"* (3: 344). Even the body's organs display the difference: the German "has the larger volume of intestines," while the Frenchman (whom Arnold also considered fundamentally Celtic, even beyond Brittany) "has the more developed organs of respiration" (3: 343). Arnold's larger purpose is to illustrate, against much philo-Teutonic and anti-Celtic opinion in England at this time, the degree to which the English have inherited elements of both racial dispositions. In *Celtic Literature*, Arnold's ethnology is in fact different from Tylor's evolutionism, though not, as Stocking observes of *Culture and Anarchy*, because it is more modern in its functionalism and relativism, but rather because it is profoundly anachronistic in its conception of national/racial "spirit." Hegel grand typologies of national *Geist* in the *Philosophy of History* (1822-31) seem no more untimely, and we should recall that in *Friendship's Garland* (1871) Arnold, referring in passing to *Celtic Literature*'s typologies, comically explains his Hellenism through Arminius's notion of Geist as "intelligence" (Arnold had been reading Hegel *Phenomenology of Spifit* [1807]; see Arnold, 5: 40-42 and 76-77).

Further difficulties of interpretation stem from the degree to which *Celtic Literature* is clearly a work of borrowed scholarship. Throughout his career, Arnold lifted ideas and terminology from continental writers whose work was less well known in England. Ernest Renan wrote essays on Marcus Aurelius and Spinoza and the Celts, and so did Arnold. On this score, however, *Celtic Literature* may be in a class by itself. Arnold's debt to Renan "*La poésie des races celtiques*", published as part of his *Essais de morale et de critique* in 1859, is well known and has long been recognized, though Renan's essay is a far more sentimental and nostalgic survey of Celtic attributes than is Arnold's attempt at ethnological science. It was from Renan, himself a Breton Celt, that Arnold took what was perhaps the germ of his essay: the belief that, in Renan's words, "le chevalrie, — cet idéal de douceur et de beauté posé comme but suprême de la vie, — n'est une création ni classique, ni chrétienne, ni germanique, mais bien réellement celtique" (*Essais*385). But as Faverty demonstrates, Arnold borrowed just as extensively from Henri Martin *Histoire de France* (1855-60), passages of which, like that on the Celt's resistance to the "despotism of fact," found numerous echoes in *Celtic Literature*. Add to this Arnold's debts to Amédée Thierry *Histoire des gaulois* (1835) for the emphasis on philology and anthropology — Arnold could have taken his sense of the main groups within the Celtic race, Welsh-Cornish and Breton (the Cymric), Scottish and Irish (the Gaëlic), from either Thierry or Renan (see Faverty 123, and Arnold 3: 498, ed. note to 292: 31-38) — and E. F. Edwards *Recherches sur les langues celtiques* (1844) for the remarks on the physiological evidence of Celtic inheritance in England (Faverty 36), and *Celtic Literature* begins to break apart into something of a scholarly collage. Is the problem then that Arnold's interest in the Celts, stimulated mainly it seems by a visit to Brittany and a subsequent visit to Wales (where he attended an Eisteddfod, or Bardic Congress, at Llandudno) was based on a hastily assembled, if comprehensive, hodgepodge of ethnological writing — for which Arnold himself can hardly be held fully responsible?

Neither a high tolerance for inconsistency nor hasty scholarship, however, is finally very satisfying as an explanation for the twists and turns in Arnold's ethnology. To tackle the second point first, Arnold's scholarship was always much broader than it was deep — which should not seem odd in a critic devoted to the idea that intellectual machinery, including the tendency to the over-specialization of thought, was the curse of his time. Indeed, Arnold is very much our contemporary in this regard, for it is precisely Arnold who should be seen as the great progenitor of the post-1968 demand for inter-disciplinary and non-systematic humanistic inquiry, at least in the Anglo-American world. Much in contemporary "cultural studies" reproduces the cursory quality of Arnold's anthropological and philological thought along with his breadth of vision. The issue, then as today, is less how to excuse this combination of qualities than to understand what it enables or overlooks, both for good and ill.

By the same token, Arnold's inconsistent approach to the concept of culture should itself be seen less as a simple failing to be explained away than as a crucial hinge in his thinking. It is far more likely that Arnold did not recognize any real contradiction between the ethnographic opinions expressed in *Culture and Anarchy* and *Celtic Literature* than that he did and ignored them. Once again, I would suggest, Arnold is our contemporary, for it is precisely his equivocations that haunt, albeit in strongly disavowed forms, contemporary humanistic reflection on culture. Both cultivated disposition and biologically rooted aptitude, both a "study of perfection," whose inwardness is itself real only if it implies "a general perfection, embracing all our fellow-men with whom we have to do" (5: 215), and a "complexion of nature" (3: 353) displayed by a racial-national stock even when blended with others in diverse physical and social environments: Arnold's sense of culture is in fact fluid and dynamic and tacks back and forth between these positions and through a number of intervening ones with some ease. This conceptual sliding or equivocation is mediated by the host of metaphors — "impulse," "bent," "force," "tendency" — that does so much work in *Culture and Anarchy*. For with such terms, Arnold can talk about a wide variety of things in either of two, often unspecified, causal sequences: either learned, if deeply rooted, sensibilities that have been cultivated by literary, philosophical, and religious traditions; or literary, philosophical, and religious traditions that are themselves primarily the consequence of racial/national "genius" or "spirit," a natural (that is, biologically given) complexion of consciousness that can be traced, in varying depths, wherever a "people" migrate and intermarry. While *Culture and Anarchy* would appear to be indebted primarily to the first causal sequence (hence its continuing viability in contemporary criticism) and *Celtic Literature* to the second (hence its relative invisibility today), it is important to recognize that both types of arguments are present in varying degrees in both essays. Once we take seriously

Arnold's claim that the new "science of origins" is indeed the foundation of "all real knowledge of the actual world," the fact that these two causal chains are inextricably linked in his thinking becomes difficult to ignore.

Perhaps the most difficult problem of all in addressing *Celtic Literature*, however, is that the essay embodies manifestly good intentions-good, that is, from the perspective of much current opinion, quite in spite of its now discredited racial assumptions. (If any piece of scholarship illustrates how far the road to hell can be paved with good intentions, *Celtic Literature* is it.) Arnold not only seriously promoted the value of studying Celtic literature and myth at a time when its mostly ill-informed proponents had been subjected to withering (and often justified) attacks, he also called at the end of his essay for a "chair of Celtic" (3: 384) at Oxford or Cambridge. (Among his listeners at the last of Arnold's Celtic lectures was John Rhys, who would be the first to occupy such a chair when established in 1877 at Jesus College [Arnold, ed. note, 3: 493]). If we are to believe figures like W.B. Yeats and Andrew Lang, Arnold's essay (along with the writings of James Macpherson and Renan) had a formative influence on the Celtic Revival (see Kelleher, and Faverty 152-53) that would soon transform — we might say re-invent — the literary history of Ireland, even if Arnold, like Joyce, displayed little of the Revival's enthusiasm for Gaelic language and folklore. Moreover, in essays like "Irish Catholicism and British Liberalism" (1879), Arnold supported the Irish Catholic demand for a Catholic University (8: 321-47), though the ethnographic grounds for his support become more clear in "Joseph de Maistre on Russia" (1879), Arnold's review of the great conservative political theorist's correspondence: 'Just as every plan of government is a baneful dream, unless it be in harmony with the character and circumstances of the nation, so it is with education" (9: 101). Whatever Arnold's shortcomings in accepting a race-culture nexus, his essay deployed such thinking toward ends that would be widely praised in the modern academy: the revival of a neglected and oppressed literary tradition, and the institutionalization of its study within the university.

Yet Arnold's brief excursions through Brittany and Wales, which reminded him of something in his Cornish mother, and presumably in himself (Renan also saw Bretagne through the eyes of his mother and his childhood), produced complicated results. His pointed interest in Celtic matters was at heart one more expression of his deeply Romantic attraction to things (like classical grace and medieval humors) that had come to seem irrelevant to the utilitarian sensibility, technological progress, and science of the modern world. This attraction could extend from solitary, sentimental melancholics, like the autobiographical hero of Etienne Pivert de Senancour's *Obermann* (1804) — "l'expression d'un homme qui sent et non d'un homme qui travaille" (i), we read in its first sentence — to entire peoples around whom the aura of lost nobility could be imagined to glow in direct proportion to their worldly disappointment: "For ages and ages the world has been constantly slipping, ever more and more, out of the Celt's grasp. 'They went forth to war,' Ossian says most truly, *'but they always fell'*" (Arnold 3: 346). This line from James Macpherson largely invented *Poems of Ossian* (1760-65), which is perhaps the single most important document for the reawakened European interest in folk culture and oral tradition throughout the late-eighteenth and nineteenth centuries, including that of German Romantics like Herder (see Chapman , *Gaelic Vision*29-52 and 83-84), also serves as Arnold's epigraph. What Arnold saw in the Celts, partly in himself, but certainly in the Irish, whom many of the English would have considered a distinctly alien race at this time, was an all but forgotten poetic sensibility, the value of which lay precisely in its manifest unsuitability for worldly success in Arnold's day. In elaborating this melancholic Celtic nobility, Arnold largely followed the lead of Macpherson, who, like Walter Scott in his popular Waverley novels, reflected more the mood of Scottish clansmen after the failed rebellion of 1745 than a heritage of Celtic poetry (see Smart 26-29). "For the sword which they were no longer able to yield," writes Faverty in summary of Macpherson's image of the Celts, "they substituted the harp. They were a dying race, but like the swan, they would sing a beautiful lament before they expired" (149). Arnold's crucial difference from Macpherson, however, lies in the fact that in *Celtic Literature* we find a mechanism, racial inheritance, by which the virtues of that beaten breed might survive in the English, if only, like so many other anthropological "survivals," in latent form.

Arnold's interest in the Celts is thus riddled with a nostalgia equal to, if more temperate, than Renan's; for Arnold, the lost cause of the Celts also becomes a salutary reminder of a "style" and "grace" and "delicate magic" (Arnold 3: 374) absent in the Teutonic (Saxon) character of the modern English Philistine. All of the attributes Arnold cites had become part of a commonly accepted Romantic discourse on the Celts from Macpherson on, though Arnold would turn that discourse to his own purposes: "The Celt's quick feeling for what is noble and distinguished gave his poetry style; his indomitable personality gave it pride and passion; his sensibility and nervous exaltation gave it a better gift still, the gift of rendering with wonderful felicity the magical charm of nature" (3: 374). In *Culture and Anarchy*, the "extraordinary grace" demanded by feudalism's "struggling society" from England's "land-holding class," whose charismatic dominance provided "cohesion" and an "ideal or standard for the rest of the community," disappears from the "luxurious, settled and easy society" of the modern aristocratic Barbarians (5: 203). But that grace, that style and magical charm, are never really lost in Arnold. They are constantly recaptured on other grounds, in phrases like "sweetness and light," in the spontaneous play of the mind that marks Hellenism, and in the racial heritage of Celtic poetry. Arnold's point is both retrospective and very much of his moment. He wants to illustrate the deep undercurrents of this often overlooked Celtic influence in English literary history: Shakespeare, Milton, Byron, Wordsworth, and Keats are all called to testify to its workings. But he also wants to demonstrate to an uncomprehending and increasingly dominant Philistine middle class that there is a vestigial "humour" of romance and poetry and magic flowing in its veins, a Celtic humor that could substitute for what aristocratic England has lost, once it is recognized as innate. The repressed "hauntings of Celtism" (3: 360) in the Englishman's character, which prompt his characteristically "self-conscious" and "embarrassed" nature, or what George Sand called his "typical awkwardness" (3: 360-61), are appropriate reproductions of the haunting, magical qualities of Celtic poetry itself — as if the poetry had been designed all along to remind the English that something intimately their own needed to be recovered from the mists of their racial past.

Unsurprisingly, it is this uncanny nostalgia that gives *Celtic Literature* its convoluted politics, for however admirable (in part) the noble Celtic sensibility might be, it remains resolutely a thing of the past, forever cursed by a worldly impotence and "feminine" (3: 347) lack of discipline that, in effect, binds it to the Empire irrevocably. In this regard, as Lord Lytton observed of Irish qualities, Arnold's treatment of the Celt bestows virtues "that win affection but never esteem" (qtd. in Faverty 146) — just like the virtues bestowed on women by a supposedly Celt-invented code of chivalry. To be sure, *Celtic Literature* (like *Culture and Anarchy*) has a distinctly ameliorative social program, demonstrating "traces of kinship, and the most essential sort of kinship, spiritual kinship, between us and the Celt, of which we had never dreamed" (3: 335).

At a time when, fifteen years after the Great Hunger in Ireland, relations between the English and Irish are at a particularly low ebb, distrust is the rule, and the rather stark choice between "coercion" and "separation" (Lloyd 142) seems to be all that is left, Arnold's essay tries to demonstrate that, "we English, alien and uncongenial to our Celtic partners as we may have hitherto shown ourselves, have notwithstanding, beyond perhaps any nation, a thousand latent springs of possible sympathy with them" (Arnold 3: 395). Arnold's grand goal is nothing less than a transformation of English character, "substituting, in place of that type of Englishman with whom alone the Celt has too long been familiar, a new type, more intelligent, more gracious, and more humane" (3: 395). And yet Arnold is in no way calling here for more Irish (much less Welsh!) autonomy; like most of the English, Arnold had no sympathy even for the maintenance of the Welsh and Gaelic languages if these challenged the hegemony of English. He demands just as great a transformation of character from "the Celtic members of this empire," who would thereby better realize "that they are inextricably bound up with us" (3: 395). In fact, Arnold's twin appeals to the English and Celts of the Empire for political moderation, however balanced they may at first seem, are in fact quite asymmetrical.

Arnold's appeal to the English presumes what to him would be historically obvious: the English are the hardier (politically and spiritually dominant) stock, both by virtue of their sound Teutonic basis (or primary humor) and by virtue of their heterosis, that is, of the various racial humors that have been bred into that basis. Like the physical hybrid, the cultural hybrid in Arnold would appear to be richer and stronger for its admixture — a fairly progressive thesis, after all, at a time of strong national and racial chauvinism: "[J]ust what constitutes special power and genius in a man seems often to be his blending with the basis of his national temperament, some additional gift or grace not proper to that temperament" (Arnold 3: 358; on the broader question of the hybrid in the nineteenth century, see Young1-28). Philology, physiology, poetry -all point toward an "affinity of race" (3: 335) between the English and the Celts, but it is only the English who seem to have benefited historically from the numerous invasions and conquests that united one race with another in Britain, precisely because the English are themselves the happy racial consequence of this earlier crossbreeding (a point made in a more satirical vein by Daniel Defoe poem of 1701, "The True-Born Englishman", on the prejudice against William III's foreignness). The Celts were the original, passive ("feminine"), and absorbed stock, "insensibly getting mixed with their conquerors" — the Saxons, the Romans, the Normans -"their blood entering into the composition of a new people, in which the stock of the conquerors counts for most, but the stock of the conquered, too, counts for something" (3: 338). It would thus appear that those Celts who fled westward into Wales, Scotland, and Ireland to avoid destruction or servitude, and who thus retained some degree of racial purity, paid a high price on the world's stage, both because of the weakness of their racial stock and because of the lack of any tempering influence. Had Arnold, when writing *Celtic Literature*, enjoyed the benefit of hearing Renan's later lecture, *Qu'est-ce qu'une Nation*, delivered at the Sorbonne in 1882, he would have found sentiments that both confirmed and usefully undermined his ideas about the Celts and the English: "Ethnographic considerations have thus been for nothing in the constitution of modern nations . . . The truth is that there is no pure race, and that to make politics depend upon ethnographical analysis is to sustain it upon a chimera. The most noble countries, the English, the French, the Italians, are those where the blood is most mixed" (Renan, *Nation*37; my translation). Arnold agreed, but only up to a point, for Renan's chimera did in fact matter to him in 1866.

Unlike the later Renan, moreover, Arnold is far from treating all forms of racial simplicity or complexity in the same way, and the only real marker of racial health is Darwinian in character — the superior worldly and spiritual success of the race. Like the Celt, for example, the German nature is "all of a piece" (Arnold 3: 361), yet the Germans have enjoyed political and cultural prosperity, in spite of their racial "Gemeinheit" (vulgarity) (3: 341), dullness, and lack of poetry, because of the relative strength of their stock, a strength based in a *"steadiness with honesty"* (3: 341) and shared by the English (in the form of *"energy with honesty"*) through Saxon conquest. The French, by contrast, are a blend in which Frankish-German and Latin have been superimposed on "an undoubtedly Celtic basis" (3: 349). But the French suffer much more from their Celtic inheritance than do the English, precisely because the Celtic humor *remained* the basis of the French stock. Once again, the final arbiter of cultural complexion is nothing less than blood: "Gaul was Latinised in language, manners, and laws, and yet her people remained essentially Celtic. The Germanisation of Britain went far deeper than the Latinisation of France, and not only laws, manners, and language, but the main current of the blood, became Germanic" (3: 338). What Arnold actually means here is unclear. Did the Romans simply not procreate much with their Celtic hosts in Gaul? Were the Saxons far more thorough in producing offspring through the Celts of Britain? Should the Saxons be considered true colonizers, settling and intermarrying among the native population that did not flee, while the Romans were mere imperialists? "They were no colonists," Marlow says of the *Romans in Heart of Darkness* (1902), "their administration was merely a squeeze, and nothing more, I suspect" (Conrad 10). It is an open question, made all the more puzzling by the fact that, following such logic, the English could be considered more Norman (that is, Latin-Celt) than anything else — a possibility Arnold, despite his rejection of all strident English philoTeutonism and his elaboration of Norman influences, does not address. Arnold endorsed the sentiment that France was "famed in all great arts, *in none supreme*" (qtd. in Faverty 137), and it seems only through its Latin (rational) humor that France had been able to overcome its Celtic flaws — though elsewhere even this Latin inheritance appears to be marked by sensuality (see Arnold, "Numbers; on The Majority and the Remnant" [1884] 10: 155). The English, by contrast, appear to have inherited only Latin virtues from the Normans, who brought with them the imperial Roman gifts for oratory and orderly administration.

The dizzying combinations of racial traits that Arnold is able to distinguish perhaps point to a salient characteristic of all such arguments: Arnold's genealogies are primarily ways of rationalizing the social and political realities of his day, of explaining (and perhaps justifying) English authority even as he contests its cruder exercise, challenges its narrowminded chauvinism, and admits — or rather, celebrates — its awkward hybrid vigor. Indeed, some current ethnological approaches to the question of the Celt deny that the term has any racial or ethnic coherence at all. Malcolm Chapman reminds us that it was only after William Jones's elaboration, in 1786, of the relation of Sanskrit to Greek and comparative philology's subsequent reconstruction of an 'Indo-European" (or "IndoGermanic") genealogy of languages that language began to be taken as a key to the genealogy of "peoples, races, nations, and cultures" (Chapman, *Celts*14-16). It was a key much exploited in an age of rising nationalism, but with little historical justification. The near-mystical Romantic link between language, race, and nation could thus be mapped in both evolutionary and geographical terms and, following Barthold Niebuhr, in terms of European history itself. For Chapman, "the Celt" is one of the most influential and persistent, but least credible, genealogical units of the age; like others before him, he finds little evidence that, for much of its supposed history, the Celt ever embodied the concatenation of physical, spiritual, and linguistic characteristics that is assumed by Romantic Celtic studies, and by Matthew Arnold. Chapman comes close to endorsing the idea that "there is no such thing as Celt" (*Celts*251), that the term may really be no more than a name for attributes like charm and grace and poetic sentiment imposed by all industrialized metropolitan societies on their "folk" (another late-eighteenth-century invention) peripheries. (For a very early predecessor of Chapman's argument, see the 1867 review of *Celtic Literature* by Fagan.)

What is clear in Arnold is that a racial "basis," a people's original "complexion of nature" or humor, will have a determining influence on its culture unless that basis has been saturated with and overcome by the blood of a conquering race. At best, a people will be able to temper the vices of its racial basis with the virtues of its racial cross-breeding. The phlegmatic Teutonism of the English can thus be enlivened by Celtic sentiment and magic; the Celtic extravagance, femininity, and eternal readiness "to react against the despotism of fact" inherited by the French can be held in check, but only barely, by Latin laws and bureaucracy. Even here, of course, the asymmetry persists, for England is blessed both with a more wholesome Teutonic "basis," despite its vices, than the French, and a greater resource, in its vestigial Celtic humor, for tempering that basis than the Germans. England's greatest danger may be too much dull, plodding rectitude, but France must constantly beware an explosive rebellion against fact — a dangerous tendency that France, with its seemingly endless political upheavals in the nineteenth century, could be said to share with the Irish Celts it was often asked to support against England.

Arnold's notions of racially based cultural traits and cultural cross-breeding might appear to be of little relevance to the larger rise of "multicultural" pedagogy in recent years and to contemporary notions of cultural hybridity and cross-cultural aesthetic practice. After all, these modern meditations on what Arnold called the "science of origins" would seem to have been amply inoculated against all that plagues Arnold's ethnology by a repudiation of the biological-racial inheritance of cultural traits and by a more thorough-going relativism. Like John Stuart Mill, Andrew Lang, Yeats, and the later Renan, most of Arnold's readers today are likely to reject the theory of "inherent natural differences" (Mill, *Principles*324) supporting *Celtic Literature* as an outmoded explanation for both individual character and cultural traditions (see also Lang, Yeats, and Renan, *Nation*37). Yet, like many people in casual conversation, then and now, these earlier writers were hardly always free in practice from using national-racial assumptions to explain cultural or political tendencies, despite their stated beliefs. Mill's attitude was primarily developmental rather than racial: his view that "despotism is a legitimate mode of government when dealing with barbarians" (On Liberty263) may be a convenient notion for imperial designs, but it need not be racially based. However, when Mill indicts the "despotism of Custom . . . over the whole East" ("On Liberty" 318) and notes that China, "stationary" for thousands of years despite earlier eras of progress, will only be "farther improved . . . by foreigners" (320), it is hard not to understand this result as a product of innate racial disposition, for it is only an unexplained and seemingly natural "diversity of character and culture" (320) that, with proper nurturing, will save European nations and individuals from a similar fate. It should thus not be surprising that highly sublimated versions of Arnoldian racial inheritance, along with what may be the practical impossibility of strict relativism, continue to haunt contemporary scholarly uses of the word culture, just as surely as the assumptions of a coherent and continuous Celtic personality have persisted in ways that critics like Chapman rightly find unwarranted.

When we refer to a culture as having a coherence based on a national or regional or group identity over time, as elaborated in a particular language, literary tradition, and set of customs — whether these are designated Irish or French or German or one of a number of newer ethnic American "communities" — does our usage in fact limit such a sense of culture to what Pierre Bourdieu calls a learned, and hence quite functionally motivated and hierarchically structured, *habitus* (see Bourdieu 167)? Do we not at times imply that it is also an expression, as Arnold put it, of a people's innate "genius" (Arnold 3: 325) or soul, a spiritual disposition composed of intellectual, emotional, and psychological tendencies passed on by blood? By the same token, when we value the cross-fertilization enabled by transnational flows of ideas and capital, and champion the discursively (rather than racially) hybrid character of cultures around the globe as a salutary form of resistance to oppressive notions of racial and cultural purity, can we always prevent our rhetoric from subtly implying something not so different from what Arnold openly stated: that there really are distinct or simpler or purer cultural "humours" to be so blended in the first place, that the heterogeneous mix of Self and Other promoted by cosmopolitan modernity, if it is to represent a salutary cultural vigor, must have begun with more uniform racial aptitudes and sensibilities? It may be impossible to speak about "culture" in any depth even today without dragging along at certain points the Romantic ghost of blood inheritance. Don't the affiliations of kinship crucial to nascent nineteenth-century nationalisms and central in turn to anti-colonial struggles for political emancipation reverberate throughout the contemporary fascination for ethnic or cultural "difference," even when this difference is anchored in language, and bald terms like "blood" and "race" are never used?

At one point, Arnold cites linguistic evidence — faulty, as Strangford's note shows — to demonstrate that "the hearth comes to mean home. Then from home it comes to mean the group of homes, the tribe; from the tribe the entire nation; and in this sense of nation or people, the word appears in Gothic, Norse, Celtic, and Persian, as well as in Scythian" (3: 331). Arnold's bad philology notwithstanding, I would suggest that clear echoes of such Romantic (and surely much older) thinking, implying that the race or nation is in fact the family writ large, can be heard throughout the Modernism that triumphs in Arnold's wake, and that vestiges of it survive well into contemporary critical thought. Current usage of the word "ethnicity," for example, as in "ethnic American literatures"—English literature no longer qualifying, of course, as ethnic, though an Englishman's ethnicity was in no sense to be taken for granted among the Victorians — at times does much of the equivocating work that Arnold's "impulse," "bent," "force," and "tendency" do. Ethnicity can enable precisely the same conceptual slippage, the same back and forth shuttle of meanings between an arbitrarily transmitted custom and a racial inheritance that manifests itself as an expression of the soul, as a vague but intractable "sensibility" passed on by blood kinship.

As Robert J.C. Young has argued, "[t]he ethnological basis of Arnold's cultural politics, and the way in which racism, ethnology and culture slide so easily into each other, might also give us pause about current ways in which we champion ethnicity, and promote a culturally defined ethnic, as opposed to a biologically defined racial, identity" (88). Indeed, in a recent issue of *PMLA* devoted to ethnicity, Sander Gilman notes: "Ethnicity as it is used in the humanities is a North American sociological concept that is defined against the categories of race and class"; it often "comes very close to definitions of race in sociology and physical anthropology" (19). Yet after Gilman, none of the essays collected in the issue openly confronts the potential problems raised by using a term like ethnicity, with its vague connotation of inherited characteristics, in a causal relation to culture. In practice, I would argue, ethnicity often allows the disavowed ghost of blood-carried cultural humors to occupy the otherwise sanitized (or non-"essentialist") precincts of contemporary cultural studies. If the rather impractical demand that we eschew the word "culture" altogether, because it supposedly designates nothing *but* ghosts (see Walter Benn Michaels), is to be answered, then the sort of Arnoldian rhetorical work that a word like ethnicity does in the analysis of culture needs to be carefully elaborated. I do not mean to claim that neither "race" nor "culture" matters, but rather that the relation between them is as arbitrary (if historically maintained or contrived) and non-natural as the relation between race and language — a fact all too easy to forget once race, language, and culture are recognized as associated instruments of social and political power.

However much I agree with readers like Lionel Gossman that Arnold's use of the words Hebraism and Hellenism would seem to be free of any overt anti-Semitism, I remain convinced that the lingering resonance of *Celtic Literature*'s view of race in *Culture and Anarchy* cannot be ignored, and that these must reflect back in turn on what Arnold meant by Hebraism and Hellenism in the first place. The Celts and the Saxons belonged, we should remember, to the same racial family tree, in spite of their differences: both were Indo-European, and it would seem that it is the Celtic aptitude for sentiment and beauty that makes the Saxon all the more truly "Hellenic." The Hebrews and English belonged to completely different racial trees for Arnold, despite the similarity of their moral tendencies. To be sure, Arnold found Gobineau's and Burnouf s vulgar caricatures of the Semite worthy of ridicule. He certainly rejected, in *Literature and Dogma* (1873), Burnouf thesis that Christ, like other northern Jews of Galilee, was really Aryan (that is, Indo-European, or Indo-Germanic). Arnold thus dismissed Bernouf s claim that Christianity was a metaphysical doctrine imported from Persia and India rather than the practical religion of the southern Jews of Jerusalem and Judea, those supposedly true Semites guided by legal literalism, incapacity for abstraction or science, and small brains (see Arnold 6: 239-40; also Faverty 172). But what cannot be disputed is the fact that Arnold followed the lead of Renan, in texts like his *Histoire du peuple d'Israel* (1889-93), in thinking of Indo-European and Semite as distinct racial groups with distinct humors, aptitudes, and complexions of nature. Arnold refused Burnouf's idea that Christianity was Aryan in origin, but he admitted "that Israel shows no talent for metaphysics," even if religious greatness arises from the fact that "he does not found religion on metaphysics" (6: 241). Renan had insisted that the Indo-Europeans excelled at intellectual, political, and military achievement, while the Semites were responsible for the development of religious belief. Arnold's own conceptions are not far off.

In language that echoes *Celtic Literature*'s "science of origins," Arnold observes in *Culture and Anarchy* that science has now made visible to everybody the great and pregnant elements of difference which lie in race, and in how signal a manner they make the genius and history of an Indo-European people vary from those of a Semitic people. Hellenism is of Indo-European growth, Hebraism of Semitic growth; and we English, a nation of Indo-European stock, seem to belong naturally to the movement of Hellenism. (5: 173)

And yet Arnold goes on to point out that there is an "essential unity of man" marked by the "affinities we can perceive, in this point or that, between members of one family of peoples and members of another" (5: 173). The racial affinity, or *likeness,* of the English Protestants and the Jews is one such affinity — Renan and Taine had also noticed a similar seriousness, strength, and simplicity of spirit (see Faverty 173)—and it is a likeness reflected in the religious continuity of Hebraism. But the thesis that

Arnold's Hebraism represents a relatively smooth continuum of transmitted religious and moral tradition from Judaism to Christianity, as implied by Trilling, Stocking, Gossman, and many others, does not at all contradict the notion that for Arnold the English and Jews represent quite distinct innate racial aptitudes. The Aryan English and the Semitic Hebrews *resemble* one another to an extraordinary degree, and they share a religious tradition, but they are hardly the same racially. It is precisely because the English are racially rooted in their Indo-European humors that Arnold can reasonably expect them, as in "St. Paul and Protestantism" (1869-70) to redress the "overHebraising of Puritanism" (6: 7), a task that includes Arnold's attempt to translate the great convert St. Paul "for us modern and Western people" (6: 23) in a way that corrects "the defect in the critical habit of himself and his [Jewish] race" (6: 22).

What seems superficially to be merely a single transmitted tradition of religious and moral ideas in Arnold's essay turns out to be instead the evolutionary emergence of a "likeness in the strength and prominence of the moral fibre" (5: 174) in the English and Hebrew people. "Eminently Indo-European by its *humour*," by its power of "imaginatively acknowledging the multiform aspects of the problem of life" (5: 174) and hence of resisting "over-certainty," the English race also has in its practical and moral life "a strong share of the assuredness, the tenacity, and intensity of the Hebrews" (5: 174). English Puritanism may be called a form of "Hebraism" because Christianity in its origins "transformed and renewed" (Arnold 5: 187) the Hebraism of the Jews. But Puritanism as the continuation of a religious and moral tradition must at the same time be distinguished from the racially-given moral complexion of the English as an Indo-European people. Puritanism is in fact the consequence, then, both of a religious law externally transmitted (with modifications) from the Jews by converts like Paul, and of a quite separate and racially given moral aptitude in the English, albeit an aptitude equal to that of the Jews. As such, the impulse or tendency toward Puritan Christianity is driven first of all by "the conscience and moral sense of our race" (5: 174), and by "our race" Arnold means "the English nation." This "moral sense" echoes, or resembles, the racial humor of the Jews only because of some much older racial connection, implied by "the essential unity of man," in pre-history. Conceived in racial rather than religious terms, Jewish morality and English (Indo-European, Hellenic) morality are not consecutive points on the same line of evolutionary descent, as are Judaism and Christianity; they are actually like two distinct, if similar, evolutionary products linked by a common, but much older and unnameable, ancestor.

Arnold may have differed from his father on the literal truth of the Bible story, but he followed him on the need to make Christianity over into a more English, or Indo-European, phenomenon. As he wrote in a letter to his mother on Christmas Day, 1867:

> Bunsen used to say that our great business was to get rid of all that was purely Semitic in Christianity, and to make it Indo-Germanic, and Schleiermacher that in the Christianity of us Western nations there was really much more of Plato and Socrates than of Joshua and David; and, on the whole, papa worked in the direction . . . of Bunsen and Schleiermacher, and was perhaps the only powerful Englishman of his day who did so . . . Perhaps the change of times and modes of action being allowed for, my scope is not so different from his as you and I often think. (Arnold, ed. note, 6: 456)

Baron Bunsen, as Faverty notes, was responsible for the theory "of the co-existence of two races among the

Jews, one black, the other of a dark color" (Faverty 172), an earlier version of the theory that Arnold had rejected in Burnouf. Arnold may have insisted on the idea that Christianity as a religion indeed originated among the Jews rather than the Aryans, and from practical moral experience rather than metaphysical speculation. After all, it is precisely Christianity as deeply experienced ethical perfection rather than as mechanical legalism, literal history, or divine intervention that earned Arnold's admiration and acceptance. But just as, in Arnold's view, it is Heine's adopted Germanic-Hellenic culture that allows him to treat his Hebraic religious and racial inheritance with an ironic freedom absent in the Jews themselves (see 3: 127-28), so it is the Hellenic humor of the IndoEuropean races that Arnold calls upon to make Christianity into the instrument of ethical perfection.

And Arnold did not hesitate when needed, as in his treatment of the Liberal proposal to allow marriage to "one's deceased wife's sister" (5: 206), to remind his readers that the worst parts of Hebraism were, in fact, Semitic: "the delicate and apprehensive genius of the Indo-European race" cannot allow itself to be "hoodwinked" by a "divine law expressed for them by the voice of any Oriental and polygamous nation like the Hebrews" (5: 208). Hebraism cannot in practice be divorced from the opposed racial bases, Semitic and Indo-European, that give it its peculiar complexions and limitations; neither, finally, can Hellenism, composed as it is of Indo-European tendencies lacking in the Semitic peoples. Culture itself, then, far from being only that inward perfection of spirit spread among the peoples of the earth by means of cultivation or education is always in Arnold anchored, whether vulgarly or vaguely, in a theory of racial inheritance, a theory that both explains culture's origins and determines the natural aptitudes of those who are to be cultivated.

REFERENCES

apRoberts, Ruth. "Frederic E. Faverty's Matthew Arnold, The Ethnologist". *The Arnoldian* (1987-88):95-98.

Arnold, Matthew. *Complete Prose Works*. Ed. R. H. Super. 11 vols. Ann Arbor: University of Michigan Press, 1960-77.

——. Culture and Anarchy. 1869. *Complete Prose Works*. Vol. 5. 85-229.

——. "Heinrich Heine". 1863. *Complete Prose Works*. Vol. 3. 107-32.

——. "Irish Catholicism and British Liberalism". 1878. *Complete Prose Works*. Vol. 8. 321-47.

——. "Joseph de Maistre on Russia". 1879. *Complete Prose Works*. Vol. 9. 86-111.

——. Literature and Dogma. 1873. *Complete Prose Works*. Vol. 6. 139-411.

——. "Numbers; or The Majority and the Remnant". 1884. *Complete Prose Works*. Vol. 10. 143-64.

——. On the Study of Celtic Literature. 1867. *Complete Prose Works*. Vol. 3. 291-395.

——. "St. Paul and Protestantism". 1869-70. *Complete Prose Works*. Vol. 6. 1-127.

Bourdieu, Pierre. *Outline of a Theory of Practice*. Trans. Richard Nice. Cambridge: Cambridge University Press, 1990.

Burnouf, Emile. *The Science of Religions*. Trans. Julie Liebe. London: S. Sonnenschein, Lowrey, 1888.

Chapman, Malcolm. *The Celts: The Construction of a Myth*. New York: St. Martin's, 1992.

——. *The Gaelic Vision in Scottish Culture*. London: Croom Helm, 1978.

Conrad, Joseph. *Heart of Darkness*. Ed. Robert Kimbrough. New York: Norton, 1988.

——. *Lord Jim*. Ed. Thomas Moser. New York: Norton, 1968.

DeLaura, David J. *Hebrew and Hellene in Victorian England.* Austin: University of Texas Press, 1969.

Edwards, W.E. *Recherches sur les langues celtiques.* Paris: Imprimerie royale, 1844.

Ellmann, Richard. *James Joyce.* Oxford: Oxford University Press, 1983.

Fagan, Henry Stuart. "Notices of Books". *Contemporary Review* 6 (1867): 257-61.

Faverty, Frederic. *Matthew Arnold, the Ethnologist.* Evanston: Northwestern University Press, 1951.

Gilman, Sander. "Ethnicity — Ethnicities — Literature — literatures". *PMLA* 113 (1998): 19-27.

Gossman, Lionel. "Philhellenism and Antisemitism: Matthew Arnold and his German Models". *Comparative Literature* 46 (1994): 1-39.

Gottfried, Leon. *Matthew Arnold and the Romantics.* London: Routledge and Kegan Paul, 1963.

Graff, Gerald. "Arnold, Reason, and Common Culture". *Culture and Anarchy.* By Matthew Arnold. Ed. Samuel Lipman. New Haven: Yale University Press, 1994. 186-201.

Hegel, G.W.F. *The Phenomenology of Spirit.* Trans. A.V. Miller. Oxford: Oxford University Press, 1977.

——. *The Philosophy of History.* Trans. J. Sibree. New York: Dover, 1956.

Joyce, James. *Ulysses.* Ed. Hans Walter Gabler. New York: Vintage, 1986.

Kelleher, John V. "Matthew Arnold and the Celtic Revival". *Perspectives of Criticism.* Ed. Harry Levin. Cambridge: Harvard University Press, 1950. 197-221.

Lang, Andrew. "The Celtic Renascence". *Blackwood's. Edinburgh Magazine* 161 (1897): 181-92.

Lloyd, David. "Arnold, Ferguson, Schiller". *Cultural Critique* 1 (1985): 137-69.

Macpherson, James. *Poems of Ossian*. 3 vols. Trans. James Macpherson. London: W. Miller, J. Murray, and J. Harding, 1805.

Martin, Henri. *Histoire de France, depuis les temps les plus reculés jusqu'en 1789*. 17 vols. Paris: Furne, 1855-60.

Michaels, Walter Bernn. *Our America: Nativism, Modernism, and Pluralism*. Durham: Duke University Press, 1995.

Mill, John Stuart. "On Liberty". *Essential Works of John Stuart Mill*. Ed. Max Lerner. New York: Bantam, 1965. 253-360.

Principles of Political Economy, With Some of Their Applications to Social Philosophy. London: Longmans, Green, and Co., 1909.

Renan, Ernest. *Essais de morale et de critique*. Paris: Calmann-Lévy, 1924.

——. *Histoire du peuple d'Israel*. 5 vols. Paris: Calmann-Lévy, 1889-93.

——. *Qu'est-ce qu'une Nation?* Paris: Pierre Bordas et fils, 1991.

Senancour, Etienne Pivert de. *Obermann*. 2 vols. Paris: Libraire E. Droz, 1931.

Smart, J.S. *James Macpherson: An Episode in Literature*. London: David Nutt, 1905.

Stocking, George. "Matthew Arnold, E.B. Tylor, and the Uses of Invention". *American Anthropologist* 65 (1963): 783-99.

Thierry, Amédée. *Histoire des gaulois, depuis les temps les plus reculés jusqu'à l'entière soumission de la Gauled à la domination romaine*. 2 vols. Paris: Hachette, 1835.

Trilling, Lionel. *Matthew Arnold*. New York: Harcourt, 1977.

Williams, Raymond. *Culture and Society: 1780-1950*. New York: Columbia University Press, 1983.

Yeats, William Butler. "The Celtic Element in Literature". *Ideas of Good and Evil*. London: A.H. Bullen, 1903. 270-95.

Young, Robert J.C. *Colonial Desire: Hybridity in Theory, Culture and Race*. London: Routledge, 1995.

6

Crowd Management: Matthew Arnold and the Science of Society

—Gage McWeeny

Through the length and breadth of our nation a sense,—vague and obscure as yet,—of weariness with the old organisations . . . works and grows. In the House of Commons the old organisations must inevitably be most enduring and strongest, the transformation must inevitably be longest in showing itself; and it may truly be averred, therefore, that at the present juncture the centre of movement is not in the House of Commons. It is in the fermenting mind of the nation; and his is for the next twenty years the real influence who can address himself to this.

Matthew Arnold, *Culture and Anarchy* (1866-69)

The destinies of nations are elaborated at present in the heart of the masses, and no longer in the councils of princes.

Gustave Le Bon, *The Crowd* (1896)

Gustave Le Bon Declared in his 1896 text that the coming age was to be "The Era of the Crowd." Matthew Arnold's own handbook to crowd control, Culture and Anarchy, published in 1869, suggests however that Le Bon merely sensationalized elements already potent enough some thirty years earlier to occasion Arnold's polemic on behalf of culture. Energizing Arnold's claims that through culture's opposition to and suppression of anarchy lies the way not only to "perfection, but even to safety," "the era of the crowd" seems already to have arrived by the middle of the nineteenth century. While Arnold's sloganeering on behalf of culture produced such phrases as "the best that's been thought and said" and "sweetness and light," culture's antagonist, anarchy, has been a less conspicuous part of Arnold's critical legacy. As the above passage indicates, however, the power of the crowd figured by the mass "fermenting mind of the nation" should rightfully be accorded a signal place in reading Culture and Anarchy, a text who se own apocalyptic tones resonate in the amplified echoes of Le Bon.[1]

The "monster-procession" of the Reform League's demonstrations for an expanded franchise in July 1866, a demonstration that turned riotous after police refused the league access to Hyde Park, inspired Arnold to revise his initial lecture's title, "Culture and its Enemies," and give his series of essays the title of Culture and Anarchy upon publication in book form in 1869. Officially relegating the anarchic crowd to a wound in the social body, Arnold insists that the "best self" of culture, "enjoins us to set our faces against" "whatever brings risk of tumult and disorder," most egregiously, the "multitudinous processions in the streets of our crowded towns" (CA, p. 100). If these multitudinous meetings are to be put down, as Arnold insists, by the soothing effects of "culture," the crowd duly disperses, but does not quite disappear. Instead, in spite of a book intended to castigate and expel it as anarchic, the crowd scatters, only to regroup. The collective character of the crowd is manifest not only in "monster processions," but also in the men of culture who are "docile echoes of the eternal voice, pliant organs of the infinite will," and our "best self" by which "we are united, impersonal, at harmony" (CA, pp. 186, 99). Even as the crowd is to be banished, Arnold acknowledges its governing power as a figure for the social realm generally, the vast "fermenting mind" of the nation. Occupying a "centre of movement" that cannot be ignored, the crowd's status as both anarchy and the future of power for years to come impels in Arnold's work figurative efflorescences of a social force that can be acknowledged officially only in its suppression.

Arnold's well-known efforts to dispel the crowd in Culture and Anarchy, however, also run the risk of eclipsing other, earlier manifestations of the crowd in his work. While Culture and Anarchy is the site of the crowd's most infamous gathering in Arnold's corpus, reading the poetry of the years prior to his critical writings reveals that Arnold's interest in crowds predates the Hyde Park demonstrations. And, though Culture and Anarchy is the site of Arnold's crowd management in its official form, it is in Arnold's poetry that the elaboration of the crowd as a manageable metonym of the social realm begins. The figurations of the crowd in the poetry present a crucial alternative to the tumultuous social realm that haunts Culture and Anarchy, offering a vision of the crowd as other than purely anarchic and illuminating Arnold's earlier and ongoing negotiations with the challenges posed by the new social forces of modernity.

The poems supplement by anticipating what is only a partial program for controlling the crowd's power outlined in Culture and Anarchy. Arnold represents culture in that text as the guardian of the social order itself, a social order that is condensed by a chain of metonymic displacements into the figure of the crowd. Men of culture, Arnold writes, must join in "repressing anarchy and disorder; because without order there can be no society, and without society there can be no human perfection" (CA, p. 181). Arnold, however, was only one of many in the mid-Victorian era whose critical practices were aimed at managing a modern social order whose complexity seemed to take on fearsome aspects through such phenomena as the crowd. Arnold's proposals for crowd management, I will argue, should be read against the background of a variety of new mid-Victorian efforts taking place under the general, emergent category of social science. These efforts sought to develop a science for understanding, conceptualizing, and governing the structures of social order in the nineteenth century. In the drive to stake rival claims for the position of best guiding mid-Victorian society, of managing a modernity whose social complexity demanded an endless series of blue books, statistics, and government studies, Arnoldean criticism and proto-sociology both asserted respective ascendancy. The crowd, as Le Bon's and Arnold's texts indicate, served as one readily available figure for the challenges of social management to which social science and criticism were responding.

The consonance of the program of crowd control outlined in Culture and Anarchy and the crowd management of the poems suggests that they might be read together as unintended referents in Arnold's claim that "without poetry, our science will appear incomplete."[2] Arnold's claims for criticism against the rising prestige of science and scientific thinking in the disciplinary developments of the nineteenth century are well known, and his use of the word science frequently indicates simply objective, systematic study.[3] In this essay, however, I want to read the "incomplete" science in Arnold's phrase specifically as an emergent nineteenth-century social science. Placing not only Arnold's critical work, but also the poetry, in the context of the burgeoning practices of social scientists in the nineteenth century illuminates the boundaries of this disciplinary contest as extending beyond its most polemical sites in the essays. In Britain, sociologist remains largely a "potential role" in the middle Victorian period, one tried on by a variety of disciplinary practices, including that of criticism. A dream of social management coalesces in the figure of the crowd throughout Arnold's corpus, I argue, a dream that will be seen both to parallel English sociology's mid-century efforts to understand and guide the social sphere, and anticipate later continental theorists who took the crowd as their special object of study.

Reading these efforts at social management together also revises some characterizations of British pre- or proto-sociology as largely uninterested in more theoretical questions of structure. Philip Abrams, for instance, argues that the incipient social science comprised in England by statistical research and ameliorist reform efforts, among other practices, lacked "any developed concept of a social system," or theorizations of social structure.[4] And, seeking to understand the nature of social order and the phenomenon of social bonds through strict scientific methods, Herbert Spencer admits a faltering first epistemological challenge for scientists of the social realm: "The phenomena [to be examined by social science] are not of a directly-perceptible kind—cannot be noted by telescope and clock, like those of Astronomy."[5] The under-theorization of social structure and the epistemological challenges of early British sociology however, find a compensatory figuration in the manifestations of the crowd in Arnold's work as it takes on the metonymic function of representing a social totality amenable to the ministrations of culture.

Between the mid 1840s and the late 1860s, Arnold elaborates first in his poetry and then his prose a vision of the crowd as signifying not simply terrifying social dissolution, but also, in the proper managerial hands, an image and instrument of social order.[6] The metonymic chain by which society's dissolution is figured by the anarchic crowd in Culture and Anarchy is also reversible: the non-anarchic, pliable crowd can function as a figure for a social realm amenable to management. Although the crowds in Culture and Anarchy have an actual, historical referent in the 1366 demonstrations of the Reform League, I trace here the modes by which the crowd in that text as well as the less historically specific crowds of the poems become figures, paradoxically, for both social order in general and its dissolution. So, while much of Arnold's poetry was produced in the years around the 1848 revolutions across Europe, the crowds in the poems extend beyond any specific historical referents and become figures for a social sphere that is alternately repellant, alluring, chaotic, and enervating. Through these poetic figurations, Arnold can suggest the transformative potential of the managed crowd which the polemical critic of Culture and Anarchy must suppress as anarchic.

The later critical work both continues and departs from the crowds of the poetry in developing the notion of culture, a structure that will be seen to be modeled on, as well as stand in opposition to, the crowd. The poetry's early figurations of the crowd complicate not only readings of Culture and Anarchy which imagine these two title terms as opposed, but also narratives that posit a sharp, clear turn from the personal to the public in Arnold's move away from writing poetry in the 1840s and 1850s to his critical prose of the 1860s and after. In reading Arnold's poetry and critical essays against a proto-sociological background, I hope to show the mutual efforts of sociology and literary study in the mid-nineteenth century to chart the social complexity, and manageability, of modernity as it is embodied by the crowd. Only by reading the crowd of the poetry with both his critical prose and the work of early sociology can we begin to comprehend Arnold's contribution to the nineteenth century's incomplete efforts to conceptualize and understand a social sphere that comes to seem at once binding and tenuous.

In Arnold's poems, we encounter versions of the crowd that are more oblique and less politically specific, as well as more openly alluring, than the eruptive Reform League demonstrators of Culture and Anarchy. IAs one reads the crowd amid Arnold's poems and essays, its representational pliability becomes apparent. The crowd can one moment figure the site of anarchic social dissolution, the next an appealingly binding social order, a salve contained within the dispersive effects of modern life. As a figure for both social disorder and a spontaneously occurring harmony, anarchic explosiveness and a suffocating, enervating social realm, the crowd becomes a testing ground in Arnold for the power of culture to manage the challenges of social complexity in modernity.

Crowd Poems

The various congregations that appear in Arnold's poems—"The armies of the homeless and unfed" in "To a Republican Friend" (1848), "the mortal millions" who live "alone" in "To Marguerite—Continued" (1849), and the "swarms of men" in "Stanzas in Memory of the Author of 'Obermann'" (1849), to cite a few invocations of the many—have been described by one recent critic of Victorian poetry as "depersonalised crowds." These crowds include not only the working class but also a creeping influx of strangers from beyond Britain, all of whom exert a "terrible pressure" on Arnold's poetry.[7] And it is difficult not to read the heart of a conflicted agoraphobe into Arnold's complaint of a world divided between living either in tormented solitude or suffering infection by "unavoidable contact with millions of small [natures]."[8] As, however, the rhetorical doubling of the offhandedly enumerated collective "mortal millions" and a solitude no less general evinces, the distinction between the crowd and the isolated subject is not always so clear in Arnold. Reading the less politically insurgent crowds of the poetry with the Reform League demonstrators of Culture and Anarchy introduces a more variegated sense of Arnold's crowds than is encompassed by "impersonal." This reading of poetry and prose together illuminates the crowd's contradictory status as a figure not only of an alienated world, but also the site of an obliquely pleasurable form of sociation in his work, as well as its emerging status as a figure for social order and dissolution.

The year preceding the publication of Arnold's first book of poetry in 1849 saw the last of the large-scale Chartist demonstrations in England, a peaceful gathering in 1848 on Kennington Common which Arnold attended. But it also was the year of a series of revolutionary movements across Europe in France, Italy, Germany, and Hungary. The events of 1848, in particular the revolutionary activity in France and the temporary installation of the poet Lamartine as the new French leader, spurred excitement in Arnold, as well as concern over the undirected violence that England's "masses" were likely to fall into in imitating their French counterparts. Arnold writes in a letter, "If the new state of things succeeds in France, social changes are inevitable here and elsewhere." But the state of England's working class is such that "their movements now can only be brutal plundering and destroying." In the opposition Arnold goes on to draw between the "intelligence of the idea-moved masses" of France and the "insensible m asses of England," the outlines of a taxonomy of collective forms that Arnold would later elaborate in Culture and Anarchy by both distinguishing and allying anarchy, the nation's "fermenting mind," and culture, come into view.[9] The contrast of "intelligence" and "idea" to describe the French with the "insensible" English, as well as Arnold's stated fears of English plundering, suggest "insensible" ought to be read as signifying lacking intelligence or irrationality: the crowd for Arnold is a kind of excitable, over-charged entity, worryingly given over to eruptions of violence.

In an instance of the characteristic reversibility of meanings that can be assigned to the crowd, however, a contradictory sense clings to Arnold's description of the English "masses" as "insensible": the quality of being unaffected, or indifferent. This quality of indifference or dullness shadows the crowds of the poetry as well as the criticism, evoking not the spectacularly violent public realm of 1866, but a social sphere at times characterized as "action's dizzying eddy," at times as the site of indifference. An indifferent, or to Use a term I will return to, disenchanted, social sphere is allied assymetrically to those more typically Arnoldean judgments of the social realm as the site of "sick hurry," the "strange disease of modern life" as his poem "The Scholar Gipsy" phrases it.

"Resignation" (1849) introduces one of Arnold's recurrent poetic themes: a self-sustaining self-repression that the speaker-poet, in describing an ideal poetic consciousness to his sister and us as readers, proclaims as an alternative to a life of unsatisfying activity amid the "something that infects the world" (1. 278).[10] Loosely following the narrative scheme of Wordsworth's "Tintern Abbey," "Resignation" tells of a return to the Lake Country by a matured poet-speaker and his sister. Occasioning a discourse by the poet-speaker on the nature of the poetic soul, this longed-for ideal is figured in the descriptions of a poet within the poem. Rejecting a romantic consonance between nature and the soul, the poet is described as stoically resigned to a world indifferent to the lives that pass through, an enervated "eternal mundane spectacle" (1. 228). The poet-speaker devotes considerable energy to elaborating upon a poetic "resigned" consciousness (1. 243), an elaboration carried out largely through a series of oppositions between the poet and the social realm.

The poet-speaker describes the figure of the poet as one who, by virtue of having been granted not "joy," but rather the compensatory "sad lucidity of soul" of a poet, nonetheless claims difference from the world of work, those "whom labours, self-ordained, enthrall" (11. 198, 14). In a quick extension of the theory of labor under capitalism as self-estrangement, even work freely undertaken "enthralls" in the sense of making one a slave. Thus, even the poem we are reading is a product of a less successful navigation of stoicism than that accomplished by the poet being described, whose signal poetic "production" is a poetic consciousness. The poet-speaker describes the poetic consciousness that is, whether through "schooling of the stubborn mind" or "birth," among those "freed from passions, and the state /Of struggle these necessitate" (11. 24-27). In a poem so desiccated of desire, the only "crav[ing]" is for a form of self-negation, to live the "life of plants, and stones, and rain" who themselves seem "to bear rather than rejoice" in life (11. 195, 270). The poem's complicated engagement of self-negation as self-preservation is imagined as a withdrawal from the social realm altogether, but this withdrawal is accomplished, crucially, without a corresponding sense of alienation.

Such assertions of detachment, however, may seem like empty boasts, and the poem enlists the test case of the crowd in order to exemplify the poet's passionlessness. The power possessed by the poet is in the maintenance of a subdued self which understands the lives of others, but remains free from an identification with those lives which might draw him into their activity:

> The poet, to whose mighty heart
> Heaven doth a quicker pulse impart,
> Subdues that energy to scan
> Not his own course, but that of man. (11.144-147)

The poet rests on a "high station" (1. 164) observing a town from above at the end of the workday:

At sunset, on a populous town;
Surveys each happy group, which fleets,
Toils ended) through the shining streets,
Each with some errand of its own—
And does not say: I am alone. (11. 165-169)

The scene regarded, significantly, is not described as that of a crowd, but rather a cluster of "group[s]," acquaintances together carrying out "same errand," that lighter, sociable version of labor that follows upon "toils." This scene of pleasurable sociability is refused by the poet who is content to "survey" rather than engage the groups, and the remote location of the poet gazing upon this happy idyll fails to engender any expected sense of disabling isolation: "And does not say: I am alone." Detachment, a value and term central to Arnold's corpus, is here valued unreservedly as both the safeguard, and the enabling condition, of a poetic consciousness that is securely distanced but not nihilistic. The lines preceding this idyll of happy groups elaborate detachment as a practice in the midst of a more crowded scene. Here, the poet

sees, in some great-historied land
A ruler of the people stand,
Sees his strong thought in fiery flood
Roll through the heaving multitude;
Exults—yet for no moment's space
Envies the all-regarded place.
Beautiful eyes meet his—and he
Bears to admire uncravingly;
They pass—he, mingled with the crowd,
Is in their far-off triumphs proud. (11. 153-163)

Two versions of the crowd as well as two distinct forms of its management appear in these lines as a measure of the poet's powers of detachment. The ruler's amplification of his thoughts through the medium of the "heaving multitude" describes a Le Bon-esque, apocalyptic ("fiery flood") version of crowd control, from which the poet maintains an admiring, but not envying, distance. Possessing no thoughts of their own, the "heaving multitude" is an image of the crowd controlled through demagoguery. By contrast, the crowd management practiced by the poet is of a piece with erotic self-management. "Beautiful eyes meet his—and he / Bears to admire uncravingly; / They pass—he, mingled with the crowd." Here, admiring without desiring, the poet enacts aesthetic disinterestedness as social practice in "mingl[ing] with the crowd" "uncravingly." Thus highlighting his own power to move within the multitude, the poet is both singled out and singles out others—in his recognition by, and judgment of, "beautiful eyes"—while remaining untouched physically and affectively. The erotic potential in the passing glances of the beautiful eyes which is deflected by the "uncraving" poet is also an erotic of potential, one that in failing to be fulfilled also fails to locate itself, to find an end, in any single individual. Endlessly potential, the serial erotic of the poet in the crowd is recouped as further evidence of a consciousness-securing disinterest defined as social management: a freedom from, purchased by being within ("mingled with the crowd"), the modem social world. The poet's detachment allows him to move in a sociable realm whose crowd character nevertheless licenses an erotic purified of "craving," an energy that can be conserved for the maintenance of a self all the stronger for being subdued. But it also is the condition for freedom from any individual social obligation, all the while remaining in pleasurable "contact" with a generalized social sphere in the image of the crowd.[11]

Carving out a zone of autonomy amid the crowd takes a more specific locale in the hybrid pastoral-urban space of the 1852 "Lines Written in Kensington Gardens." Arnold's revision of romanticism transfers the "air-stirr'd forest" (1. 16) of a bucolic lake country scene to an "open glade" (1. 1) of a London park, a refuge encircled by the "girdling city's hum." In this ersatz forest, the buzzing multitudes of people in the populous city that surround the speaker as he lies in the park are placed at a double remove. They first are flattened into mere background noise, a "hum," which is then attributed to the city itself rather than any human presence. Against the peopled world, which has been generalized to noise, is a natural world all the more able succinctly to individuate itself: "Birds here make song, each bird has his,! Across the girdling city's hum" (1. 5). The lyric opposition between self and world becomes here an opposition between noise and individuating music or meaning. Both the bird's songs and the speaker's thoughts come into focus only against the contrasting world of the "hum." A child occasionally crosses the glade, but even this human presence is (temporarily) elided by the speaker's gently self-mocking engrossment in the miniaturized country idyll: "Here at my feet what wonders pass,! What endless, active life is here! / What blowing daisies, fragrant grass!" while "the huge world, which roars hard by" engrosses the multitude outside the glade (11. 13-15, 21).

Arnold's lyric negotiation of the self's relation to the world, a meditation that both reduces the crowd to a hum and structures its own claims to meaningfulness against this necessary noise, is seen to be only momentarily sustainable as the speaker's reverie is broken off by direct supplications for peace toward the end of the poem. Abandoning the elaboration of the trope of an ersatz, depopulated, sylvan retreat, the speaker cries:

> Calm soul of all things make it mine
> To feel, amid the city's jar,
> That there abides a peace of thine,
> Man did not make, and cannot mar. (11. 37-40)

This abrupt move into direct address breaks the lyric mode, a fragmenting not untypical of Arnold. But the lyric condition of a self both constituted by its remove from the world, and yet painfully longing for contact with that world, remains.[12] Reversing the earlier translation of the people of London to a mere noise, sympathy is now enlisted to compensate for an unsustainable peace: "The power to feel with others five! / Calm, calm me more! nor let me die / Before I have begun to live" (ll. 42-44). The speaker both desiring to feel and not feel, to know and not know, the generalized social world that began as a crowd's hum is here vainly called back into individualized, sympathy-ready form in order to reclaim his peace. Arnold's lyric mode of securing the self, albeit only momentarily, by opposition to or difference from a more crowded world also bears with it a counter-possibility of alienation, a self not secured but enervated by its difference. "In the deserted, moon-blanched street, / How lonely rings the echo of my feet!" begins "A Summer Night," which speaks of "the old unquiet breast . . . Never by passion quite possessed / and never quite benumb'd by the world's sway" (ll. 27-33): dispassion is less a satisfactory mode of poetic consciousness, as it was in "Resignation," than a feature of an insufficiently energized social realm. While the crowd has been the problem against, or the medium within, which a poetic subjectivity might be secured in the above poems, I want to turn finally to a poem in which the crowd might also be read as the solution for the ambivalent negations of the social sphere brought on by this self-securing Arnoldean subjectivity. If the crowd does not precisely show its face in "The Buried Life" (1852), its force is registered as all the more powerful for its dispersion in the text as the governing presence of "the world's most crowded streets" (l. 45). The allure of these streets, I will argue, renders the lyric binary of lovers at a pleasurable remove from the social world ambiguous. I want to suggest that "The Buried Life" enacts an Arnoldean fantasy of social management by staking out a middle territory between the self and the crowd through a plunge into the "world's most crowded streets," and in doing so, momentarily achieves the type of reconciliation precluded elsewhere.

"The Buried Life" invokes a characteristic gesture of withdrawal in its lyric scene of lovers residing in a space of intimacy sheltered from all other social relations: "Give me thy hand, and hush awhile, / And turn those limpid eyes on mine" (ll. 9-10). Even this scene of pleasurable isolation, however, may be dangerously consonant with a troubling self-alienation that characterizes modernity: "long we try in vain to speak and act / Our hidden self," "But hardly have we, for one little hour, / Been on our own line, have we been ourselves" (ll. 64-65, 59-60). With the silencing of the beloved, the pleasurable exile of the lyric pair shades into, and is doubled by, the complaint of the speaker's own intrapsychic exile. The "light words" and "gay smiles" of the beloved bring "no rest," "no anodyne" to a nameless sadness within (ll. 7-8). The complaint of a love that can speak only its occlusion—"Are even lovers powerless to reveal / To one another what indeed they feel?"—occasions a turn inward to "a something in this breast," a turn ostensibly propelled by the exquisite pain of the erotic pair's love beyond words (11. 14-15, 6).

The turn inward, however, is more precisely the precipitant of a turn away from the zone of erotic sequestration and into the streets of men. The exquisite pain of unspeakable feelings that first places the speaker/ beloved pair in pleasurable isolation is, in the next stanza, generalized to the common lot of men:

> I knew the mass of men concealed
> Their thoughts, for fear that if revealed
> They would by other men be met
> With blank indifference, or with blame reproved.
> (11. 16-19)

The particularity of the speaker/beloved pair with which the poem opens is mitigated by the increasing investment of the narrative energies of the poem instead in the "mass of men." The intimate scene of lover and beloved first presented as the spur to the inward turn, the yearning for perfect knowledge, "let me read there, love! thy inmost soul," is shadowed by what would appear to be opposed to the private space of the lovers, the urban crowd:

> But often, in the world's most crowded streets,
> But often, in the din of strife,
> There rises an unspeakable desire
> After the knowledge of our buried Life.
> (11. 45-48)

The overall movement of the scenes of the poem, from private pair to public streets and back again in the final stanzas, forecasts a trajectory in which the din of public life is merely a foil to the deeper pleasures of the sequestered erotic pair. This movement, however, is complicated both by the centrality of the crowd experience to the mining of the "hidden self," and by the vastly greater rhetorical energy of the desires that arise in the crowd over the uninflected "something in this breast" of the erotic pair. The opening invocation of the socially dense space of the crowd in the sixth stanza locates the public, urban anonymity of the crowd as the experiential ground that produces the most energized turn, "an unspeakable desire," toward the hidden self. It is not just the buried self that is inaccessible even to a lover's language, as is argued in the opening of the poem, but the desires induced by the crowd are themselves unspeakable. Unspeakability, then, might be less symptomatic of self-alienation than of the lyric poem's necessary disavowal of its investment in the power of "the world's most crowded streets" over that of the lyric pair. After all, what kind of nineteenth-century English love lyric would take "the streets of men" as the site of a desire stronger than that of the speaker for the beloved? The public, urban anonymity of the crowd in this poem drives the strongest desire to know the hidden self, thus suggesting that the desire for identity itself, the desire to discover one's "buried life" may be stronger than any erotic desire for the beloved. And it is only by immersion in the tumultuous "mass of men," rather than simply in detached retirement, that "the buried life" can be known.[13]

The poem's return from the scene of crowded streets to the sequestered lyric couple in the final stanzas is a return to a realm that has been transformed. The social sphere of the crowd's "din of strife" rezones the intimate space of the lyric couple:

> Only—but this is rare—
> When a beloved hand is laid in ours,
> When jaded with the rush and glare
> Of the interminable hours,
> Our eyes can in another's eyes read clear,
> When our world-deafened ear
> Is by the tones of a loved voice caressed—
> A bolt is shot back somewhere in our breast,
> And a lost pulse of feeling stirs again. (II. 77-84)

The first person address of the opening stanza, "Give me thy hand and hush awhile," changes here to a third person narration of exempla, mitigating its immediacy: "When a beloved hand is laid in ours . . . A bolt is shot back somewhere in our breast! And a lost pulse of feeling stirs again." The transformation that enables the release of the buried self takes place not in the first-person present tense of dramatic address; rather, it is in the generality of example. At the moment of claiming love's power to redress the alienation of the buried life, the speaker's invocation of "a beloved" in which "Our eyes can in another's eyes read clear," the specific beloved addressed in the first stanza vanishes (11. 78, 81). Installing the anonymity of a case ("A beloved," "another's eyes") in place of the particular lyric pair, the poem despecifies the agent that unlocks the bolt in the breast, as if the individuality-annulling spirit of the crowd has descended upon the formerly private couple. With the transformative power of the specific erotic pair's love mooted by generality, we can read the social world's effects—"the rush and glare / Of the interminable hours," "our world-deafened ear"—not as the wearied defeat by, or noisy interference of, the social realm. Instead, these conditions are the necessary and crucial inflection of the "tones of a loved voice." The specific erotic pair's dispersion into generalities is not the frustration but the expansion of the paradise of pure communication from the lyric pair to a fantasized generality of society. Not in spite of, but rather due to, "the rush and glare of interminable hours," can the speaker enter into the field of pure communication: "what we mean, we say, and what we would, we know" (1. 87). The collective deliverance which takes "we" rather than "I" as its point of reference, annuls the specificity of the individual speaker by dispersing him into the plurality of an expansive social realm.[14] The poem's incorporation of the encounter with the crowd as a condition for the revelation of what is less a deep privacy than a collective communion blurs the lines of division between the crowd and the erotic pair that the poem seems to set out to amplify. Relieving the burdens of subjectivity imposed by "the buried life," the "crowded streets" drive a social fantasy of generalized linguistic communion and transparency. The crowd appears obliquely in these lines in its productive, managed form, an image of a social realm unburdened by separation and alienation.

Such lyric expansiveness, however, can be sustained only momentarily. The final lines returns us to the singular pronoun, "And then he thinks he knows / The hills where his life rose, / And the sea where it goes," as well as to a less assured condition of communication—"he thinks he knows" (11. 96-98, my emphasis). While maintaining the generality of the exemplum of "a man" who "becomes aware of his life's flow," these lines qualify this field of pure communication, suggesting that the effects of the crowded streets might be, like the crowd on those streets, only passing.

Culture and Anarchy

Arnold's turn to critical prose and increasing neglect of poetry in the late 1850s and after was not a turn away from the concerns that had occupied his verse. As the more general crowds of the poems give way to the specific Reform League crowd castigated in Culture and Anarchy, Arnold continues to elaborate an understanding of the social realm against the background of nascent sociology's efforts to do the same. While sociology identified the crowd as an instance of the aggregate behavior that was its scientific object, culture alone, Arnold would seem to claim in critical prose aimed at quelling mass eruptions, could speak its language. In its various transformations, begun in the poetry, from anarchic figure to an image of the social order upon which culture will act, the crowd is recast as the proper object of control for the literary critic rather than the sociologist. A more efficacious manager of sentiment than science or politics, culture alone claims to be capable of addressing and controlling the anarchic crowd, of speaking to the vast "fermenting mind" of the nation. The crowd can be seen here to underwrite Arnold's attempts to chart a role for culture that places it neither as mere inward aesthetic self-involvement, nor as allied with the stultifying "machinery" of public life. Arnold's aesthetic and political program of detachment, in which culture must remain aloof from the "fetish" of activism, enlists the coercive, public power of the crowd in an effort to resolve the contradictory elaboration of culture as both an "inward condition" and the shaping force of a social sphere.

Arnold invokes the anarchic crowd of the 1866 Hyde Park riots in Culture and Anarchy in order to array culture against what he famously calls "doing as one likes." Culture will be a palliative and constraining force on the "strong individualism" so prevalent in modern society, a mode of shaping the "unrestrained swing of the individual's personality." (CA, p. 63). In the essay "Democracy," Arnold warns of the singular individual as dangerously inchoate, being possessed by an incompleteness that threatens violence unless the individual is molded by the shaping, forming effects of culture: "character without culture . . . is something raw, blind, and dangerous" (CPW, 2:24). In Culture and Anarchy, culture is not only the sum of great aesthetic and scientific works, the "best that's been thought and said," but a power enlisted to shape the "unrestrained swing" of the individual, a social force with all the coercive and imperative potency ascribed to the crowd by later sociologists. "Then we have got a practical benefit out of culture . . . a principle of authority; to counteract the tendency to anarchy which seems to be threatening us" (CA, p. 89).

The individualism that culture will restrain, however, looks paradoxically like collectivism later in Arnold's book. In the chapter entitled "Doing as One Likes," a blind faith in freedom leads directly to anarchy: "this and that man, and this and that body of men, all over the country, are beginning to assert and put in practice an Englishman's right to do what he likes; his right to march where he likes, meet where he likes, enter where he likes, hoot as he likes, threaten as he likes, smash as he likes" (CA, pp. 84-85). Presenting a continuum between rampant individualism and the coercive collectivism of a mass riot, "doing as one likes" inverts the poles between the individual and the crowd. Dangerous individual freedom appears not as a cause, but an effect of anarchic crowd behavior in this passage. Arnold moves without remarking from the singular "this and that man" to the plural "this and that body of men." The "unrestrained swing of the individual" becomes a crowd "march[ing] where he likes," "meet[ing] where he likes." Arnold's syntactical maneuvers in utilizing the singular pronoun "he" with verbs, "meeting" and "marching," associated with collective behavior underscore the degree to which it is in fact the collective that sets the terms for his pillorying of individualism. "Doing as one likes" could be more accurately phrased as "doing as the crowd likes."

Alongside the indictment of individualism, Culture and Anarchy also insists that the apostles of culture refrain from directly intervening in the public sphere. In abjuring any concrete activity, the men of culture for whom "public life and direct political action" are not "much permitted," "must keep out of the region of immediate practice" (CA, pp. 183-184; CPW, 3:42). The temporary retreat of the critic stages a retreat to safety from a violent public sphere dominated by "tumult and disorder," "multitudinous processions in the streets of our crowded towns" (CA, p. 100). The violence of the social sphere is one force that drives the critic's retreat from the public realm in order more ably to apply the "fresh stream" of critical thought to it. Invoking a word with a complex array of meanings in his vocabulary, Arnold insists the man of culture withdraw from the realm of social action and instead practice a detachment he names "disinterest."

The effort to establish a realm of social autonomy is doubled into a subjective autonomy by Arnold's pointed placement of culture's effect inside an individual: culture, as Arnold repeats throughout his essay, is "above all, an inward operation" (CA, p. 190). The effects of culture are primarily those of bildung, or self-development, as many of his commentators have remarked. Self-development, Arnold is careful to stress, is always oriented toward a more general ideal, a point ignored by many of his critics: not a withdrawn aesthete, but a "best self." It is this combination of inward orientation and withdrawal from the social sphere, however, that troubles Arnold's claims of culture's social beneficence. The cultivated inaction of the man of culture appears to Arnold's critics as less a contribution to the social good than a form of effete subjectivity, characterized by an "effeminate horror" of political reform (CA, p. 162).

If a violent social sphere is one precipitant of criticism's spatial and subjective retreat, however, another is something like its very opposite: a social sphere characterized not by chaotic tumult, but by an enervating, constrictive "bondage to machinery," and unthinking attachment to the fetish of politics and freedom (CA, p. 83). This characterization of the current social realm both accompanies and opposes its more tumultuous timbre: its "external and mechanical rule" creates the need for a culture that will impart flexibility in our thinking, thus allowing the cultured person to turn a "fresh stream of thought" upon stock notions and habits (CA, pp. 128, 167).

Culture is elaborated by Arnold partially as a more limber understanding and response to the complexities of a social world than that of a British science of society interested largely in statistical averages and direct, legislative instruments of reform. As part of an increasing rationalization of the state and the roles of individuals within it in the nineteenth century, statistical analyses of society could provide a measure of social conditions. Such statistical social data, however, could also take on an air of determinism for those individuals within this state. The apparent social forces governing life, and death, in the French sociologist Emile Durkheim's famous analysis of the predictability of the number of suicides in a given society, would in later years provoke terror.

Such an understanding of the social realm in the modern era inspired new strategies for securing a sense of self-determinism. Frances Ferguson has described a romantic "aesthetics of individuation" that emerges under a more and more rationalized social realm which takes on a systemic, deterministic aspect to those living in it: "with the notion of system emerged an antitype to the notion of society as a collection of individuals."[15] While culture's aesthetic self-development might be one version of individuation, Ferguson's formulation of society as system also suggests some of what is at stake in Arnold's vocabulary of "machinery" and "fetish" in describing the current social sphere.

As a characteristic feature of a nineteenth-century society experiencing the growth of government agencies and scientific techniques for charting and controlling the social realm, rationalization is allied with what Max Weber has called the "disenchantment" characteristic of a rational, scientific world's self-understanding.[16] Scientific understanding banishes the supernatural forces that seemed once to rule society from this disenchanted world of modernity, a world that the science of society is instrumental in both illuminating and constructing. As the quasi-mystical descriptions of the binding powers of social statistics in Durkheim, and Arnold's own appropriation of mystical tones in describing the powers of culture, suggest, however, the banishing of disenchantment is always an incomplete project. A social realm characterized by "machinery," a realm studied for the purpose of governing through scores of statistical analyses and government agencies, is for Arnold a disenchanted world. Society as a system threatens not just the autonomy of the individual, but also the malleability of a social realm that Arnold argues culture will shape in guiding England's future. Society as a crowd, however, suggests a solution to the problem of this modernity. Culture's role of crowd management allows Arnold to describe a public, non-bureaucratic, non-parliamentary sphere for its effects, a sphere of the crowd that escapes the enervation attending social rationalization. The volatile energies of the anarchic crowd might be marshaled into an image of a re-enchanted social realm freed from the machinery of modern bureaucracy and politics. This re-enchanted social realm, purified of anarchy but retaining the potency of the crowd, will be managed by a culture which is thus granted in Arnold's scheme "the future of powers for years to come."

Theodore Adorno's analysis of lyric poetry's doomed utopian urges describes the dream and nightmare of the relations figured by the crowd: a world of people "between whom the barriers have fallen."[17] It is this fantasy of an unmediated but manageable relationship to the social order for the agents of culture that pushes Arnold toward the crowd. Perhaps more flaneur than Carlylean prophet, Arnold, impelled by sociology, performs a negotiation of the opposing poles of engagement and autonomy, social actor and "inwardness" for the critical agent of culture on the terrain of the crowd. Unlike the flaneur, however, Arnold must manage rather than simply bathe in the crowd, shaping it from anarchy into the vehicle for culture. Enabling a sustaining fantasy of social order, the crowd in Arnold's texts is a power that is everywhere, so diffusive that it is difficult to pin down. At once "anarchy," "the centre of movement," the mass mind, and the fantasized pliant addressee of culture, the collective figurations of the crowd in Arnold can only be managed.

NOTES

1. Matthew Arnold, *Culture and Anarchy and Other Writings*, ed. Stefan Collini (Cambridge: Cambridge Univ. Press, 1993), pp. 185-186. All subsequent citations will be from this edition and hereafter abbreviated as CA. Gustave Le Bon, *The Crowd: A Study of the Popular Mind*, 2nd ed. (Georgia: Cherokee Publishing Company, 1982), p. xv.
2. Matthew Arnold, *The Complete Prose Works of Matthew Arnold*, ed. R.H. Super, 11 vols. (Ann Arbor: Univ. of Michigan Press, 1960-77), 9:161. Hereafter abbreviated as CPW in the text and noted by volume and page number.
3. Arnold's summary argument on behalf of literature in this early version of a contest of the faculties can be found in "Literature and Science" (1882)(CPW, 10). See also Wolf Lepenies, *Between Literature and Science: The Rise of Sociology*, trans. R.J. Hollingdale (Cambridge: Cambridge Univ. Press, 1988).

4. Philip Abrams, *The Origins of British Sociology: 1834-1914* (Chicago: Univ. of Chicago Press, 1968), p. 48; on sociologist as "potential role," see p. 5.

5. Herbert Spencer, *The Study of Sociology* (1872-73; London, 1880), p. 71.

6. The history of writing on crowds as a new phenomena of modem urban life does not, of course, begin with Arnold. Space does not allow for a more thorough account than I can give briefly here of the variety of literary, historical, and social scientific texts on the crowd that inform Arnold's own warnings. Le Bon's claim in 1896 that the "Era of the Crowd" had arrived registers a panic about the political power of crowds that emerges, largely in the wake of the French Revolution, over the course of the nineteenth century. Reaction to the bread riots, the deaths of working-class demonstrators at Peterloo in 1819, and the dawning of the era of the Mass Platform in England with the organized, national Chartist congregations of the late 1830s and 40s underscore the long history of crowd politics that Le Bon registers only belatedly. John Plotz marks the crowd's radical new representational claims in the years of the Chartist movement, one development of which was that the congregation of bodies in public became visible as itself a coherent demand for political power on behalf of a larger group, that of the working class. By 1839, Plotz argues, "the age of the organized crowd had arrived" (*The Crowd: British Literature and Public Politics* [Berkeley: Univ. of California Press, 2000], p. 130). Most important for my own discussion is the transformation of the conditions in which crowds of earlier decades that were viewed as isolated eruptions of irrational, undirected fervor could by the 1840s successfully represent by metonymy a broader social order-in the case of Chartism, that of the working class. Only after the crowd comes to be understood as metonymic of social order, its disruption as well as its maintenance, can it then become the crucial object of, and offer opportunities for, the theorizations of the social realm that sociologists undertake later in the nineteenth century.

7. Isobel Armstrong, *Victorian Poetry: Poetry, Poetics and Politics* (New York: Routledge, 1993), p. 173. Arnold's formations under the "pressure" of colonial others, and in particular the centrality of racial difference to Arnold's formulations of culture, are detailed in instructive fashion by Robert Young in *Colonial Desire: Hybridity in Theory, Culture, and Race* (London: Routledge, 1995), chap. 3, "The Complicity of Culture: Arnold's Ethnographic Politics." The most complete study of Arnold's poetry remains A. Dwight Culler's imaginative *Reason: The Poetry of Matthew Arnold* (New Haven: Yale Univ. Press, 1966).

8. Letter to Arthur Hugh Clough, cited in Nicholas Murray, *A Life of Matthew Arnold* (London: Hodder and Stoughton, 1996), p. 99.

9. Letter from March 10,1848, *Letters of Matthew Arnold*, ed. George W.E. Russell (New York: Macmillan, 1900).

10. *The Poems of Matthew Arnold*, ed. Kenneth and Miriam Allott (New York: Longman, 1979). Subsequent citations of poems will be from this edition.

11. The multitude's lack of any specific markers of class, political interest, or nationality—its condition as a general rather the particularized crowd—further position it here as a proving ground for Arnoldean detachment.

12. For a more complete consideration of Arnold's lyric "moments," see Virginia Carmichael, "The Moment of Lyric in Matthew Arnold's Poetry," *VP* 26 (1988): 61-73.

13. In this respect, "The Buried Life" departs from the text it seems to be echoing, Book Seven of Wordsworth's The Prelude. There, the speaker also plunges into the London crowd: "How often in the overflowing streets! Have I gone forwards with the crowd and said / Unto myself 'The face of everyone f That passes by me is a mystery! "'(7:626-629). Rather than propelling a desire for self-knowledge, as in Arnold, the confusion induced by "Living amid the same perpetual flow / Of trivial objects, melted and reduced f To one identity by differences / That have no law, no meaning, and no end" is identified with a self-dissolution brought on by the crowd (11. 701-704).

14. "The Buried Life" rewrites the terms of the encounter with the modern world envisioned in "The Scholar-Gipsy." There, in "isolation" sequestered from the "strange disease of modern life" in which "each half lives a hundred different lives," the legendary scholar-gipsy has "one aim" "one desire." The envied autonomy and concentration of the individual, however, are allied again with the immersion in a collective, here the ahistorical group of the "gipsy-tribe."

15. Frances Ferguson, *Solitude and the Sublime: Romanticism and the Aesthetics of Individuation* (New York: Routledge, 1992), p. 97.

16. Max Weber, *The Protestant Ethic and the Spirit of Capitalism*, trans. Talcott Parsons (London and New York: Routledge, 1992).

17. Theodore Adorno, "On Lyric Poetry and Society," trans. Shierry Weber Nicholsen, *Notes to Literature*, ed. Roif Tiedemann, vol. 1 (New York: Columbia Univ. Press, 1991), pp. 37-54.

7

"Unhackneyed Thoughts and Winged Words": Arnold, Locke and the Similes of Sohrab and Rustum

—Daniel Kline

But hardly have we, for one little hour,
Been on our own line, have we been ourselves—
Hardly had skill to utter one of all
The nameless feelings that course through our breast,
But they course on for ever unexpressed.

—Arnold, "The Buried Life"

How needful it is for those who are to discuss any matter together, to have a common understanding to the sense of the terms they employ,—how needful and how difficult.

—Arnold, "Literature and Science"

Sohrab and Rustum is no ordinary poem. Such is the judgment of George Henry Lewes in his review of Matthew

Arnold's 1853 volume, Poems, for the Leader on December 3, 1853. Lewes goes on, however, to add that we should have an easy task to show that its excellencies are not derived from the Greek, although most of its defects are. More than this, its defects are often the mere defects of rude art, which are copied from Homer; such, for example, as the practice of conducting the narrative through lengthy similes, elaborately circumstantial, positively retarding and encumbering what they are meant to accelerate and lighten.[1]

Virtually all critics agree that Sohrab and Rustum marks an important shift in Matthew Arnold's poetic career as he haltingly abandons the melancholic post-Romantic explorations of the self that characterize his first two published volumes of poetry. At the same time, the increasingly etiolated classicism that comes to occupy a prominent place in much of the poetry written after 1853 and that is, in part, inaugurated by Sohrab and Rustum has won over very few modern readers just as it failed to impress many of Arnold's mid-Victorian contemporaries. While the poem does have notable apologists, including Arnold's Oxford friend J.A. Froude, the preponderance of Victorian critical opinion is aligned with Lewes's mixed estimation. It is against this ambivalent heritage that mixes critical acknowledgment of the poem's import for an adequate understanding of the development of Arnold's poetic oeuvre accompanied with critical disapprobation of the poem's apparent aesthetic inadequacies that I wish to put forward some additional claims for the importance of Sohrab and Rustum, specifically its importance for a fuller understanding of Arnold's language. Lewes's comments are also prescient in that they focus on the similes in the poem and thus anticipate a persistent question related to Arnold's poetic style that I will take up here, namely why he has such frequent and strategic recourse to the simile in his poetry. Indeed, some of Arnold's most memorable poetic touchstones are similes, including the comparison of the metaphorical Sea of Faith to a furled, bright girdle in "Dover Beach" (11. 2 1-23) and the unfair likening of Clough's debilitating indecisiveness to the inconstancy of the early June cuckoo in "Thvrsis" (II. 51-60).[2] Critics have long acknowledged the importance of the simile and its often critical role in the interpretation of particular poems, most notably the Tyrian trader simile that concludes "The Scholar-Gipsy.[3] And, of course, the most commented upon rhetorical feature of Sohrab and Rustum is its collection of sixteen epic similes. Although these similes have largely attracted critical derision, I think they are crucial in assessing the important role that Sohrab and Rustum plays in Arnold's lifelong struggle with language.[4] More particularly, I argue that the similes are the most evident manifestation of Arnold's previously unacknowledged indebtedness to the linguistic philosophy of John Locke—specifically the ideas from his lesser known Of the Conduct of the Understanding—and represent Arnold's concerted yet ultimately unsuccessful effort to solve the problem, raised in the two epigraphs above, of how the communicative efficacy of his writing might be obviated by the referential inadequacy of words. This problem, which had been occupying Arnold throughout much of his early career, was brought into focus through his repeated and various excursions in Lockean philosophy (which I outline below), but it is also the specific occasion of Arnold's virulent reaction to the Spasmodic poets that leads him to a sustained attempt at using the similes of Sohrab and Rustum as a site to apply the insights derived from Of the Conduct of the Understanding.

My argument here is initiated by a letter that is of consequence for constructing a genealogy of Arnold's interest and subsequent employment of the simile in his poetry. In the autumn of 1850, Arnold wrote to Arthur Hugh Clough discussing his immediate reading plans while fulfilling the less than arduous duties required of him as private secretary to Lord Lansdowne. Park Honan cites the letter as evidence that Arnold was reading An Essay Concerning Human Understanding along with Spinoza's Ethics,[5] but it would be advantageous to pause and examine the relevant part of this letter:

> I go to read Locke on the Conduct of the Understanding: my respect for the reason as the rock of refuge to this poor exaggerated, surexcited humanity increases and increases. Locke is a man who has cleared his mind of vain repetitions, though without the positive and vivifying atmosphere of Spinoza about him.[6]

Interestingly, Arnold distances himself here from the main current of Victorian disapprobation and misinterpretation of Locke. His opinions on the philosopher reveal that Arnold has not imbibed the argument against Locke made by Victor Cousin, who, in a series of lectures within his popular course in philosophy that Arnold read, claims that Locke subordinates reason to sensation.[7] Most importantly, though, the letter suggests that Arnold is already familiar to some degree with Lockean philosophy and is preparing to build on this knowledge not by rereading An Essay Concerning Human Understanding but rather by reading Of the Conduct of the Understanding.

Arnold's very words, "Conduct of the Understanding" allude not to An Essay Concerning Human Understanding but to a much shorter, lesser known yet still popular text by Locke entitled Of the Conduct of the Understanding.[8] These two works, while closely related, should not be confused with each other. Of the Conduct of the Understanding is a kind of special appendix to the Essay and recapitulates some of that text's main points, but it also introduces some new material and significantly amends some of Locke's ideas on language from the Essay at a moment when Arnold's own thinking about language was moving in new directions.

Two chapters from the Conduct, "Words" and "Similes," are germane to Arnold's developing thoughts on language and the similes of Sohrab and Rustum. In An Essay Concerning Human Understanding, Locke contrasts the natural imperfections of words with those conscious and unconscious abuses which increase the opacity of language and the tenuousness of successful communication. The chapter entitled "Words" from the Conduct restates what Locke considers in the Essay to be one of the chief abuses of language: "They who would advance in knowledge . . . should lay down this as a fundamental rule, not to take words for things . . . till they can frame clear and distinct ideas of those entities . . . Words are not made to conceal, but to declare and shew something" (Of the Conduct, pp. 65-66). This confusion of the relations between words, ideas, and things is, for Locke, the prime source of linguistic ambiguity—a result that is clearly at odds with Locke's repeatedly stated ideal of clarity and precision in the handling of words. Consequently, the guiding principle behind Locke's catalogue of remedies for the abuses of language is grounded in a desire to reduce such obscurity and sloppiness in the use of words. In the Essay, the most highly criticized abuse of words is rhetoric, partially because it is the most deliberate, and while Locke does admit that rhetoric is effective, his famous attack at the end of Book III of the Essay concludes:

> I confess, in Discourses, where we seek rather Pleasure and Delight, than Information and Improvement, such Ornaments . . . can scarce pass for Faults. But yet, if we would speak of Things as they are, we must allow, that all the Art of Rhetorick, besides Order and Clearness, all the artificial and figurative application of Words Eloquence hath invented, are for nothing else but to insinuate wrong Ideas, move the Passions, and thereby mislead the Judgement; and so indeed are perfect cheat.[9]

Such an estimation of rhetorical language hardly endears Locke to poets of any age and obviously poses immediate and practical problems for any poet, including Arnold.

Locke makes a crucial revision, however, in the Conduct's chapter "Similes," when he comes to reexamine figurative language:

> For those are always more acceptable in discourse, who have the way to let in their thoughts into other men's minds with the greatest case and facility . . . Nothing contributes so much to this as similes . . . Well chosen similes, metaphors, and allegories, with method and order, do this the best of anything, because being taken from objects already known and familiar to the understanding, they are conceived of as fast as spoken; and, the correspondence being concluded, the thing they are brought to explain and elucidate is thought to be understood too . . . Figured and metaphorical expressions do well to illustrate more abstruse and unfamiliar ideas which the mind is not yet thoroughly accustomed to. (Of the Conduct, pp. 72-73)

Ultimately, Locke's ideal of a stabilized sign relation and the efficacious and rational exchange of ideas in communicative acts is enough to overcome his earlier dogmatic rejection of tropes as questionable means to such an end. He does, however, place certain important restrictions on figurative language, namely that its adoption be used in the service of some essential functions of language, including the "dispatch" of communication, and that it be used with "method and order."

Locke's discussion of the relative value of the simile as a linguistic resource returns us to Arnold's poetry, since

Arnold appears to enlist it as a poetic resource. It is surely more than a coincidence that similes begin to feature prominently in Arnold's poetry following the announcement of his intentions to read Locke's Of the Conduct of the Understanding in October 1850, most notably in "Dover Beach" and "Stanzas from the Grande Chartreuse," which employ similes that seek to elucidate the at times abstruse and unfamiliar ideas (to appropriate Locke's terminology from the Conduct) that the poems turn upon. Locke's qualifications of "method and order" in the use of metaphors, allegories, and similes also offer provocative connections with Arnold's well-known practice of concluding a poem with a simile, most famously in "The Scholar-Gipsy." However, it is also Locke's begrudging acknowledgment that the effective employment of the simile can be of use in the service of inter-subjective communication, whether that communicative act is conceived of as occurring between two speakers or between poet and reader, that will lead us back to the similes of Sohrab and Rustum, which, as I will suggest, are not merely Homeric ornamentation but are at least partially indebted to the view of the trope that Arnold encountered in Of the Conduct of the Understanding.

Arnold's exposure to Locke's revised view of language in Of the Conduct of the Understanding occurs at a particularly fortuitous moment as Arnold was in the process of intensely rethinking his medium as a major component of the reformulation he was making to his poetics in the late 1840s and early 1850s. Arnold's increasing commitment to write a didactic poetry appropriate for an aspiring commentator on the age (an aspiration that Arnold eventually realizes in critical prose) has been much discussed, but Arnold, perhaps, indicates his basic motives in a letter to Clough:

> I am glad that you like the Gipsy Scholar—but what does it do for you? Homer animates—

> Shakespeare animates—in its poor way I think Sohrab & Rustum animates—the Gipsy Scholar at best awakens a pleasing melancholy. But this is not what we want.
>
> The complaining millions of men
>
> Darken in labour and pain
>
> —what they want is something to animate and ennoble them—not merely to add zest to their melancholy or grace to their dreams—I believe a feeling of this kind is the basis of my nature—and of my poetics. (1:282)

Arnold, here, is drawing a distinction between the kind of poetry that "animates" and "ennobles"—a didactic poetry that communicates ideas, which for Arnold are the bedrock of all good poetry-and the kind of poetry that "awakens" emotions such as "a pleasing melancholy"—a suggestive poetry of emotion. In this sense, Arthur Henry Hallam's distinction between the poetry of sensation and the poetry of reflection is useful.[10] Arnold increasingly comes to align himself with the Wordsworthian poetry of ideas and statement as opposed to a Keatsian or Tennysonian tradition of a poetry of sensation, association, suggestion, and emotion. If what Arnold wants is a poetry that animates and ennobles through the communication of ideas rather than simply awakening a pleasing melancholy—a poetry that would have an appreciable and more direct influence that as Hallam notes is not available to the poet of sensation—then a new attitude to language or new type of linguistic efficacy is also required. Locke's thoughts on language, and the simile in particular, offer Arnold the rudiments of such an efficacy, but to really appreciate the force and the fortuitousness of the Conduct's precepts for Arnold, it is necessary to recount, briefly, Arnold's struggle with this issue (the efficacy of words) and the role played by his earlier exposure to Locke.

That Arnold had been musing about the effectiveness of his language is evident when we consider his indebtedness to Locke prior to reading Of the Conduct of the Understanding. Indeed, as I have been suggesting, Arnold's reading of the Conduct takes on significance in part because he had already turned to Locke's An Essay Concerning Human Understanding earlier in his career, and it is this earlier exposure to the Essay that at least partially contributes to the melancholy and at times pessimistic reflections on language that form a leitmotif in Arnold's first two volumes. The exact extent of that influence is subject to debate, but Arnold's invocation, in the 1850 letter to Clough, of Locke's central principle of reason and his reference to Locke as "a man who has cleared his mind of vain repetitions" (in order to set up the gently witty comparison with Spinoza) suggests a previous exposure and acquaintance with Lockean philosophy. It is surprising, considering the attention that has been paid to the eclectic nature of Arnold's intellectual influences, that the importance of the British empirical tradition, and Locke in particular, has been but perfunctorily acknowledged by Arnold's critics.[11] Arnold encountered An Essay Concerning Human Understanding and the philosophy of language contained in it while he was a student at Rugby or as an undergraduate at Balliol College. Furthermore, he may well have been coming at these ideas indirectly in two very different ways through the work of Locke's eighteenth-century admirer Condillac and the aforementioned Victor Cousin, one of his harshest nineteenth-century critics and an important arbiter of Victorian attitudes to Locke.

In the third book of An Essay Concerning Human Understanding, Locke makes an important distinction about language that he refers to as the "double use of words." In many ways the entire discussion or language that occupies Book III is organized around this distinction as it moves from a thorough investigation of how words are used to record thoughts to how they are used in communicating thoughts. To put it another way, the discussion of language gradually shifts from an investigation of the relation between words and ideas to an analysis of the possibilities and difficulties in the exchange of signs between speakers in acts of communication. In working his way through the arguments on language to be found in An Essay Concerning Human Understanding, there is much that Arnold probably found amenable, especially Locke's discussion of the functional offices language performs in the organizing, abstracting, abbreviating, and consolidating of ideas and mental processes.[12] Increasingly, however, the communicative possibilities and problems between speakers come to dominate Locke's interest in the final chapters of the third book of An Essay Concerning Human Understanding, where Locke makes explicit a note of skepticism that has underwritten the entire discussion of language:

> The chief End of Language in Communication being to be understood, Words serve not well for that end, neither in civil, nor philosophical Discourse, when any Word does not excite in the Hearer, the same Idea it stands for in the Mind of the Speaker. (Essay, 3.9.4)

Because words are the arbitrary signs for ideas in the mind according to Locke, and every person's ideas remain to a certain extent particular, the chance for a perfect correspondence of ideas between speaker and auditor through language is negligible-the odds of achieving or even approaching the semantic idealism that is crucial for Locke's epistemology are impossibly long. Paul Guyer neatly summarizes this dilemma:

> If our words immediately signify only our ideas, and stand for outer objects as well as the ideas of others at best indirectly, then indeed, we can never

> be quite sure that another means exactly the same thing we do ourselves, or is saying the same thing about an object that we are, and we had better be careful about hastily assuming he does. But this skeptical consequence is hardly a refutation of Locke's view: instead, it is exactly the practical lesson that he wishes us to learn from his theoretical inquiry.[13]

It was this generally pessimistic view and not the specific advice on similes in the Conduct that Arnold first encountered. Arnold's exposure to Locke's Essay and the hopeless semantic idealism that issues from its discussion of language certainly adds a linguistic dimension in the persistent theme of human isolation and alienation in Arnold's poetry in the late 1840s and early 1850s. The "confused alarms" that characterize communication on the darkling plain at the end of "Dover Beach" or the "lovely notes" that pour across the channels and sounds dividing the isolated human islands in "To Marguerite—Continued" are not simply anxious and wistful expressions respectively of Arnold's understanding of a mid-Victorian ontological predicament characterized, long ago, by J. Hillis Miller as "disconnection between man and nature," others, and himself (p. 2). They are also thinly veiled fears that, as a poet, he will not be heard or will be misunderstood at best: admissions of "the extreme difficulty of communication from one mind to another" (Riede, p. 8).

This problem, so wistfully expressed in the "Switzerland" series, seems to reach a climax in Empedocles on Etna, which as a meditation on the plight of the poet and the reception of poetry is as troubling as "The Lady of Shalott." More generally, Arnold's concerns with communication and how to speak to his audience—concerns which the self-reflexivity of his first two volumes had been voicing with increasing intensity—are baldly stated in Empedocles on Ema. The dramatic structure of the poem with the competing and cacophonous voices of Empedocles, Callicles, and Pausanias focuses attention on the problems and inherent ambiguities of ordinary, daily human communication. Speaking of Empedocles on Etna in this vein, David Riede points out:

> The exchange [between Empedocles and Pausanias], though trivial, demonstrates the general inconsequentiality of human speech, which may be too easily believed, too uninformed, or simply "thrown away, but seems never to have its intended effect. But the drama is designed to emphasize failed communications in more obvious ways as well. The two central characters, Callicles and Empedocles, never see each other, and at no point does Callicles even hear what Empedocles is saying. Empedocles, at the top of the mountain, does hear Callicles' songs and they seem at first to have the desired effect of soothing him (1.2.483), but in the end they vex him and help drive him to suicide. Indeed, Empedocles' consistent misunderstanding of Callicles' songs wonderfully epitomizes the problem of the modern poet who can never make himself properly understood, cannot communicate by poetry. (Riede, p. 81)

This was the dilemma that Arnold had reached upon completion of Empedocles on Etna. Locke's generally pessimistic view of language in the Essay had served Arnold well in the melancholy explorations of the first two volumes, but with Empedocles on Etna he had reached something of a dead end.

Increasingly, however, Arnold's interests lie not in exposing and exploring, but rather in solving some of the challenges and obstacles of inter-subjective communication in a didactic poetry that, in employing an accessible language that is concerned with audience, will be, to invoke the terms of John Stuart Mill, not overheard but rather in the nature of oratory.[14] It is at this point, in the early 1850s, as he begins to reformulate his poetics in the ways discussed above, that Arnold encounters Locke's revised view of language in the Conduct. As Arnold's thoughts about what poetry should do for readers and how it should do it change, there is a parallel and necessary permutation within his conception of language. Locke's revised view of language from the Conduct has much to contribute to this permutation. Locke's revived possibilities for language, and particularly similes as a way to reduce the vagaries of communication, inform Arnold's own casting about for language strategies in service of a newly emerging poetics. Empedocles on Ema had demonstrated how "it is impossible to say exactly what one means, and to be precisely understood' (Riede, p. 89), but Locke's Conduct had offered a strategy, via the simile, to reduce the imprecision in the use of words. The word 'precisely" is of critical importance here. Communicative efficacy comes to reside in accuracy and precision as Arnold, undoubtedly influenced by the emerging ascendency of scientific discourse in Victorian England, looks for more uniform and limited relations between signifier and signified that will distinguish his work from what he perceived to be the vague, affective emotionalism of his Romantic predecessors and especially a great many of his Victorian contemporaries. It is, then, somewhat fortuitous that at a moment when Arnold was deeply concerned about employing language more accurately and precisely that he finds a seemingly unlikely ally through his return to John Locke's philosophy of language, but in this case the ideas expressed in Of the Conduct of the Understanding.

Perhaps the most interesting and immediate evidence of Arnold's evolving attitude to his medium is revealed by examining the linguistic self-reflexivity of Sohrab and Rus Rustum to complement what has already been said in this vein about Empedocles on Erna. Both poems are examples of failed communication, although the attitude that *Sohrab and Rustum* takes to language is different in tone, I think, than its predecessor. The poem is filled with verbal parleying, challenges, boasts, orders, decrees, and rumors that ultimately bring Sohrab and Rustum to the battlefield. The actual physical trial between Sohrab and Rustum is bracketed by lengthy verbal exchanges, and the physical combat is frequently punctuated with traded insults and taunts, themselves often about words and language such as Rustum's sneer to Sohrab: "Curled minion, dancer, coiner of sweet words' (1. 458), in many respects, the poem's martiality is as much verbal in its war of words as it is physical in its clash between the Tartar and Persian warriors. Paradoxically, the poem's dramatization of the efficacy of language is simultaneously balanced by its dramatization of the failure of speakers to control or realize the implications and effects of the words they employ. The tragedy of Sohrab and Rustum, such as it is, is generated by a failure of language, namely the mistaken rumors which lead Rustum to believe he is without a son as well as the successive moments of non-recognition throughout the poem's central incident. Yet, by eschewing the dramatic form for *Sohrab and Rustum*, Arnold also creates a very different situation from *Empedocles on Etna*. Empedocles and Callicles are physically separated, and the poem holds Empedocles' arid, scientific, logical language in contrast to the lyrical and mythical language of Callicles. In this sense, the poem looks backward to Arnold's early career and his exploration of the various kinds of authoritative language that seem fated to communicative impasse. In *Sohrab and Rustum*, on the other hand, the two central characters meet face to face and speak to each other oratorically—gone is Callicles' poetry, overheard by Empedocles—and still misinterpret each other with disastrous consequences. All this serves to foreground the growing intensity of Arnold's interest in the dynamics of communication propelled by an emerging poetic creed and facilitated by Arnold's various reading engagements in Locke's language philosophy.

Yet the similes of Sohrab and Rustum are the site in the poem where the Lockean insights of the Conduct are applied and adapted in poetic practice. Moments after his realization that he has mortally wounded his son, Rustum's suicide attempt is stayed by Sohrab who, as the narrator of the poem notes, "saw his thought" (1. 706). This moment is, l think, emblematic of Arnold's idealized, and perhaps utopian, reader response. In fact, a few years earlier, Arnold had complained to his future wife Frances Lucy Wightman in the poem "Calais Sands" that he could only "guess thy thoughts" (1. 32). Locke suggests in the Conduct that similes become the most effective vehicles for the transmission of new and unfamiliar thoughts, and as Arnold seeks to write a poetry that will acculturate his readers to the nobility and enduring value to be found in the classics, the similes of Sohrab and Rustum become a way of investing the language of the poem with accuracy and precision at key moments in that momentous and, for Arnold, vitally important task.

Perhaps the most famous simile in the poem, the Victorian lady simile, makes this strategy most evident. Sohrab initially appears, unknown, before his father, and Rustum's internal reaction is documented through an epic simile:

> As some rich woman, on a winter's morn,
> Eyes through her silken curtains the poor drudge
> Who with numb blackened fingers makes her
> fire—
> At cock-crow, on a starlit winter's morn,
> When the frost flowers the whitened window-
> panes—
> And wonders how she lives, and what the
> thought

> Of that poor drudge may be; so Rustum eyed
> The unknown adventurous youth. (II. 302-309)

The mental state that is externalized in the simile is curiosity. For Arnold, however, that word is far too vague and ambiguous. Everyone's (especially the reader's) idea signified by the word "curiosity" is particular to a certain extent. As Amrollah Abjadian has shown, there are several important similes in Sohrab and Rustum, and they "are not only active similes, underlying, and mingling with the action of the poem, but they also externalize or objectify the internal states of the character."[15] Yet, Arnold has a very specific type of curiosity in mind that he is attempting to communicate to the reader, and the fact that this simile is not orientalized is important. The images of the trope belong more to mid-Victorian England than to ancient Persia. The simile dramatizes an encounter between the middle and lower classes and adds a specific note of social disparity to Rustum's curiosity—a curiosity, furthermore, that is itself intriguingly mixed with the vexed issues, anxieties, and ambivalences that congregate around the Victorian notion of sympathy.[16] If Arnold were to eliminate the simile, however, and simply state that Rustum views Sohrab with condescending curiosity (or some other adjective-noun combination), the reader would be more arrested by such words than the simile. The figure not only externalizes the mental state, but it points to the fine shading and coloring of that emotion which an adjective and noun might not be able to communicate with ease, accuracy, and even adequacy. The simile is an attempt to overcome the dilemma which the poet confronts, armed with the imperfect medium of language which struggles to communicate accurately and effectively, "The nameless feelings that course through our breast." It is a means to present the particularities of that specific idea that Arnold wants to show the reader. Paradoxically, then, the simile, which calls attention to itself in various ways (its epicness, allusiveness, etc.), also seeks to alleviate the obtrusiveness caused by vague words and ease difficulties in conveying to the reader an idea that may not in itself be easily expressible or even nameable. While Arnold is certainly not the first to use a simile in this way, his use of the simile in such a way in the aftermath of his exposure to Of the Conduct of the Understanding and his exploitation of the elaborateness inherent in the epic simile as opposed to its more humble relation, the simple simile, suggest that Arnold is interested in Sohrab and Rustum in using the epic simile to invest his language at crucial moments in the text with precision and accuracy in delineating the mental states of his various characters so that the didactic force of the tragic fragment will be both more obvious and effective to Arnold's imagined audience. In suggesting that the similes should be read as the results of Arnold's adoption of Lockean ideas on language in the service of an evolving poetics, I am at least partially calling into question the traditional ways that the similes, and by extension Sohrab and Rustum, have been read. The majority of readers have sought to read the poem in concert with the 1853 "Preface" to the Poems. Taking their cue from the 1853 "Preface," which received as much if not more comment than the poem itself, most of the reviewers focused on the poem's use of classical subject matter and style. Most critics disliked Arnold's insistence on the classics and charged both poem and poet with impiety, as John Duke Coleridge did in a review which angered many of Arnold's friends, or elitism, as in Coventry Patmore's review.[17] Critics who have written specifically on the similes of the poem have also judged them according to the terms laid out by Arnold's "Preface."[18] The aesthetic inadequacies of Sohrab and Rustum are certainly discernible, but they are often exaggerated by the tendency to hold the poem to the letter of the precepts of the "Preface." Yet the tendency to turn to the "Preface" in this manner overdetermines, I think, the relation between the poem and this problematic essay.

The 1853 "Preface" to Arnold's Poems is certainly one of the most commented on and debated prose essays in Arnold's collected works, and it is also one of his most frustrating pieces, filled with contradictions, inconsistencies, untenable positions, and a variegated intellectual indebtedness to modern and ancient European literature and literary theory. By replacing Empedocles on Etna with Sohrab and Rustum Arnold was, inevitably, going to draw the response that the poem and "Preface" were interconnected. To some extent they are, but it is interesting how often it is assumed that Arnold necessarily wanted the two pieces to be so closely linked—the relationship seems to me to be more fluid than is generally acknowledged. Critics, beginning with the poem's first reviewers, have assumed a more intimate relation between Sohrab and Rustum and the 1853 "Preface" than Arnold would likely accept. Arnold wrote the 1853 "Preface" after he had composed Sohrab and Rustum. His initial hopes for the poem were high and, writing to his mother in the midst of composition of the poem, he noted with pleasure and anticipation that

> all my spare time has been spent on a poem which I have just finished, and which I think by far the best thing I have yet done—and that it will be generally liked-though one can never be sure of this. I have had the greatest pleasure in composing it-a rare thing with me, and, as I think, a good test of the pleasure what you write is likely to afford to others. (1:266)

However, as he composed the "Preface" in the second half of 1853, his letters in the late summer of that year point to an interesting qualification of his earlier halcyon descriptions of the poem to friends and family such as the one to his mother cited above. He reveals to Clough after writing out the poem for the printer's fair copy: "I have written out my Sohrab & Rustum, and like it less" (1:270).

In many ways Arnold remained happy with the poem, but his unease with it reveals that his thinking was already moving in new ways, and the first real outlet for this would be the "Preface." Rather than demanding an unswerving fidelity of "Preface" to poem simply because they appear in print together and Sohrab and Rustum seems to replace Empedocles on Etna, we might consider the possibility that Sohrab and Rustum had to be written first in order for Arnold to write the "Preface" to which it has been linked. Those looking for greater correspondence between the dictates of the "Preface" and an Arnoldian poetic performance would be advised to look forward in Arnold's career to Balder Dead and Merope. Indeed nowhere in the "Preface" does Arnold suggest that Sohrab and Rustum is, as Culler phrases it, the "Exhibit A" of a new poetics (p. 205)—he only repeatedly stresses that Empedocles on Etna certainly falls short. By considering the relation between Sohrab and Rustum and the "Preface" as much less determined than is usually assumed, one sees more clearly the palimpsestic nature of the similes. The similes, taken as a group and in some cases individually, are palimpsestic in the sense that I read the key similes in the poem as the culmination and flowering of Arnold's indebtedness to Locke. At the same time, other similes come to anticipate some of the requirements outlined in the 1853 "Preface," such as the need for accurate construction even as they actually hinder others including Arnold's repeated call in the "Preface" for the subordination of expression. The poem is transitional—situated at a great remove from Empedocles on Etna but not achieving the polish of Balder Dead—a poem that Arnold ranked even more highly than Sohrab and Rustum for a time after he had composed it. Rather than reading the similes by looking forward to the "Preface," it is instructive to read them as emerging from Arnold's reading in Locke's philosophy of language as well as from the specific occasion for the poem.

In this sense, the general spirit the "Preface" is more useful than its specific precepts. The "Preface" is written by a poet for poets and thus despite its appearance in a volume for the general public, Arnold does have a specific subsidiary audience in mind. As much is indicated in the text's repeated insistence on action and the proper choice of subject matter, but Arnold also shares Aristotle's concern for the affective power of literature, finally making explicit the gradual shift in Arnold's poetry that I have already mentioned. Despite the references to Schiller and Goethe that bracket the essay, the "Preface," following in the tradition of Aristotle's Poetics, seeks to align mimetic and rhetorical theoretical orientations to combat the excesses of the dominant expressivist tendencies of the early Victorian period. So the "Preface" is for poets but it is about the kinds of effects literature can and should have on readers. The animation and ennoblement of the readers was to be accomplished, in Arnold' s view, through the representation and effective communication of a reformulated subjectivity. A frequent charge against the "Preface" and the poems that surround it is that they constitute a turn away from the subjective emphasis of Arnold's early poetry to the more objective stance embodied in the narrative and dramatic forms of Sohrab and Rustum, Balder Dead, and Merope. Lionel Trilling characterized the "Preface" as a "renunciation of subjectivity,[19] but it is not so much that the Preface and especially preceding poems such as Sohrab and Rustum seek to renounce subjectivity as that they seek to redefine it, to delineate it more precisely, to communicate it more clearly, and in broader if somewhat cruder strokes for a perceived larger audience. If the "Preface" and Sohrab and Rustum are Arnold's response to the morbid introspection of Empedocles on Etna, then Arnold was not quite ready to abandon subjective explorations in his poems, especially in his first major effort after Empedocles, Sohrab and Rustum.

He was, however, quite ready to forgo "the modern English habit (too much encouraged by Wordsworth) of using poetry as a channel for thinking aloud, instead of making anything" (Letters, 1:141). This was the approach of the Spasmodic poets and, as Sidney Coulling and others have pointed out, Arnold was responding in the "Preface" to this specific literary phenomenon. The Spasmodics, as the early Victorian disciples of the later Romantics, had extended and expanded a Romantic exploration of the self and exercised, as J. H. Buckley notes, an impressive influence over early Victorian taste.[20] It was the extended, self-absorbed, solipsistic work of poets such as Philip James Bailey and Alexander Smith, and even his own earlier work, including Empedocles on Etna, that Arnold is dogmatically attacking in the "Preface." So far from renouncing subjectivity in the 1853 "Preface," Arnold's interests have shifted to reformulating, perhaps simplifying it so it can be communicated with precision and accuracy in order t o serve a more effectively didactic social function. An emerging neo-classical poetics, then, would be well served by an attitude toward language that had grown increasingly neo-classical; regarding language as the vehicle for pre-existing thoughts to be used in the service of accurately and exhaustively elucidating a reformulated subjectivity, which sacrificed Romantic complexity and the nebulosity of Spasmodic subjectivism but also avoided their solipsistic and perceived socially evasive tendencies as well. The first place these ideas are raised, explored, and tentatively worked out is in Sohrab and Rustum. This interest in a reformulated subjectivity and the "Preface"'s concurrent concerns with the effects of poetry on audiences works in concert with Arnold's increased concern with the communicative efficacy of language—a concern that intensified and evolved from his exposure to An Essay Concerning Human Understanding and later to Of the Conduct of the Understanding. The similes have both a general and a specific local dimension. They are Arnold's attempts to incorporate the Lockean insights on language he had encountered in the Conduct to give his language greater precision and accuracy at a time when he felt this was a necessary component for his new poetics.

At the same time the similes are nor simply direct importations of Locke's ideas into Arnold's poetic practice. In this particular case the precision and accuracy that Locke's insights offer Arnold through the simile are brought into contact with Arnold's gradually clarifying desire to present a reformulated subjectivity. Thus, the similes are evidence of a general intellectual development in Arnold's thinking on language (his complicated indebtedness to Locke) brought to bear on a specific poetic issue (the reformulated representation of subjectivity that is a crucial component of Arnold's poetic transition, finally codified in the "Preface"). It was not enough for Arnold to lament with Tennyson "Vague words! But ah how hard to frame / In matter-moulded forms of speech" or proclaim as Tennyson did that his words enfolded an emotion or state of mind that could be "given in outline and no more."[21] For Arnold the effort had to be made to be more precise in tracing out the thoughts and ideas that were for him the basis of modern poetry. Otherwise his poetry would simply express that "congestion of the brain" which he so frequently complained about and which might be a fitting label for the excesses of the Spasmodic movement. The problem then becomes for Arnold, to use the words of Locke from Of the Conduct of the Understanding, "to know the right way to lay our thoughts before others with advantage and clearness." The problem with a Spasmodic poem such as Tennyson's Maud is not that the sensibility it represented was mad but rather that the means by which it was represented rendered it "mud."[22] The success of the Spasmodics gave new impetus to their opponents, including Arnold, who discerned a need for accuracy and precision in communication—a direction that Arnold's poetry was already moving in as I have previously suggested and which may have accelerated this general development.

The similes are Arnold's attempt to put into practice the advice on the trope he encountered in Of the Conduct of the Understanding to assist in reworking his medium in a way more amenable to the new poetic creed that was taking shape and that demanded a more precise, accurate use of words to effect the kind of didacticism that Arnold increasingly saw as the object of poetry in the modern age—particularly in the light of the praise bestowed upon such garish, Spasmodic poems as Festus or A Life Drama. A closer look at some individual examples from Sohrab and Rustum reveals that the similes achieve such ends, if only incompletely.

Arnold himself seems to have been aware that the similes of the poem held the potential to be jarring and distracting, and he defended their quantity in a letter to J.D. Coleridge: "Homer sows his [?] similes very thick at times" (Letters, 1:279). Two of the more memorable similes in Sohrab and Rustum concern the assembled hosts of Tartar and Persian troops, and the feelings of the two armies when Peran-Wisa makes known Sohrab's offer of a single combat:

> As, in the country, on a morn in June,
> When dew glistens on the pearled ears,
> A shiver runs through the deep corn for joy—
> So, when they heard what Peran-Wisa said,
> A thrill through all the Tartar squadrons ran
> Of pride and hope for Sohrab, whom they loved.
> But as a troop of pedlars, from Cabool,
> Cross underneath the Indian Caucasus,
> That vast sky-neighbouring mountain of milk
> snow;
> Crossing so high, that, as they mount, they pass
> Long flocks of travelling birds dead on the snow,
> Choked by the air, and scarce can they
> themselves
> Slake their parched throats with sugared

mulberries—
In single file they move and stop their breath,
For fear they should dislodge the o'erhanging
snows—
So the pale Persians held their breath with fear.
(II. 154-169)

The contiguity of the similes, in this case, raises the issue of other employments of the trope, alluded to above, and while I would not deny the point that the similes can be considered as a kind of intratextual network that employs a condensed array of symbolic images, or that they contribute to the structural symmetry of the text, I would suggest that the similes are primarily Lockean. The epic similes make visible and concrete what is inevitably invisible and abstract. This might be seen as a questionable tactic since J. Douglas Kneale, arguing in a different context about Wordsworth, has pointed out that the epic simile presents problems that threaten its intended clarifying and instructional effectiveness: The conventional "as . . . such" or "as . . . so" structure, elaborated over several lines, clearly demarcates the splitting of the figure into its constituent parts of vehicle and tenor, respectively, and it distinguishes between the subordinate "as" and the dominant "such." But here is the paradox of epic simile: while the vehicle is meant to be in service of the tenor—in other words, while the poet temporarily turns from the subject in order to trope it through comparison with something else—the comparison itself becomes foregrounded, amplified, elaborated, its ironies sounded, its potential for foreshadowing explored.[23]

In contrast, Arnold's conception of the figure is rooted in Locke's estimation of the trope as a potential agent of clarification in communication. The usurpation of the tenor by the vehicle that is the hallmark of all epic similes, which might lead to the very obfuscation that Arnold is trying to avoid, is elided as Arnold uses the vehicle specifically to define rather than to elaborate on a clearly understood tenor. The "epic" status of the similes allows Arnold to exploit all the resources of narrative and imagery to present the fine subtleties of the ideas and subjectivities he wishes to represent with vividness and concrete precision in what is an almost taxonomic manner. In the Conduct Locke does not create a hierarchy of the various types of figures, but I think that Arnold's preference for the simile over metaphor and allegory as a technique for linguistic precision is in line with a recent estimation of the trope:

> Unlike metaphor, which requires the reader to do the work of constructing a logic of categories and analogies, a simile states explicitly that two terms are comparable and often presents the basis for that comparison. "Her lips were red as wine" does not leave the reader with the work that a metaphor requires. The simile is therefore in general a more controlled figure than metaphor producing less excess of meaning.[24]

It is precisely this excess of meaning that Arnold is attempting to combat with a new attitude to language that focuses on precision and accuracy. The epic simile is specific and controlled and has a specific appeal to the poet as facilitator, and, of course, in the case of Sohrab and Rustum it fits in especially well with the epic posturing of the poem.

The same process is at work later as Rustum approaches the front of the Persian army. The narrator attempts to elucidate the emotions felt by the Persian troops:

> And dear as the wet diver to the eyes
> Of his pale wife who waits and weeps on shore,
> By sandy Bahrein, in the Persian Gulf,
> Plunging all day in the blue waves, at night,
> Having made up his tale of precious pearls,

> Rejoins her in their hut upon the sands—
> So dear to the pale Persians Rustum came.
> (II. 284-290)

The same attempts to convey the particularities and fine shading of the emotions and feelings are evident. The mental state delineated is easily identified in a general sense as relief, but again Arnold is interested in communicating a precise shade of that relief in the simile. The personal narrative that the simile depicts adds an exactness and a precise dimension to the general mental state which otherwise might be interpreted in any variety of ways (and in a sense still is, but to a lesser degree). This is further accomplished by the domestic elements in the simile, which transfer the reader's thoughts from the alienating world of the battlefield to the familiar atmosphere of the family. The Persian setting of such a scene undermines its complete familiarization, but Arnold also admitted in a letter that the simile originally lacked such a specific locale, further confirming the palimpsestic nature of the use of the figures in this poem. We should also remember that Locke argues in the Conduct that part o f a simile's effectiveness is its use of the familiar and the known (Of the Conduct, p. 73). Arnold's domestication of the subject matter might be read as an attempt to achieve such familiarity. The use of the epic simile as a way of investing language with the accuracy and precision necessary, as it is here in the specific instance of Sohrab and Rustum, for a particular delineation of subjectivity is, however, subject to all sorts of interesting tensions which emerge most clearly if one examines one of the most elaborate of the similes in the poem. As Rustum begins to have uneasy doubts mixed with a kind of anger, the emotion is described in a lengthy epic simile:

> As when some hunter in the spring hath found
> A breeding eagle sitting on her nest,
> Upon the craggy isle of a hill-lake,

And pierced her with an arrow as she rose,
And followed her to find her where she fell
Far off; anon her mate comes winging back
From hunting and a great way off descries
His huddling youth left sole; at that, he checks
His pinion, and with short uneasy sweeps
Circles above his eyry, with loud screams
Chiding his mate back to her nest; but she
Lies dying, with an arrow in her side,
In some far off stony gorge out of his ken,
A heap of fluttering feathers-never more
Shall the lake glass her, flying over it;
Never the black and dripping precipices
Echo her stormy scream as she sails by-
As that poor bird flies home, nor knows his loss,
So Rustum knew not his own loss, but stood
Over his dying son, and knew him not. (II. 556-575)

In this simile the concurrent use of the trope as part of an intratextual network to reinforce the "accurate construction" of the poem and the various intertextual echoes of Milton and Shelley make themselves most obvious.[25] But, as in the other similes that have been discussed, Arnold is also attempting to delineate a particular kind of tragic ignorance. This simile and the others are witness to the referential inadequacy of language while at the same time they attempt to delineate an idea with precision or clarity. The similes attempt to efface the ambiguity from an unnamed, vague, or shadowy signifier by a multiplication of signifiers via the form of the epic simile. Arnold confronts the referential adequacy of his medium in the similes, but this confrontation is much more than the ubiquitous poetic topos. It is rooted in Arnold's interest in investing his language with accuracy and precision through the trope. A constructive contrast can be seen later in the Victorian era, when Thomas Hardy would confront the same problem. But while Hardy resorts to the historical insights provided by the new philology in England, Arnold turns to philosophy.[26] Confronted with a poverty in language, Arnold responds with gestures, in the similes, of linguistic abundance and plenitude. Faced with the lack of a precise word, Arnold compensates with an extended wealth of words—a dubious strategy at best. George Eliot, echoing the ambivalence of Lewes and others, may well have been thinking of this effect of the similes when she described Arnold's poetry in an unsigned review for the Westminster Review in 1855: "The thought is always refined and unhackneyed, sometimes new and sublime, but he seems not to have found the winged word which carries the thought at once to the mind of the reader."[27] Arnold perhaps unconsciously realizing that such a "winged word" did not exist, was willing to sacrifice communicative dispatch for a perceived semantic accuracy, precision, and clarity. Further, it was precisely the hackneyed, vaguely cliched thoughts and dilettantism of the Spasmodics that Arnold was seeking to distance himself from, beginning with Sohrab and Rustum. In the end, however, we share Eliot's discomfort, as the similes never quite seem to work. I think this is in part because Arnold asks them to do too much. While my focus here has been on the ways that the similes contribute to Arnold's evolving concept ion of language at a time when his poetics demanded a renewed medium, I have gestured, in passing, to some of the ways that critics have seen the similes operating in Sohrab and Rustum. The division of critical opinion about the similes of the poem suggests that they must be read as palimpsests, to which I have added yet another philosophical/linguistic layer. The similes ultimately are not as successful in an overall sense because the various layers of the palimpsest clash too readily and obviously with each other, in being forced to bear structural, intertextual, and mimetic responsibilities (often within a single simile), they can be easily dismissed when the focus is on one of these functions alone. The similes buckle under the weight of too many responsibilities. Despite the fact that they increase the amount of language in the poem, they are in a curious way an ultimate attempt at the subordination of expression by gesturing to a word that does not exist as Arnold struggles with this problem of referential inadequacy. The buried life may well be inaccessible, but the similes trace in outline for an audience that is perceived in need of animation and ennoblement what is there, and they do so with a kind of authoritative and scientific precision.

The best discussions of Arnold's language, applying the insights of post-structuralism, have effectively demonstrated the inconsistencies, inadequacies, and ambivalence in Arnold's conceptions of language and in his various linguistic performances in poetry and prose. Neither Locke nor Arnold ever asserts that a perfectly transparent, adequate, precise, and effective medium is attainable, and David Riede is certainly right when he argues that "Arnold's ideal of a transparent language is, of course, simply impossible to attain or even approach" (Riede, p. 97). Yet, in adopting Locke's qualified endorsement of the simile as a strategy for transparency, Arnold did try to approach it. While "doubt," "distrust," and even "disillusionment" remain the watchwords for characterizing Arnold's attitude toward language, examining the way in which Arnold struggles with the communicative efficacy and referential inadequacy of his language—as he does through the similes of Sohrab and Rustum—is of particular importance. It reveals, among other things, that Arnold's distrust of his medium was not so debilitating as to drive him to a despairing passivity about his use of words. It does not preclude him from casting about for potential solutions to particular linguistic problems such as the ones he confronts in Sohrab and Rustum.

NOTES

1. Matthew Arnold, *The Poetry: The Critical Heritage*, ed. Carl Dawson (London: Routledge and Kegan Paul, 1973), p. 84.

2. Matthew Arnold, *The Poems of Matthew Arnold*, ed. Miriam Allott (London: Longman, 1979). All quotations from Arnold's poetry are from this edition.

3. See, for example, C. Wilson Knight, "'The Scholar Gipsy': An Interpretation," *RES* 9 (1955): 55-62; or more recently, Sidney Coulling, "The Grave Tyrian and Merry Grecian Once More," *VP* 26 (1988): 11-24; and E. Warwick Slinn, "Experimental Form in Victorian Poetry," *The Cambridge Companion to Victorian Poetry*, ed. Joseph Bristow (Cambridge: Cambridge Univ. Press, 2000), pp. 46-66.

4. Critics who have found reason to censure the similes of Sohrab and Rustum with varying degrees of intensity include A. Dwight Culler, *Imaginative Reason: The Poetry of Matthew Arnold* (New Haven: Yale Univ. Press, 1966), pp. 212-214; and David Riede, *Matthew Arnold and the Betrayal of Language* (Charlottesville: Univ. of Virginia Press, 1988), pp. 104-105.

5. Park Honan, *Matthew Arnold: A Life* (Cambridge: Harvard Univ. Press, 1981), p. 279.

6. Matthew Arnold, *The Letters of Matthew Arnold*, ed. Cecil Y. Lang (Charlottesville: Univ. of Virginia Press, 1996), 1:176-177. All further quotations from Arnold's correspondence are from this edition.

7. Locke's fortunes in England throughout the nineteenth century have been documented by Hans Aarsleff, who points out that, despite the presence of important apologists including Dugald Stewart and John Stuart Mill, the preponderance of opinion as it was effectively marshaled by Coleridge and Whewell in England and Cousin in France stood in opposition to Locke, particularly his An Essay Concerning Human Understanding, and that "the Essay as the central document of British empiricism was continually subordinated to the German

transcendental philosophy championed by Coleridge and others" (p. 121). Aarsleff's investigations also suggest that the often virulent reaction to Locke is a fair index of his well-established and pervasive position within nineteenth-century British schools and universities, such as Cambridge where An Essay Concerning Human Understanding was required reading. See Hans Aarsleff, "Locke's Reputation in Nineteenth-Century England," From *Locke to Saussure: Essays in the Study of Language and Intellectual History* (Minneapolis: Unix'. of Minnesota Press, 1982), pp. 120-145.

8. Although the Essay was for most nineteenth-century readers the crucial Lockean text, Of the Conduct of the Understanding was the second most published of Locke's works, going through ten editions in the century. Henry Hallam speaks approvingly of it, and there is evidence that Gerard Manley Hopkins was familiar with it. The heyday for the Conduct was not the nineteenth but the eighteenth century, as W.S. Howell has noted: "The Conduct of the Understandıng and its parent work, An Essay Concerning Human Understanding, were without question the most popular, the most widely read, the most frequently reprinted, and the most influential, of all English books of the eighteenth century" and, Howell continues, the Conduct "was often used in British universities as a textbook on logic." It is certainly possible then that Arnold was familiar with the work while a student at Oxford and prior to his Lansdowne employment. See Aarsleff; Henry Hallam, "Preface," *Of the Conduct of the Understanding*, ed. Thomas Fowler, 2nd ed. (New York: Burt Franklin, 1971), p. v; Gerard Manley Hopkins, *The Note-Books and Papers of Gerard Manley Hopkins*, ed. Humphry House, (London: Oxford Univ. Press, 1987), p. 8; W.S. Howell, *Eighteenth-Century British Logic and Rhetoric* (Princeton: Princeton Univ. Press, 1971), pp. 277-279.

9. John Locke, *An Essay Concerning Human Understanding*, ed. Peter H. Nidditch (Oxford: Oxford Univ. Press, 1975), 3.10.34. Hereafter cited as Essay. For a succinct and general summary of the main points of Locke's theory of

language, see Donald S. Hair, *Robert Browning's Language* (Toronto: Univ. of Toronto Press, 1999), pp. 12-13.

10. Arthur Henry Hallam, "On Some Characteristics of Modern Poetry, and the Lyrical Poems of Alfred Tennyson," *Tennyson's Poetry*, ed. Robert W. Hill, Jr. (New York: Norton, 1999), pp. 581-588.

11. See, for example, Honan, p. 96. Howard Fulweiler attributes a good deal of Arnold's "shattering disillusionment" with the creative power of language to his unavoidable misfortune of living belatedly in a post-Lockean era, and while Fuiweiler is one of the few critics who examines Locke's importance to Arnold in detail, his exploration does not extend to Sohrab and Rustum and Locke's Of the Conduct of the Understanding. See also William Buckler, who notes Lockean epistemology informing "The Future" and J. Hillis Miller who, writing on Empedocles on Ema, has noted that Arnold's concept of the soul is "like the tabula rasa of Locke and the sensationalists." Howard Fulweiler, *Letters from the Darkling Plain: Language and the Grounds of Knowledge in the Poetry of Arnold and Hopkins* (Columbia: Univ. of Missouri Press, 1972); William E. Buckler, *On the Poetry of Matthew Arnold: Essays in Critical Reconstruction* (New York: New York Unix'. Press, 1982), p. 102; J. Hillis Miller, *The Disappearance of God: Five Nineteenth-Century Writers* (Cambridge: Harvard Univ. Press, 1963).

12. Along these lines, we might profitably read the act of naming that the Youth in "The Strayed Reveller" performs in identifying Ulysses (11. 99-112) as a poetic rendering of this taxonomic function of language that is a large part of Locke's treatment of words in Book Ill of An Essay Concerning Human Understanding, particularly Locke's discussion of the names of complex ideas or mixed modes (3.5.10).

13. Paul Guyer, "Locke's Philosophy of Language," *The Cambridge Companion to Locke*, ed. Vere Chappell (Cambridge: Cambridge Univ. Press, 1994), p. 121.

14. John Stuart Mill, "What is Poetry," *The Broadview Anthology of Victorian Poetry and Poetic Theory*, ed.

Thomas J. Collins and Vivienne J. Rundle (Pererborough: Broadview Press, 1999), pp. 1212-1220.

15. Amrollah Abjadian, "Arnold and the Epic Simile," *Etudes Anglaises* 12 (1989): 414.

16. See Audrey Jaffe, *Scenes of Sympathy: Identity and Representation in Victorian Fiction* (Ithaca: Cornell Univ. Press, 2000). Jaffe's arguments on Victorian sympathy and its connections to Victorian liberalism and ideologies of identity lie beyond the scope of this essay, but offer provocative connections with this particular simile with its dramatization of a scene between the well-off and the poor drudge of modern life.

17. For the reviews of Poems, which contained Sohrab and Rustum, see Dawson, pp. 77-156.

18. See, for example, Riede, pp. 102-112; Mark Siegchrist, "Accurate Construction in Arnold's Sohrab and Rustum," *PLL* 14 (1978): 51-60; and, more recently, James Najarian, "'Curled minion, dancer, coiner of sweet words': Keats, Dandyisin, and Sexual Indeterminacy in Sohrab and Rustum," *VP* 34 (1997): 23-42.

19. Lionel Trilling, *Matthew Arnold* (New York: Columbia Univ. Press, 1949), p. 150.

20. Sidney Coulling, "Matthew Arnold's 1853 Preface: Its Origin and Aftermath," *VS* 7 (1964): 233-263; J. H. Buckley, "The Spasmodic School," *The Victorian Temper: A Study in Literary Culture* (Cambridge: Harvard Univ. Press, 1951).

21. Alfred Lord Tennyson, *In Memoriam, The Poems of Alfred Lord Tennyson*, ed. Christopher Ricks (London: Longman, 1987), Section 94, II. 45-46 and Section 5, 11. 9-12.

22. Two years after Arnold's Sohrab and Rustum appeared, a review of Mand in the "Morning Post" noted that there was an extra letter in the title of that poem, and it would have been more appropriately titled "Mad" or "Mud." Sir Charles Tennyson relays this apocryphal anecdote in his biography of the poet: "One critic commented that one of the two vowels should be omitted

from the title, and that it didn't much matter which was chosen for the purpose" (Charles Tennyson, Alfred Tennyson [New York: Macmillan, 1949], p. 286). See also Edgar F. Shannon "The Critical Reception of Tennyson's "Maud," *PMLA* 68 (1953): 397-417.

23. J. Douglas Kneale, *Romantic Aversions: Aftermaths of Classicism in Wordsworth and Coleridge* (Montreal: McGill-Queen's Univ. Press, 1999), p. 86.

24. Thomas McLaughlin, "Figurative Language," *Critical Terms for Literary Study* (Chicago: Chicago Univ. Press, 1995), p. 83.

25. For a good discussion of the use of the similes as "structural signposts" see Siegchrist bot also Culler's comments on the economy of Arnold's symbolic vocabulary and the contribution of the similes to the poem's "symbolic topography" (p. 212). Examples include the repeated comparisons of Sohrab to a lion (II. 91, 177, 216) and the simile describing the cry of Rustum's horse Ruksh (11. 501-506) or the association of Sohrab with flowers and trees (11. 313-318, 633-639) and Rustum with pillars (II. 336-338, 859-864). For comments on the allusiveness, epic origins, and oriental nature of the similes see J.R. Broadbent, "Milton and Arnold" *EIC* 6 (1956): 404-417; Culler, p. 214; Riede, pp. 104-106. For the mixed quality of the content and form of the similes see Gabriel Pearson, "The Importance of Arnold's Merope," *The Major Victorian Poets: Reconsiderations*, ed. Isobel Armstrong (London: Routledge, 1969), pp. 225-252. Pearson discusses the "seepage" of contemporary ideas and images into the poem's classical ethos-an idea related to my claim of the palimpsestic nature of Arnold's use of the trope in Sohrab and Rustum.

26. See Dennis Taylor, *Hardy's Literary Language and Victorian Philology* (Oxford: Oxford Univ. Press, 1993), pp. 298-299. See particularly Taylor's chapter "Hardy's Minute Way of Looking at Style and Idiom" for Hardy's approach to dealing with the "referential inadequacy of language" (p. 298).

27. George Eliot, in *Matthew Arnold, The Poems: The Critical Heritage*, pp. 129-130.

28. In addition to Riede and Fulweiler, see also W. David Shaw, *The Lucid Veil: Poetic Truth in the Victorian Age* (Madison: Univ. of Wisconsin Press, 1987), pp. 141-147, and J. Hillis Miller, *The Linguistic Moment* (Princeton: Princeton Univ. Press, 1985).

8

Matthew Arnold: Poetry, Ideas and the Age

—Vincent Buckley

Matthew Arnold: Poetry, Ideas, and the Age Arnold is no more interested than are the modern critics I am considering in writing a treatise on the value of poetry or on poetic values. He is a practising critic, with a variety of approaches to his central concern; and that concern shows itself not as a fully formulated doctrine but as a constant preoccupation, held with the utmost intelligence and sensitivity. The same is true of Leavis and Eliot. They hold their views in as personal a way as it is possible to hold them, but they do so with as great an objectivity as they can. All three of them work towards the greatest degree of impersonality consistent with an inward, personal engagement with the real issues. And Arnold can be more naturally associated with Leavis and Eliot than with the majority of the critics who preceded him. He is a recognisably modern critic in a sense in which Dr Johnson, for example, was not, and in which even Coleridge was not fully modern. This modernity consists largely in what we may call his representative self-consciousness, in his sense of the age in which he lives as an age both special and historically important. Most sensitively alert men develop this sense when they live in the kind of age which is loosely known as transitional. Arnold has it in a high degree, and is anxious to estimate and represent the spirit of his age, the *Zeitgeist*. In this he is a Romantic; his Romantic apprehension of and concern with the *Zeitgeist* makes of course against provincialism, for it involves a broad and noble desire to derive important ideas from every available source, not to remain content with old forms of thinking and of social organisation, and to co-operate, as it were, with history in making truth effective.

All this is trite enough, when it is stated so baldly; accounts of the nineteenth century are full of this kind of analysis; and I remark this quality here not only because of the positive formulations to which it drives men like Arnold, but also because of its limitations. It generates, in a curious way, a provincialism of its own, a provincialism not of place but of time. Arnold is too avidly of his time, as his generalisations about religion show so clearly. Whereas he hits justly and spiritedly at the provincialism of contemporary England, the provincialism which is really middle-class insularity, he is nevertheless provincial in his own thought in a different way. I have already commented on his deficiency in metaphysical awareness, his reluctance to raise, at any but a social level, the deepest issues of human life as they are represented in poetry. But the deficiency also shows itself in his actual placing of poets. His famous judgment on Pope and Dryden, that they are 'classics of our prose', and that they attempt to compose 'in their wits' that genuine poetry which can only be composed 'in the soul', has become notorious to an age like our own which has a good deal more to learn from Pope than from Gray.[1] Then, the list which he gives of the chief English poets of three hundred years is a significantly anomalous one. It includes Gray and Goldsmith, Cowper and Scott and Campbell, but it makes no mention of Dunbar or Donne, Ben Jonson or Marvell, Blake or Christopher

Smart.[2] To have made precisely those inclusions, precisely those omissions, is to have been, and in a limiting sense, too much of the age. Living so intensely in the historical present, Arnold lives too exclusively in it, and he reinforces it too eagerly with the stoic past. Thus he says of Wordsworth:

> . . . then we understand what constitutes a European recognition of poets and poetry as contradistinguished from a merely national recognition, and that in favour both of Milton and of Shakespeare the judgement of the high court of appeal has finally gone.[3]

Here it is the appeal to the finality of the present which is slightly alarming, while in the case of his list of poets it is the complacent use of the conventional evaluations of the present. In both cases, the note of provincialism is faintly but unmistakably sounded; and it is the result of the intensity of Arnold's attempt to engage with the historical present and to win its meaning. Arnold the progressivist is here in evidence.

These elements in his critical thinking have, therefore, a negative side; but it is more than compensated for by the alertness, the positive sense of life and hope, which his historical intelligence leads to. In an age such as that which Arnold inhabited, and which he was unusually aware of inhabiting, it is necessary for the critic to think more critically and clearly than ever; and it is necessary for the poet to have a highly developed critical apprehension of his work.[4] Arnold's awareness of the needs of the age makes him a modern.

It does not make him what is often called an intellectual, and sometimes an 'intellectualist', or even an 'egghead'. The misconception, however, is often made. If one of the commoner mistakes is to regard him as merely a romantic, involved in a dream of restoring the world's lost innocence through a fusion of elevating sentiment with the fervent dutifulness of Rugby, it is a mistake hardly less common to see him as an intellectual relying on poetry to solve, in more or less abstract terms, the problems of the age. Certainly, as we shall see, he regards poetry as confronting a world of ideas; and he sees those ideas springing up from the meeting of alive modern minds with the problems of a specific age. But he does not regard poetry as solving intellectual problems, or even as directly confronting them. His famous reproof to Clough is relevant here:

> to *solve* the Universe as you try to do is as irritating as Tennyson's dawdling with its painted shell is fatiguing to me to witness . . .[5]

and

> but you know that you are a mere d — d depth hunter in poetry and therefore exclusive furiously. You might write a speech in Phèdre — Phedra loquitur — but you could not write Phèdre.[6]

These judgments are from a very early stage of Arnold's literary life, but the great movement of his criticism shows that he has never revoked them. He is not an intellectual at all in the Clough sense; nor is he an intellectual in the sense in which Eliot is one; he is driven by no urge to formulate analyses and account for causes; his is not an analytical mind in any full sense; and consequently he does not ask poetry for an *analysis* of society, or an assignment of philosophic and social causes. On the contrary, he is concerned to get people to see the virtue of one central insight into the world, and to see the value of poetry as the best pledge of that insight. That insight is one which demands, in Arnold's formulation of it, to be expressed in terms of sentiment rather than of philosophical analysis. Certainly he finds the universe recalcitrant to his moral sense as also to his imagination.[7] Certainly, too, he sees poetry in the elevated style as a way of transcending, or even of evading, this recalcitrance. But poetry is valuable to him largely because it turns insight into animating sentiment.

The mention of insight brings up the rôle of ideas in poetry, and Arnold's view of poetry as somehow representing the best ideas of the age. His two important essays, 'The Function of Criticism at the Present Time' and 'On the Modern Element in Literature', give us his view. He sees poetry in certain eras as having a special task, that of stabilising and advancing contemporary insight into the significance of a contemporary situation. Such a poetry would need to have special qualities, to be 'modern' in a profound sense; and it would need, as the condition of its 'adequacy' (an important word for Arnold), special qualities of alertness and strength in the characters of its authors. Here is the didactic strain in Arnold's thinking coming out in a very subtle form; it is a didacticism not of the traditional moralist but of the social evolutionist.

We have already seen him criticised for the belief that a poetry which deals with life, life in its deepest reality, is a poetry which deals with moral ideas. Now, in 'The Function of Criticism', we find the remark clarified and justified: poetry deals with moral ideas not directly, as though they were debatable judgments or mere counters of abstract intercourse, but in their social aspect, as an animating atmosphere in which the poet is stimulated to focus his attention on his primary subjects, the life of man and the life of nature:

> Now in literature, the elements with which the creative power works are ideas; the best ideas on every matter which literature touches, current at the time; at any rate we may lay it down as certain that in modern literature no manifestation of the

> creative power not working with these can be very important or fruitful. And I say *current* at the time, not merely accessible at the time; for creative literary genius does not principally show itself in discovering new ideas, that is rather the business of the philosopher; the grand work of literary genius is a work of synthesis and exposition, not of analysis and discovery; its gift lies in the faculty of being happily inspired by a certain intellectual and spiritual atmosphere, by a certain order of ideas, when it finds itself in them; of dealing divinely with these ideas, presenting them in the most effective and attractive combinations; making beautiful works with them, in short. But it must have the atmosphere, it must find itself amidst the order of ideas, in order to work freely; and these it is not so easy to command. This is why great creative epochs in literature are so rare . . .[8]

Two points in this passage may be assented to at once: the notion that a poet in a complex age can be an important poet only if he is alert and responsive to that complexity and its causes; and the notion that where that complexity is the result of a people's growth in social and spiritual energy, it can be a stimulation, a help to the poet, rather than a hindrance. But Arnold makes the poet sound like a privileged sponger on the fortuitous bounty of other men's thought, or like a middleman between 'advanced' philosophers and a public which would otherwise prove impervious to them. As I say, there is a curious sort of provincialism here; and a man of our own day might well enquire of those 'best ideas' whether they are *true* as well as stimulating for poetry. Arnold has not made himself clear; and the reason, I think, is that he does not know precisely what it is he wants. He wants modernity, a fully modern responsiveness; but just how that is to manifest itself in the stimulating of poetry through contemporary thought, he cannot say. Nor does he appear certain whether or not he wants to apply his notion of modernity as a criterion for judging the works of all ages. He sees the Greece of Sophocles, and the England of Shakespeare, permeated with thought in this way. But what of the England of Chaucer, the France of Racine, the England of the later eighteenth century? And why, we may ask, is it necessary to define this stimulation in terms of *ideas*? As soon as you choose to do that, you are necessarily involved in questions of truth. Arnold, of course, is intimately concerned, here as elsewhere, with the advancement of truth. But he often seems to find it quite as persuasive, and a great deal easier, to develop his case in terms of modernity rather than of truth.

We are brought back to the word 'life'. In being concerned with the modernity of ideas, and shying off the question of their truth, Arnold is really paying tribute to their freshness, their life. And his insistence on 'ideas' is valuable if we take him to mean that any poetry cannot be adequate for its age unless it has the vigour which comes from the existence in the age of fresh and lively ideas. For this life to be realised in poetry it is necessary for society to have accepted the ideas at a mature level, and for the poet to be inwardly ready for them. So Arnold charges the English Romantics with being, in their inward grasp of their personal experience, unready for the task of converting contemporary ideas into poetry. They were not ready, and the age was not ready. Consequently, they were lacking both in the material and in the stimulation which a fully awake society provides for the poet; and 'a thorough interpretation of the world was necessarily denied to it'.[9]

The English Romantics lacked an intellectually mature world, and they lacked a sufficiently mature personal experience of their world in terms of ideas. These were the opportunities which Goethe had pre-eminently:

> . . . the grand business of modern poetry — a moral interpretation, from an independent point of view, of man and the world -it is only German poetry, Goethe's poetry, that has, since the Greeks, made much way with.[10]

And

> Goethe's task was — the inevitable task for the modern poet henceforth is — as it was for the Greek poet in the days of Pericles, not to preach a sublime sermon on a given text like Dante, not to exhibit all the kingdoms of human life and the glory of them like Shakespeare, but to interpret human life afresh and to supply a new spiritual basis to it.[11]

Very few people nowadays would be so optimistic, so irresponsibly optimistic, as to expect poetry to 'supply a new spiritual basis' to human life; but this is the sort of position to which a writer may be driven in following out the logic of demanding not only a poetry adequate to its age (as Dante's and Shakespeare's surely were) but a poetry whose adequacy comes from dealing with ideas 'from an independent point of view'. And, again, what Arnold demands is that the point of view be independent, not that it be true. It is very hard to disentangle the positive insights from the provincial confusions in these passages. Generally, Arnold seems to want the modern poet to use ideas, to be stimulated by them, rather than — as he puts it himself — to 'discover' them. But here, with his emphasis on 'an independent point of view', he seems to expect poets to be their own philosophers, and original ones at that; for surely there is an important sense in which all good poetry is the expression of 'an independent point of view', and that is a sense which Arnold plainly intends to surpass.

But a later essay gives us a hint that the difficulty with these passages comes chiefly from the peculiar nature of his attachment to Goethe, and not from an irremediable confusion in his attitude. His gratitude to Goethe as a 'liberator' is so great that it tends to become confused with a judgment on Goethe's greatness as a poet. In 'A French Critic on Goethe', we find that ' Goethe is the greatest poet of modern times' because he is 'in the width, depth, and richness of his criticism of life, by far our greatest modern man'.[12] Goethe is 'the clearest, the largest, the most helpful thinker of modern times.'

I cannot help finding this very odd. It is the tendency to think in maxims appearing again, but on a new level. Goethe is seen as a sage, a liberator, a poetic philosopher, the archetypal modern man. And Arnold is content to rely on the assettion of these qualities in representing him as a great poet; he never once shows us how this sagacity, freedom, philosophy, representativeness, are made *actual* in poetry. It is, in a way, a literary-critical judgment; but it is made in such a way as to raise a literary issue the relevance of which Arnold seems to see only in the vaguest terms.

But he is interested in affirming whatever in modern poetry is capable of liberating man from the deadness of 'routine thinking'. So he presents Heine as, after Goethe, the most important liberator of the century; and it is in his treatment of Heine that the dual nature of his interest comes out; it is an interest in 'intellectual deliverance' and in 'moral deliverance' together. It is true that an intellectual deliverance is, in a sense, moral, in that it frees Man from the routine thinking which tends to deaden him for perfect moral action. But Arnold can never get far away from his own didactic tendency; he wants poetry to free man in a more direct way as well — to free his sympathies, his moral feeling. Heine, while being a great intellectual liberator, does not offer 'moral deliverance'.[13]

He cannot offer it, because he is lacking in 'self-respect, in true dignity of character'.

Here is a typically Arnoldian stress which I shall want to consider later. At the moment, it is more important to try to make sense of his view of ideas in poetry. One of the most interesting things in the essay on Heine is the criticism of the English Romantics for their comparative lack of modernity, their failure, partly because of a lack in society, partly because of a lack in themselves, to 'apply the modern spirit'. The result is a kind of spiritual and moral immaturity which can be traced in their works as well as in their lives: a tendency to be overwhelmed by the world, to fail to *master* it, or to withdraw from it.

What, in fact, was the career of the chief English men of letters, their contemporaries? The greatest of them, Wordsworth, retired (in Middle-Age phrase) into a monastery. I mean, he plunged himself in the inward life, he voluntarily cut himself off from the modern spirit. Coleridge took to opium, Scott became the historiographer-royal of feudalism. Keats passionately gave himself up to a sensuous genius, to his faculty for interpreting nature; and he died of consumption at twenty-five. Wordsworth, Scott and Keats have left admirable works; far more solid and complete works than those which Byron and Shelley have left. But their works have this defect, — they do not belong to that which is the main current of the literature of modern epochs, they do not apply modern ideas to life; they constitute, therefore, *minor currents,* and all other literary work of our day, however popular, which has the same defect, also constitutes but a minor current.[14]

Now, this is in direct contradiction to Arnold's later estimate of Wordsworth, in which he applies a criterion of value which is of a directly aesthetic-moral kind, of a kind which I looked at in the last chapter. You cannot use two criteria which lead to conflicting results in your estimate of the one poet. Wordsworth is either of pre-eminent value, or he is not. But Arnold developing a general case is always very much Arnold the advocate, the sophisticated and self-convinced barrister of literature. And he is concerned, at the moment, to contrast the relative unreadiness of the English Romantics to the modernity of Heine:

> Heine's intense modernism, his absolute freedom, his bitter rejection of stock classicism and stock romanticism, his bringing all things under the point of view of the nineteenth century, were understood and laid to heart by Germany, through virtue of her immense, tolerant intellectualism, much as there was in all Heine said to affront and wound Germany.[15]

But he does not offer moral deliverance.

It is an impressive conception of the necessity for a new freshness, a new responsiveness, a new intellectual vigour, in modern poetry; but not only can it not be used as a criterion for the judgment of *all* poetry (as Arnold's own critical practice testifies), it does not recommend itself as an analysis in these terms. A modern responsiveness seems to me to have less to do with the *modernity* of *ideas* than Arnold will admit. And he presses so strongly for his own conception because he is so concerned to press a view of the relation of poetry to society, and of the inner integrity of the poet which becomes more than usually necessary in a complex transitional age. There is in it, too, a personal drive towards a kind of contemplative detachment from the spectacle of life, a spectacle which otherwise would prove oppressive and imaginatively unmanageable. All of these facets are more or less in keeping with the aspects of his thought which I have outlined in the previous chapter; but there is a certain amount of confusion, and even of contradiction; Arnold is a much more complex literary personality than has often been recognised.

Nevertheless, the driving interest, in his discussion of the rôle of ideas as in his discussion of the healing and animating spiritual influences of poetry, runs towards the necessity of serenity, detachment, freedom in the contemplation of human destiny. It is in the achievement of some such state that Arnold sees man's readiness for perfect moral action. Moral and intellectual deliverance come, in the finest poetry, to the same thing. He recognises this in his discussion of modernity, in 'On the Modern Element in Literature':

> An intellectual deliverance is the peculiar demand of those ages which are called modern . . .

But first let us ask ourselves why the demand for an intellectual deliverance arises in such an age as the present, and in what the deliverance itself consists? The demand arises, because our present age has around it a copious and complex present, and behind it a copious and complex past; it arises, because the present age exhibits to the individual man who contemplates it the spectacle of a vast multitude of facts awaiting and inviting his comprehension. The deliverance consists in man's comprehension of this present and past. It begins when our mind begins to enter into possession of the general ideas which are the law of this vast multitude of facts. It is perfect when we have acquired that harmonious acquiescence of mind which we feel in contemplating a grand spectacle that is intelligible to us . . . [16]

The whole work of this comprehension does not, of course, devolve upon the poet; he is, in a sense, the servant of 'current' ideas as well as their controller; we have seen this already. But the work of reconciling man to the universe becomes here the work of reconciling him, in a serene and detached understanding, to the movements of his contemporary society. It is still a moral task, in the distinctively Arnoldian sense which I have noted. However, as we see in the case of Goethe, it is possible for him, in developing this particular aspect of his critical position, to confuse poetic greatness with greatness as a sort of practical moral philosopher. And this in the midst of his heartening returns to such words and phrases as 'instructive fulness of experience', 'life', 'development', ''vigour', and of his outright rejection of ennui and overweening depression in literature as elements which make against vitality, both in literature and in life. Lucretius is thus seen as inadequate to a 'modern' age because of the strain of morbidity and defeat in him.[17]

The whole essay deals with poetry as the finest interpreter of an age; it interprets through grasping the central problem of that age, and through employing all possible human energies as agents of that interpretation. It is an interpretation of society, not in any narrow sense, but in the sense of historical forces working on society in the shape either of ideas or of aspiring energies. So it comes to be an interpretation of the nature and needs of man as a given age reveals them.

To our contemporaries, such an analysis may seem vague and naóve to the point of wilfulness. But if a man chooses to speak of this subject at all, how can he escape being vague? Arnold's attitude arises, after all, from his intimate personal sense of the complexity and needs of the age; and his expression of it is plainly intended, not to produce a logically perfect thesis, but to persuade his readers of the greatness of their own age, both in its tasks and its possibilities. He is trying to stimulate an attitude of mind, and it is the attitude which is important. On this question, he stands, I suppose, on the opposite side to Eliot; but, though he often seems rather callow compared with Eliot, he is here on the right side. His attempts to deal with the question of a 'true point of view' from which to contemplate the spectacle of modern life get nowhere. But the attitude he is trying to inculcate is a valuable one. And it is fairly closely in harmony with his view of the moral reality of poetry, announced elsewhere. The intellectualism which he seems to press for has a non-intellectual root and effect; the detachment which he recommends is a contemplative detachment which is in itself a readiness for moral action.

The real force of his view, the constant stress, is seen if we complete the foregoing analysis with his remarks about Leopardi, Byron, and Wordsworth. It is precisely in the 'sure and firm touch of the true artist', and in intellectual clarity and maturity, that Leopardi is seen to surpass Byron, and even Wordsworth:

> . . . he has a grave fulness of knowledge, an insight into the real bearings of the questions which as a sceptical poet he raises, a power of seizing the real point, a lucidity, with which the author of *Cain* has nothing to compare.

Yet he is deficient in energy, compared with Byron; and, compared with Wordsworth, he is deficient in joy, in hope:

> But as compared with Leopardi, Wordsworth, though at many points less lucid, though far less a master of style, far less of an artist, gains so much by his criticism of life being, in certain matters of profound importance, healthful and true, whereas Leopardi's pessimism is not, that the value of Wordsworth's poetry, on the whole, stands higher for us than that of Leopardi's, as it stands higher for us, I think, than that of any modern poetry except Goethe's.[18]

There is a certain sleight-of-hand here, in the rapid and persuasive linking of 'healthful' and 'true'. And I feel, as so often with Arnold, that the true is seen as a consequence of the healthful, and not the other way round. The pragmatic moralist is at work, not the sternly scientific observer of contemporary currents, not the dedicated philosopher trying to wrest from an historical era the understanding of its laws. By what criterion could Arnold decide that Leopardi's *criticism of life* is less true than Wordsworth's? He offers none, and I think he could offer none. The sense in which 'true' is used is, it seems to me, an utterly pragmatic one. Leopardi is less 'true' because he has the inferior effect upon the reader. He does not stimulate the best sentiments, does not conduce to a state of mind in which there is a readiness for virtuous action and a desire to make that action perfect.

And the question of 'modernity' is, in effect, jettisoned. When it comes to an assessment of the worth of most poets, even contemporary poets, Arnold cannot use it to any purpose. What he is after, in his talk about intellectual deliverance, is the release of a current of ideas which can stimulate a current of sentiment and sympathy — the *right kind* of sentiment and sympathy. Intellectual deliverance and moral deliverance lead eventually to the same result. But they lead there only when the intellectual encourages and fosters the moral deliverance. And the estimate of Goethe is not so much that he is a great modern thinker, but that he is a thinker-poet whose work is healing, healthful, for a modern age. It is in that sense that he is adequate and Leopardi is not. And, when all is said and done, Arnold does see Wordsworth as being in the major current of the age: at least, in the current which Arnold, with his constant moral preoccupation, really regards as major.[19]

This interpretation of Arnold's position is confirmed time and time again in his writings, by open statements, habitual stresses, uses of phrase. It is seen as early as 1848, when his reference to '*an* Idea of the world' shows what he is after. The much later phrase '*the* true point of view', with the definite article unobtrusively guiding the tone of the discussion, is simply a sign that Arnold has himself come in the meantime to fix on the attitudes which appear to him 'healthful' for the modern age. And they are attitudes, not ideas in any very definite sense of that word. So he writes to Clough:

> They will not be patient neither understand that they must begin with an Idea of the world, in order not to be prevailed over by the world's multitudinousness; or if they cannot get that, at least with isolated ideas: and all other things shall (perhaps) be added unto them.[20]

What he here calls 'an Idea of the world' seems to be very nearly what some critics of our own day prefer to call a 'myth'. It is a structure of belief or of imaginative attitude by reference to which the experience of an individual or a people is seen as patterned and significant. Our contemporary critics, it is true, are generally individualistic in their demand for it: or, at least, they demand it for the sake of 'the poet', so that he may have a centre of significance for his writing. And that, too, seems to be Arnold's emphasis, at an early stage of his thinking. Later, as I say, his view becomes more stable and assured through his mature conviction of the moral reality of poetry, a conviction which comes very largely from his view of the moral effects of poetry.

The rôle of society in the stimulation of poetry has been mentioned. It is a point on which Arnold is rather indefinite (as he can't help being); and he seems, in any case, reluctant to insist on it. But, such as it is, it is one side of the coin of which his view of the *inwardness* of the poet is the other. Arnold's view of society is in some sense an organic one; and his analysis of the relation of poetry to society always includes a sharp sense of the way in which society affects the individual: not externally, by a merely mechanical process or set of pressures, but interiorly, in the individual's sensibility as well as his character and intelligence.

The social orientation of his criticism has always been recognised. Twenty years ago, his name was often invoked in support of one side-the Marxist or quasi-Marxist side — in the literary controversies of the day. He was invoked because he had said that poetry was a 'criticism of life'; and because of his social leanings, he was assumed to have meant that it was a critical analysis of society. It was a gross misreading, both because Arnold's 'criticism' means nothing approaching that conception at all, and because he stands, if anywhere, on the opposite side of that controversy — on the side of individual perfection leading to social justice. I have already quoted the passage in 'The Function of Criticism at the Present Time', in which he speaks of poetry as having its unique contact with life through the use of ideas, modern ideas. There, he says

> the grand work of literary genius is a work of synthesis and exposition, not of analysis and discovery; its gift lies in the faculty of being happily inspired by a certain intellectual and spiritual atmosphere . . . But it must have the atmosphere, it must find itself amidst the order of ideas, in order to work freely . . .[21]

That atmosphere, that order of ideas, is patently a social thing; it is society under one of its aspects, its aspect of a spiritual commonwealth. We know that Arnold holds poetry to have the effect of helping to purify society by purifying the sensibilities of those men who are, in reality, the leaders of society, who are men of affairs and who engage most intensively in moral action. It is a semi-Platonic idea. And we know that he sees society under its aspect of a spiritual commonwealth rather than an economic one. Consequently, a concern for poetry is also a concern for society, and a concern for society a concern for poetry. We may expect Arnold to be interested in analysing society to see what it can offer the poet in the way of stimulating influences, which he calls an atmosphere, an order of ideas. So we get the idea that poets can work at their highest pitch only when the 'spiritual atmosphere' of society is favourable, as it was in Elizabethan England, in the Germany of Goethe, and, above all, in the Greece of Sophocles. A body of poetry can be 'adequate' to represent and interpret its society only when that society is adequate in its interpretation and representation of the nature of man.

This is a generalisation with which most modern critics would agree, in a loose way. But, as it bears on the moral reality of poetry, it can be treated only in an empirical way; and we lack the kind of experience of most past societies which would enable us to make with any confidence an empirical analysis. Many statements about Elizabethan society, for example, contain a wistful and rather question-begging note. And if we want to reach a conclusion about the spiritual energies of Elizabethan England, we can do so largely through a grasp of Elizabethan poetry. The reasoning tends to be circular, and it is a field of enquiry in which it is possible to talk a great deal of nonsense. Arnold does not. He treats the whole question by estimating what disabling effects are had on the range and quality of a poet's work by its being composed in a plainly limited society. So he says of Burns, in 'The Study of Poetry', that he suffers from a different defect from that which limited Dryden and Pope. They lived in an 'age of prose', in a society which needed for its stabilisation the virtues of, as it were, prose thinking, not of poetic exaltation. Burns, on the other hand, suffered from a defect of 'substance', deriving from a deficiency in the world which provided his subject-matter. He suffered from the crudity of the actual social world he inhabited, and which came quite naturally to inhabit his poetry:

> But this world of Scotch drink, Scotch religion, and Scotch manners is against a poet, not for him, when it is not a partial countryman who reads him; for in itself it is not a beautiful world, and no one can deny that it is of advantage to a poet to deal with a beautiful world; Burns's world of Scotch drink, Scotch religion, and Scotch manners, is often a harsh, a sordid, a repulsive world; even the world of his *Cottar's Saturday Night* is not a beautiful world.[22]

The word 'beautiful' has an unsettling effect. But this is not a mere aberration on Arnold's part, a wandering of his attention or wavering of his pen. Nor is he making the irritating suggestion, which we have met so often, that there are certain things which are 'unpoetical', which cannot be mentioned in poetry. It is true that, in the 1853 Preface to his poems, he presses a view of the intrinsically poetic nature of some subjects in poetry; but we can regard that essay as marginal to his work, and a piece of specious self-defence. What he is more usually concerned with, what he is concerned with here, is the necessity of getting a point of view above the chaos of life, an elevated insight into it. And his complaint against the Ayrshire of Burns amounts to a complaint that it could not assist the poet to get such a point of view from which to interpret it, to make his 'criticism of life'.

Yet we may ask in what way Burns' world was insufficient, and in what way it was too repulsive to be represented in great poetry. Burns was not a social realist, and it may seem that the condition of his social world is irrelevant to the quality of his poetry. It may also be that

Arnold's phrasing is seriously at fault, that the terms in which he puts his position, and in which we are forced to pose our questions, prejudice the answers. Eliot flatly denies the whole position: 'is it so important', he asks ironically, 'for the poet' to deal with a beautiful world? Beauty in society, or so he seems to be suggesting, merely serves to hide the metaphysical tensions in the lives of the people who live in it.

Eliot may well be right, but it seems to me that he is not engaging Arnold's real position at all. They are speaking of utterly different things. And an answer to the dilemma which Arnold raises must be attempted, for he is making an important criticism, a criticism which gives point to the analysis of English society undertaken in *Culture and Anarchy* and *Friendship's Garland*. We can see that in those works he is making a reservation about that society from the point of view of the poet as well as from that of the man of general culture.

The answer is this: that the aspirations and values of society are expressed in its 'manners', in a visible pattern of action, preoccupation, and desire; and that the poet, in attempting to penetrate to the hidden aspirations, must take account of the overt manners, and must indeed use them as in some sense his sensible medium. It is from them that he will draw much of the imagery, much of the local detail of his poetry; it is from them that he will draw much of the emphasis, the body, which gives his poetic speech a distinctive quality. And, of course, in them he will find his image of human destiny. Arnold is here being very like Yeats. Yeats' predilection for the Irish landed gentry was due not to their open political rôle in an unstable society, but to the way in which the rhythm of their life established a pattern of manners in itself stable and stabilising: in itself fit to be reflected in poetry of the most exalted kind.

It is a question of *manners*, not of any vague surface loveliness. In criticising Burns, Arnold is acting not as a sociologist of a somewhat priggish kind, but as a literary critic in the strict sense. He is noticing the local detail of Burns' poetry, estimating the degree to which it constitutes a poetic world, and attributing its crudities to the real world which it so obviously expresses. There is no more involved than that; and that seems to be an eminently sensible exercise of the critical habit.

Arnold's view is more robust and satisfying than he perhaps realised himself. The rôle of society in the generation of poetry is not merely the provision of a current of ideas, but is also something of a more direct, a more *sensible* kind. For the ideas, as we see in 'On the Modern Element in Literature', come themselves to take a palpable form, to exist in society as a pattern of manners as well as an order of ideas. It is a *medium* of living and behaviour as well as of ideas; and it is significant that the word 'medium' should have been used at all.

> Burns is a beast, with splendid gleams, and the medium in which he lived, Scotch peasants, Scotch Presbyterianism, and Scotch drink, is repulsive . . .[23]

Living in such a society, Burns could not attain the point of view, the elevated yet concerned detachment, which would lead to a 'criticism of life' of the highest kind. He could not produce, under those conditions of the imagination, a poetry which would in the full sense console and inspirit the reader. It is not that he could not, or that a poet in a similar circumstance cannot, write good poetry; but it would be only by transcending the limitations of his world that he could do so. And he transcends those limitations by bringing into poetry his inner integrity as a man, by realising and representing in poetry his 'genuine self'. Burns does so at times:

> No doubt a poet's criticism of life may have such truth and power that it triumphs over its world and delights us. Burns may triumph over this world, often lie does triumph over his world. . . .[24]

But he triumphs over his world only at times, and then not in the passages which his admirers laud most fervently. The obstacles of his environment have been too big for consistent poetic greatness.

Our experience of poetry, and of the conditions under which it is produced, would seem to bear out Arnold's contention, though the matter is probably more complex than he would allow. On Arnold's own showing, the substance of a poet's work is life and ideas-life as interpreted and evaluated through the focussed lens of ideas; and both life and ideas are available to the poet generally in a social form, as his society shapes and mediates them. And he cannot, with full imaginative power and insight, reach the 'great primary human affections', the laws of human nature, if they are not adequately represented to him by his society.

Rather, if his society is inadequate, and if he is great enough, he can reach them as they exist in himself. The quality which enables him to 'triumph over his world', the transcendent quality, is a quality of his own interior life. It is an elusive quality. It is not simply poetic or personal energy; it is not simply intelligence; it is not simply goodness in the ordinary sense. Yet it is energetic, and intelligent, and above all moral. We might call it genius under its moral aspect. It is not an attribute of personality, in the sense in which personality is the man as his friends and biographers love to reveal him. It is an attribute of something deeper in him. Arnold calls it by various names. It is 'sincerity'; it is 'high seriousness'; it is a 'voice from the very inmost soul of the genuine (man)': and when the poet does not speak to us with his real, his deepest voice, there is bound to be something 'poetically unsound' in his work. He will not merely miss the accent of the greatest poetry, the 'accent of high seriousness'; he will also introduce into his work touches or notes — of bravado, or hectoring, or preaching, or sentimentality — which ring false, muffle his general tone, and deflect the reader's attention from what is potentially healing and morally stimulating in his meaning. But when the poet holds these virtues, the most profound virtues of his own being, apart from the limitations of his society, he can use them to triumph over those limitations:

> The world of Chaucer is fairer, richer, more significant than that of Burns; but when the largeness and freedom of Burns get full sweep, as in 'Tam o' Shanter', or still more in that puissant and splendid production, 'The Jolly Beggars', his world may be what it will, his poetic genius triumphs over it. In the world of 'The Jolly Beggars' there is more than hideousness and squalor, there is bestiality; yet the piece is a superb poetic success. It has a breadth, truth and power . . . here we have the genuine Burns . . .[25]

Of course, Arnold is not postulating any essential opposition between the poet and society, an opposition which has been dearly held by many writers in the past century. Even in having a world to 'triumph over', the poet represents that world. 'The accent of high seriousness, born of absolute sincerity',[26] is a quality of poetry, not of human conduct. But it can exist in poetry only because it exists, in a different form, in the inner life of the poet. It may exist, too, in society; because it is in the personalising of social values (that is, of values held socially, and given a form in *manners*) that the 'substance and matter' of poetry normally arise; it is in a poetry of high seriousness that that process of personalising issues. The mark of the 'genuine' man becomes the mark of the poetry and the guarantee of its genuineness. When it does so, we find a quality of 'diction and movement', a note, a mark, an accent. It is in such strictly 'literary' characteristics that we recognise the moral force of the poet's utterance: his self-utterance.

Now, this is plainly an exalted view of the poet's function, of his relationship to his society and his age, and of his relationship to the depths, the moral possibilities, of his own nature. It is very far from Eliot's idea of poetry as a report on the essential human condition; it is, rather, an idea of poetry as realising the best part of the poet's nature for the consolation and animation of other men. It is a profoundly moral idea; it is an idea of the poet as performing a function which is nearly priestly, hieratic; it is an idea of the great value of style; and it is an idea of poetry as *utterance,* not as *form.*

At this point of his thinking, when he reaches the interior moral dignity of the poet, Arnold is able subjectively to resolve all the elements of his thought which otherwise would be in danger of contradicting one another. In a way, it is the terminal point of his thinking: here the concern for the moral effects of poetry leads back to, and is justified by, a concern for the moral stature of the poet. Anyone who is interested in tracing out the development of this essay, '*The Study of Poetry*', will find with what subtle naturalness Arnold's dealing with the various elements of poetry leads up to his vision of the poet as the representative, the priestly man, the liberator of his own deepest sentiments and of his reader's. That is why Goethe is assessed so highly. It is Goethe's inner personality pervading his work that is morally important to us. And that is why the 'high seriousness' of the finest poetry is held in such high esteem by Arnold, and why he sees in it a quality almost of ritual.

Such an approach is obviously in danger of being at once too optimistic and too narrow: too optimistic in its view of the value of poetry in general, too narrow in its assignment of greatness to particular works. It is also in danger of using, instead of an objective view of each poet, the 'personal estimate' which, in this very essay, Arnold deplores. If poetry can be seen as utterance, and if its value as utterance can be traced with such confidence back to the inner life of its author, then there is no reason why we should not leave the attempt to learn from the poetry and try to learn from the life of the poet — or, at least, from what we can speculatively assume of the life of the poet. Whatever we learn, it is something affirmed and affirmative, not something which is a mere analysis of facts or states. It affirms something of the essence of human life, of that life which is 'at bottom' moral. The poet can affirm values because, at some depth of his personality, he lives them. The stress is on interiority, on the poet as discoverer, not so much of ideas or truths, but of values in himself. As I say, it is not merely for Arnold (or for us) a question of the poet's public personality. Wordsworth may be a prig, Villon a ruffian, Byron a selfflagellating exhibitionist; they are not to be judged on such an estimate, but on whatever is true and valuable 'in the very inmost soul of the genuine (man)'.

I have suggested that there is a certain limitation in this noble view of the poet's powers and function: it is the limitation which shows itself in Arnold's tendency to treat poetry as utterance, and to see the greatest poetry characterised by the use of the 'grand style', the impressive *saying,* the ennobling manner and diction. This tendency is associated with, even consequent upon, his stress on the inward personal life of the poet: as though we could ever detect *that,* except as it appears in poetry; and as though we could ever estimate it, even when we did detect it in poetry. In other words, I am suggesting that Arnold's judgments about the personal dispositions of specific poets are not properly literary-critical judgments at all; and that his recurrent liking for such judgments shows, first, an evasion of the business of estimating each poem as a fully *formed* experience or thing, and, second, an unwitting desire to seek poetic virtue in other places besides poetry. These two tendencies together account for his failure to analyse any fairly substantial passage in detail: a surprising failure, in a way, since even Johnson and Coleridge were interested in, and capable of, such an analysis.

It is, again, a quasi-religious emphasis. The very language in which he speaks, in '*The Study of Poetry*' and elsewhere, has strong religious overtones; it is the language of spirituality and of redemptive power. The poet is seen as the true representative of his age, his specific society, his readers and, finally, his own inner potentialities; and Arnold speaks of him in terms of the transcendence of personal and environmental limitations. Again, it is not precisely a case of poetry being seen as a religion, but of poetry being expected to do the work, to enact and establish the values, which are usually considered to be the business of religion, and to have a religious justification. The poet is the true representative, but in an almost hieratic sense. He is not a 'legislator', acknowledged or otherwise; Arnold does not possess the mind of the political campaigner, as Shelley does. He is something more than a legislator; and in Arnold's view of his vocation, it is a vocation not merely to *do* something but to *be* something.

Thus we have the open association of personal character with style: and an association in which they are seen as more than mutual analogies — as forces of a moral kind exerting a mutual influence. The judgment on Keats is instructive here. It is a judgment which passes from an estimate of Keats the man to an estimate of Keats the poet, and back again, always employing the same terms:

We who believe Keats to have been by his promise, at any rate. if not fully by his performance, one of the very greatest of English poets, and who believe also that a merely sensuous man cannot either by promise or by performance be a very great poet, because poetry interprets life, and so large and noble a part of life is outside of such a man's ken, — we cannot but look for signs in him of something more than sensuousness, for signs of character and virtue. And indeed the elements of high character Keats undoubtedly has, and the effort to develop them . . .[27]

But since Keats died young:

> What we should rather look for is some evidence of the instinct for character, for virtue, passing into the man's life, passing into his work.[28]

It would be as well for Arnold to add the word 'consequently' after that second 'passing'; for that is what he means. Keats has clearsightedness and lucidity; 'and lucidity is in itself akin to character and to high and severe work'.[29]

If we take the stresses revealed in my last chapter, and look at them beside the implications of these judgments on Keats, we can see the real limitation better. Arnold is, in fact, limited by being too much a moralist, and by expecting of poetry too immediate a moral effect. Here, we find not only an exalted view of the poet's task and opportunities (which a defeatist age like our own might well take notice of, and meditate on), but a virtual identification of the man with his poetry. We have already seen Arnold slipping unwittingly, like an alcoholic, to an inflated opinion of the literary-moral value of Marcus Aurelius' maxims, of Goethe's power to liberate the modern world, of isolated lines of poetry which have the power not only of examples but also of sentiments complete in themselves, and of Guérin's quasi-moral renderings of Nature. Similarly, in all of the later estimates of particular writers, we find Arnold inviting us to learn as much from the man as from his poetry. Why are the accounts of Byron and Keats, of Tolstoi and Amiel, so pervaded by the sympathy with them as persons? Surely because we are being invited to be edified by them as men as well as by their poetry. And if this is so, why should we need the poetry at all? Why can't we simply praise famous men? Is it because the essential virtue which they possess as persons is merely more compressed, more public, and more accessible in their poetry?

That one can even ask such irritated questions is a sign of a weakness in Arnold's grasp. But, to be fair, his own practice as an analyst of poetic value directs us away from this weakness in him-even if much of his actual criticism suggests the weakness to us. In Arnold's view, there can be no substitute for poetry, for poetry is quite *nodal* in its holding, or summing up, of all relevant values. In the first place, if 'character' is a necessary condition of poetic greatness, it is not a sufficient condition. In the second place, if character is in question at all (and it is), it is nevertheless character in a broad and profound sense; it is not, for example, a question of a trained will; it is, rather, a fusion of moral maturity with that serene contemplative detachment by means of which one can 'master' the chaos of the world, both in oneself and for the sake of others. Arnold's practical judgments operate negatively as well as positively. In his estimate of Keats, where he is trying to indicate a direct relationship between hidden qualities in the man and valuable potentialities in the poetry, he may strike us as naéve and misleading. It is there that his weakness emerges most nakedly. But in his 'limiting judgment' on, for example, Byron, or on *Villette,* his instinct for the relationship between spiritual attitude and artistic value is much sounder, more realistic:

> Why is Villette disagreeable? Because the writer's mind contains nothing but hunger, rebellion, and rage, and therefore that is all she can, in fact, put into her book. No fine writing can disguise this thoroughly, and it will be fatal to her in the long run.[30]

In fact, in Arnold's view, the presence of 'fine writing' under such conditions would be an irrelevant decoration over the unpleasant spiritual facts. It would certainly not constitute 'style', in his sense, though it might be loosely described as 'a style'. His judgment on Byron's weaknesses is also illuminating:

> Some of Byron's most crying faults as a man, — his vulgarity, his affectation — are really akin to the faults of commonness, of want of art, in his workmanship as a poet.[31]

'This kind of judgment is fairly common in literary criticism. We may compare Arnold's view of Byron, for example, with Eliot's remarks on the artistic greediness of the Elizabethans. And, indeed, there is a great similarity, even in the phrasing, between certain of their judgments. So Arnold continues his account of Byron:

> [Goethe] saw the constant state of warfare and combat, the negative and polemical working', which makes Byron's poetry a poetry in which we can find so little rest; he saw the *Hang zum Unbegrenzten,* the straining after the unlimited, which made it impossible for Byron to produce poetic wholes such as the *Tempest* or *Lear;* he saw the zu viel Empirie, the promiscuous adoption of all the matter offered to the poet by life, just as it was offered, without thought or patience for the mysterious transmutation to be operated on this matter by poetic form.[32]

Eliot's recurrent emphasis on the inordinate aspirations which modern literature has so often fostered is strongly foreshadowed in these passages. Yet Arnold's remarks are very much in keeping with his own general preoccupations, and are coloured by them. He does not, as Eliot does, see poetry as representing, and evaluating, a state of almost metaphysical tension in the world or in the human soul. He is very far, too, from having any sympathy with the insight which made Yeats declare that, while rhetoric came out of the quarrel with others, out of the quarrel with ourselves we make poetry. He raises the question of the 'daemonic' element in life and literature only to shrug it into a practical irrelevance.[33] In his judgment on Byron and others, the stress is on *character,* and on poetry as possessing an authority and integrity similar or equivalent to that of virtuous human character; and, as we have seen, his interest in virtuous character is closely associated with the virtues of serene, informed detachment from the chaos of the merely factual world. It is this which constitutes a readiness for perfect moral action; it is this which comes into poetry as the accent of high seriousness, of perfect sincerity. And it is precisely this, of course, that Byron lacks. He does not have the virtue of rest, and so his poetry is lacking in restfulness. The emphasis is plain. Poetry *teaches* in a way very like that in which we learn from a man's life: by example, as it were. And Byron cannot reconcile his readers to the universe, for he is not himself reconciled with it. Neither, as we have seen, is the author of *Villette.*

It would be as well, at this point, to return for a moment to the notion of the *Zeitgeist* as favouring some poetical epochs while limiting others. The relative immaturity of the Romantics was as much a result of the era as of the individual. Byron lived in a time unfavourable to the greatest poetry; and so, Arnold suggests, does he himself:

It is only in the best poetical epochs, (such as the Elizabethan), that you can descend into yourself and produce the best of your thought and feeling naturally, and without an overwhelming and in some degree morbid effect.[34]

It is at this point that the question of form and style is thrust upon us. At first sight, in a critic of Arnold's open-heartedness and comparative simplicity, such a question may seem to have little to do with the question of the moral value or reality of poetry. But Arnold speaks of style much in the same way as the Bloomsbury critics spoke of form, or as some of our contemporaries speak of 'myth' and symbol: as though virtue, or revelation, or the *mana,* resided in the style itself. For Arnold, style is the pledge of character, and its imaginative equivalent.

This seems natural enough, if we grant Arnold's moral conceptions and his sense of the way in which poetry works on the reader to increase a capacity, and to produce a readiness, for moral action. But few modern critics would want to speak about style in this sense at all; and I feel that their reluctance is reasonable; to speak in such a way is surely an unreasonable limiting of the integrity of poetry, of that very integrity which it is Arnold's intention to promote. But he sees integrity as coming directly from the moral integrity (in the ordinary sense) of the poet himself, and as appearing in poetry in a form which allows of a tracing back of influence from the poetry to the poet: so that it is the glimpsed moral life of the poet, as well as the palpable life of the poem, which is an example and inspiration and solace to the reader. Such a conception almost inevitably involves a reliance on style which is no longer of much use to us; the man is the style, and the style creates manliness in the reader. There is certainly a weakness here, and the choice of his touchstones reveals it; it is open to the same objections as I have already advanced against his view of the way in which poetry has its moral effect. The whole position may be summed up by saying that it is a recurrent tendency in Arnold to see poetry not as an incarnational act and art, but as a kind of utterance which has something in common with eloquence, something in common with maxims.

A recurrent tendency, but not, fortunately, an invariable one-as we shall see. What is fluctuating, however, in his placing of emphases is caused by his reluctance ever to make up his mind about the relationship between substance and form in poetry. In speaking of them, he always sees poetry as an adjustment of style, of tone and movement and diction, to the 'substance', the meaning; but he does not indicate the nature of the relationship between them. This is obviously unsatisfactory, and it is the cause of much that is unsatisfactory, even question-begging, in the famous Preface to the 1853 edition of his poems. But that is an immature essay, which cannot rank with his great pronouncements, and it is in 'The Study of Poetry' that some attempt is made to account for the quality of a poetic style — 'high seriousness' — by finding its source and pledge at once in the subject of the poem and in the inner moral integrity — the 'sincerity' — of the poet.

Still, we are not told anything of the nature of the relationship even here; we are only told that a relationship exists. Poetic substance and poetic style are complementary qualities. After citing Aristotle for his remark that poetry is superior to history in high truth and high seriousness, Arnold goes on:

> Let us add, therefore, to what we have said, this: that the substance and matter of the best poetry acquire their special character from possessing, in an eminent degree, truth and seriousness. We may add yet further what is in itself evident, that to the style and manner of the best poetry their special character, their accent, is given by their diction,

> and, even yet more, by their movement. And though we distinguish between the two characters, the two accents, of superiority, yet they are nevertheless vitally connected one with the other. The superior character of truth and seriousness, in the matter and substance of the best poetry, is inseparable from the superiority of diction and movement marking its style and manner. The two superiorities are closely related, and are in steadfast proportion one to the other. So far as high poetic truth and seriousness are wanting to a poet's matter and substance, so far also, we may be sure, will a high poetic stamp of diction and movement be wanting to his style and manner. In proportion as this high stamp of diction and movement, again, is absent from a poet's style and manner, we shall find, also, that high poetic truth and seriousness are absent from his substance and matter.[35]

Well, it is unequivocal enough, in its way; and we may reflect that it is the first time that such a firm and lucid statement of an important truth has been made in English criticism. It is on this depth or aspect of Arnold that both Eliot and Leavis draw, though they turn it to other and more subtle analytic uses. And we should not be too scandalised by Arnold's characteristic reluctance to tell us what he means by truth, that truth which presumably guarantees the 'seriousness' of the substance and matter. I have already suggested where he locates the value of that substance; and I have suggested that, since he is a sort of pragmatist in these matters, the value exists in an effectiveness, a moral, inspiriting effectiveness, which he would not want to submit to the judgment of reasoning. The substantial value of poetry exists, for Arnold, in the moral nature of the poet's contact with reality-whether that reality seems to be merely natural, as in the case of Guérin, or in itself moral, as in the case of Shakespeare. The moral nature of this contact with reality is characterised by a broadness of view, a serenity and detachment, and a consequent animation or joy. It is the contact with reality of a soul mastering the world, becoming reconciled with the universe; and its effectiveness as poetry is connected with its doing the same service for the reader.

In other words, whatever the 'character of truth and seriousness, in the matter and substance' may mean, it is not simply a current of liberating ideas or a special moral faculty in the poet. These things are necessary for great poetry, particularly in the modern age; but they are necessary as *conditions* for the reaching of the moral contact with reality; they lie beneath that contact, enable and stimulate it; but they do not comprise it. Consequently, it should be clear that by 'substance and matter' Arnold does not mean what is often very loosely called the 'subject-matter' of an actual, achieved poem. It is something deeper than these, and it is a blend of elements. In the greatest poetry it is transmuted into — we may almost say it becomes — 'style'.

It should also be clear that style does not mean what it is often very crudely assumed to mean: a polishing of the surface of a work or a decoration of tensions, or a gilding the pill of meaning. Certainly, it is part of the exercise of a conscious and deliberate act, but it is not arbitrary and detachable; it is, rather, an equivalent and expression of the 'content'. It is, in fact, the means of giving its true poetic stature and meaning to the 'thing said'—a way of evaluating it:

> —Style, in my sense of the word, is a peculiar recasting and heightening, under a certain condition of spiritual excitement, of what a man has to say, in such a manner as to add dignity and L distinction to it.[36]

There are many remarks on style, on the 'grand style', on high seriousness as a mark of verbal movement; and we are not so much concerned with his conception of the grand style; it is simply symptomatic of his whole approach, and does not add much to what we already know of that approach. But his constant preoccupation with style can be seen in his early letters perhaps as well as anywhere. In the letters to Clough we get, at any rate, a clear statement that Arnold conceives style as not only having a moral source in the deepest integrity of the poet, and so being a verbal equivalent of moral character, but as having, of itself, a moral effect upon the reader:

> Nay in Sophocles what is valuable is not so much his contributions to psychology and the anatomy of sentiment, as the grand moral effects produced by *style*. For the style is the expression of the nobility of the poet's character, as the matter is the expression of the richness of his mind: but on men character produces as Lgreat an effect as mind.[37]

I have said that this passage is representative; and so it is in essentials. It is true that, in 'The Study of Poetry' and in others of his late essays, poetry is seen as a more complex and organic thing, and he is incapable of making quite such simple distinctions as he does here. But the passage shows the constant direction of his mind. He does not see style merely as an extra, a decoration; but he does see it as having an effect in its own right. This effect will only be validly and lastingly made when the style is an adequate embodiment of the substance and matter. So that Arnold would presumably consider it absurd for critics who are revolted by the whole attitude, the whole pretension, of such a writer as André Gide to call him a great writer because of his 'style'. The notion of style implied in such a judgment is a notion of something produced in a nearly schizoid way, with the mind and sensibility working on words in a very different way, perhaps a contradictory way, from that in which they work on their experience of the world. And, if it is proper to talk of style at all, we must speak of it as the rhythmic exercise of the mind and sensibility upon an adequate object of experience. If style is anything, it is surely the medium through which a whole personality comes to centre itself on its intelligence, and so to express its insight and perception. It is not merely a result of the artistic process, but part of the process itself. It is, therefore, in Arnold's terms, a moral thing. If a poet apprehends the moral reality of his experience, it is through his style as much as through anything else that he does so.

But I have said that Arnold would *presumably* agree; and I have added the reservation 'if style is anything at all'. In fact, one must be uneasy about Arnold's reliance on style. He is speaking, after all, primarily of one style — the 'grand style', the accent and movement of elevated and elevating sentiment — as the one most suited to great poetry. And this in itself is suspicious. It seems to me that, if my remarks are acknowledged, then the term 'style' becomes misleading. It is still the subject of, or the excuse for, certain gross misunderstandings of the nature of literature and of its value. And Arnold does see a poet's style as in some way detachable, if only for the purposes of explicit criticism, from his substance and matter. There is almost a suggestion that style *is* moral value. Arnold is always in danger of wanting to get the moral meaning and effect of poetry too easily; and we may feel that the composing and elevating effect produced by style alone cannot be really valuable and lasting to a contemporary reader in the great complexity of our time. However backed it is by 'the power to survey the world from a central, a truly human pointof view',[38] the grand style in poetry is not enough nowadays, if it ever was, to 'make moral action perfect'.

It is true that we are not asked to rely for the moral effects of poetry on style alone, though we are certainly asked to give it an inordinate respect. There is also an insistence (less constant, less noticeable) on what Arnold calls *architectonicé,* on what we may call builtjorm, as distinct from the *organic form* which Sir Herbert Read has inherited from Coleridge. This power of building is not a matter of mere 'technique'; it too is akin to character, and in some sense a product of character:

> . . . but the true art, the *architectonicé* which shapes great works, such as the *Agamemnon* or the *Divine Comedy,* comes only after a steady, deep-searching survey, a firm conception of the facts of human life, which the Celt has not patience for. So he runs off into technic, where he employs the utmost elaboration, and attains astonishing skill; but in the contents of his poetry you have only so much interpretation of the world as the first dash of a quick, strong perception, and then sentiment, infinite sentiment, can bring you. Here, too, his want of sanity and steadfastness has Lkept the Celt back from the highest success.[39]

We see that *architectonicé,* built form, is considered as the equivalent and pledge of certain artistic qualities which are as *moral*-in Arnold's sense — as those which find their outcome in style. Just as style is the product of an inner sympathy and nobility working on the substance and matter, so form is the product of 'steadfastness', spiritual and emotional stamina, a kind of artistic fortitude. No doubt Arnold regards poetic form as in some way delightful, as giving us what someone has called the sense of a completed movement; but that is not the aspect of it which he chooses to emphasise. He chooses to emphasise its capacity, as it were, to give moral example. Burgum, in his trenchant and hostile analysis, certainly accuses him of ignoring aesthetic values, and consequently of ignoring form altogether:

> He was more sensitive to style because it is the style and not the form of a poem which is rhetorical and therefore by its nature influential upon conduct.[40]

And

> Since he has refused to discuss design or plot, emotion has ceased to be an end in itself in poetry, and has become praiseworthy in proportion to its tonic effect upon the reader's moral system.[41]

There is some truth in these judgments; but they are not quite fair. For one thing, Burgum's term 'moral system' is ambiguous; and even if it is taken in the sense of moral capacity, it does not do justice to Arnold's delicate apprehension'of the issues. He certainly does not see men as having a moral system in the same way that they have a nervous system or a digestive system-a set of responses simply waiting to be 'toned up' by a good verbal shock or a good dose of poetry. Burgum. is certainly right in considering him to insist on style as the carrier and pledge of virtue; but, as we have seen, it is virtue in a fairly complex sense: a flow of feeling, a condition of sentiment and sympathy which in itself constitutes a readiness for action. There is, as well, the interest in form, though his later criticism does not take enough account of it. But it is in the matter of form that Burgum's interest declares itself. Arnold conceives form as *architectonicé,* as built form. He is not a devotee of form as Burgum apparently understands it: the organic form of Coleridge and Read. In his view of form he claims to be a follower not of Coleridge but of Goethe. And it is an open question whether or not the term *organic form* is itself a misnomer.

The point is, that even in the relatively immature Preface to the first edition of his Poems, he associates *architectonicé* with greatness of subject-matter and depth of feeling. So he says of Shakespeare that he was 'penetrated with' his subject. *Architectonicé* may be a limited conception, but it is not a mechanical one. It too teaches; it too is an element in the moral effectiveness of the poetry. It teaches not only through delighting us as form-a most infrequent stress in Arnold's writings-but also because it displays certain other qualities of the soul: fortitude, steadfastness, a readiness for the 'prolonged dealing of the spirit with matter'.

It seems to me idle to debate in the abstract the relative importance of 'style' and 'form'. The only conceivable reason for dwelling so much on them here is that they reveal so much of Arnold's view of the moral reality of poetry. His great strength as a critic seems to his in his awareness that poetry has its roots in a kind of wisdom — which is what he means by 'truth and seriousness' — and its effect in the animation of the reader for the daily business of life: in the encouragement of 'disinterested' intelligence and of the flow of feeling and sympathy. But his weakness as a critic, at least for our time, lies in his account of what intervenes between those roots and that effect. What intervenes, of course, is the poetry itself. And he accounts for this too much in terms of elevated sentiment, of truth turned too easily into feeling, of style. Because of the limitations of his actual vision of poetry, he tends to estimate it too much in terms of its presumed effects; and he can know those effects only as they occur in himself. However he may try to reach a point of complete disinterestedness, his demands are basically subjective, as well as personal. Hence the frequent desire for a consoling sentiment. And I feel also that he sees poetry as reaching a great effect in too simple and easy a manner — by directly stimulating a readiness for virtuous action.

Life is conduct; poetry leads to conduct by stimulating a certain kind of life, which is itself a readiness for conduct.

That is why he is, in a sense, a didactic critic. He is quite as much a moralist as Johnson was; but his view is more complex and sophisticated than Johnson's. And that is also why Burgum is able to insist that he echoes Sidney, but that in place of the courtier he puts his idea of the 'Christian gentleman'. He is a moralist of a quasi-religious kind; and I don't think it would be unfair to say that he sees the poet as a priest of the religion of elevated naturalism: a religion in which any supernatural dimension is simply not available to the imagination. It is from some such view that his whole critical position comes; it is such a view which seriously weakens his great critical achievement.

NOTES

1. *Essays in Criticism*, Second Series, *op. cit.* pp. 24 and 56-7.
2. *Ibid.* p. 79.
3. *Ibid.* p. 78.
4. The essay, *The Function of Criticism at the Present Time*, is a masterly elaboration of these related points.
5. *Letters to A. H. Clough*, *op. cit.* p. 63: Letter of 1847.
6. *Ibid.* Letter of May 24, 1848, p. 81.
7. Vide, in this connection, an interesting comment by G. H. Bantock: *Scrutiny*, Vol. XVIII, No. 1, pp. 39-40.
8. *Essays Literary and Critical*, *op. cit.* p. 3.
9. *Ibid.* pp. 4-6. The relevant passage is far too long to quote in full, and it cannot be quoted at lesser length without distortion.
10. *On the Study of Celtic Literature* (Everyman's Library edition), p. 128.

11. *On the Study of Celtic Literature* (Everyman's Library edition), p. 130. These two quotations practically summarise the whole intention of that other essay of Arnold, *On the Modern Element in Literature.*
12. *Mixed Essays* (1880 edition), pp. 311-12.
13. *Essays Literary and Critical, op. cit.* p. 125.
14. *Essays Literary and Critical, op. cit.* pp. 115-16.
15. *Ibid.* p. 6.
16. *Essays* (Oxford University Press, 1914), pp. 453-6.
17. *Essaysop. cit.* p. 469.
18. *Essays in Criticism*, Second Series, *op. cit.* pp. 111-14.
19. v. J.B. Orrick, *op. cit.* p. 30. Goethe is a 'dissolvent', whose work stimulates the reader to attain a full and easeful personality in a schizoid and rapidly changing world. He interprets the facts of the world in such a way as not so much to falsify them but to draw consolation from them.
20. *Letters to A. H. Clough, op. cit.* p. 97: Letter of after Sept. 1848-9.
21. *Essays Literary and Critical, op. cit.* p. 3.
22. *Essays in Criticism*, Second Series, *op. cit.* p. 26.
23. *Letters, op. cit.* Vol. II, p. 184: Letter to Miss Arnold, Nov. 1880.
24. *Essays in Criticism*, Second Series, *op. cit.* p. 26.
25. *Essays in Criticism*, Second Series, *op. cit.* pp. 30-1.
26. *Ibid.* p. 29.
27. *Essays in Criticism*, Second Series, *op. cit.* pp. 62-3.
28. *Essays in Criticism*, Second Series, *op. cit.* pp. 63-4.
29. *Ibid.* p. 67.
30. *Letters, op. cit.* Vol. 1, p. 29: Letter to Mrs. Forster.
31. *Essays in Criticism, op. cit.* pp. 105-6.

32. *Essays in Criticism*, *op. cit.* p. 109.

33. See p. 56, note 2, Chapter II.

34. *Letters*, *op. cit.* Vol. I, p. 52: Letter to Mrs. Forster. V. also *Letters to A. H. Clough*: Letter 10, p. 73.

35. *Essays In Criticism*, *op. cit.* p. 13.

36. *On the Study of Celtic Literature* (Everyman's Library edition), p. 107.

37. *Letters to A.H. Clough, op. cit.* pp. 100-1.

38. *Essays in Criticism, op. cit.* p. 16.

39. *On the Study of Celtic Literature, op. cit.* p. 83.

40. E. B. Burgum, *op. cit.* p. 105.

41. *Ibid.* p. 103.

9

The Times, the Crimean War and "Stanzas from the Grande Chartreuse"

—D.S. Neff

Some thirty years ago, A. Dwight Culler suggested that the "Thunderer" seen as "fulminat[ing]" at Arnold's persona "to join the modern world" near the conclusion of "Stanzas from the Grande Chartreuse" (lines 163-68) be identified as the voice of The Times (27). Since "Stanzas" was composed between September 1851 and March 1855, and since The Times, whose "circulation in 1853 and 1854 was far greater than that of all its rivals put together" (History 167), did its most resounding and-memorable thundering during that period about the Crimean War (1854-1856), an analysis of the possible role played by The Times pronouncements on the Crimean seems to be a way in which to augment Culler's very suggestive observation. Indeed, it appears that the famous newspaper whose coverage of and commentaries on the Crimean War brought down a government not only offers deeper insights into what might have made the persona of "Stanzas" seek refuge in the world of the Carthusians, but also provides a tantalizing clue as to the identity of "Achilles" in "Achilles ponders in his tent" (115), Arnold's famous allusion to a central tragic figure and motif in the Iliad that has puzzle dreaders of "Stanzas from the Grande Chartreuse" ever since that poem was published.[1] A specific candidate for Arnold's "Achilles" who has managed to escape critical notice is a person who was the focus of intense criticism by The Times when Arnold may have been putting the finishing touches on "Stanzas": Lord Fitzroy James Henry Somerset Raglan, Commander-in-Chief of the British forces during the Crimean War.

The Crimean War resulted from a series of irresolute, wrongheaded, and duplicitous maneuvers by Britain, France, Russia, and Austria as those great powers attempted to employ balance-of-power diplomacy to cope with the dissolution of the Ottoman Empire.[2] In Friendship's Garland (1866-70; 1871) Arnold, looking back on the causes of the Crimean War, has Arminius von Thunder-ten-Tronckh, his satirical spokesperson, single out the informal talks on the ultimate fate of Turkey held between Tsar Nicholas I and British Ambassador Sir Hamilton Seymour in January of 1853:

> I always suspect that your sly old Sir Hamilton Seymour, in his conversations with the Emperor Nicholas before the Crimean war, had at last your Philistines and your press, and their unmistakable bent, in his eye, and did not lead the poor Czar quite straight. If ever there was a man who respected England, and would have gone cordially and easily with a capable British minister, that man was Nicholas . . . Nicholas wished nothing better. Even if you would not thus settle the question, he would have forborne to any extent sooner than go to war with you, if he could only have known what you were really at. To be sure, as you did not know this yourselves, you could not

> possibly tell him, poor man! Louis Napoleon, meanwhile, had his prestige to make. France pulled the wires right and left. (CPW 5.336)

According to Arminius, Nicholas I could not have gained a realistic assessment of British reactions to provocative Russian moves in the Crimea because the British government was little more than "the mouthpiece of . . . Philistines." Even though the "best" foreign governments would have liked to "deal with England seriously and respectfully," they had instead been compelled to deal with those "dozen men sitting in devout expectation to see how the cat will jump,—and that cat the British Philistine!" Arminius, goes on to assert that such a dependence upon shifting Philistine opinion "demoralises your Ministers themselves in the end, even your able and honest ones, and makes them impossible to deal with" (5.335-36).

Turkey, having been influenced at least partially by British Ambassador Stratford de Redcliffe's irresponsible and ill-considered assurances of European support, declared war on Russia on 23 October 1853. On 30 November 1853, the Russian fleet from Sebastopol destroyed a Turkish naval squadron lying off the town of Sinope (located on the southern shore of the Black Sea in Asia Minor), and then bombarded Sinope itself. The British Government, pressured by public opinion at home and by French and Austrian desires to punish Russian adventurism, finally agreed to forward an ultimatum to Russia, insisting that the Tsar's forces withdraw from the Danubian Principalities (a situation that was of major concern to Austria, but had nothing to do with Sinope or Turkey). On 19 March 1854, the Tsar communicated his refusal to obey the ultimatum, and little more than a week later war was declared on Russia by France (27 March) and England (28 March).

In a leader of 2 January 1854, a month after news of the slaughter at Sinope had reached Constantinople, The

Times offered its wholehearted support for England's entrance into the Crimean conflict, exclaiming that "we are persuaded that the people of England were never more able or more ready to support the Government in an energetic display of our national power to protect the world against an unprovoked attack" (6). Following public opinion that The Times had helped to inflame, a leader of 15 June 1854 argued for an invasion of the Crimea, asserting that since "the two great nations of the West [England and France] . . . have taken up arms in this quarrel [they] have a right to anticipate results conformable to the magnitude of these expeditions." Consequently, "the taking of Sebastopol and the occupation of the Crimea are objects which would repay all the cost of the present war, and would permanently settle in our favour the principal questions now in dispute" (8). An appeal to patriotism was powerfully expressed in a leader of 30 September 1854, which proclaimed that "with all its sacrifices and with all its horrors, War teaches in irresistible language the force of that bond which makes us a people and ennobles us as Englishmen" (6).

In Friendship's Garland, Arnold has a friend of Arminius blame The Times in particular for both catering to and irresponsibly inciting modem, middle-class misjudgments in its efforts to shape the course taken by the British nation:

> [W]hat is the Times but a gigantic Sancho Panza, to borrow a phrase of your friend Heine;—a gigantic Sancho Panza, following by an attraction he cannot resist that poor, mad, scorned, suffering, sublime enthusiast, the modern spirit; following it, indeed, with constant grumbling, expostulation, and opposition, with airs of protection, of compassionate superiority, with an incessant byplay of nods, shrugs, and winks addressed to the spectators; following it, in short, with all the incurable

> recalcitrancy of a lower nature, but still following it? (CPW5.29)

Arnold, who did not agree with The Times's position on the invasion of the Crimea, has Arminius say that Lord Aberdeen "knew better" than to invade the Crimea, but that Aberdeen's "eye was nervously fixed on the British Philistine and the British press. The British Philistine learnt that he was being treated with rudeness and must make his voice heard 'with promptitude and energy.'" Therefore, according to Arminius (and Arnold), the Crimean War was the result of "the usual explosion of passions, prejudices, stock-jobbing, newspaper articles, chatter, and general ignorance" (CPW 5.336). In "The Nadir of Liberalism" (1886), Arnold called the Crimean conflict "a foolish and prejudicial war for England" (CPW 11.59), and did not blame the aristocracy for it. In "My Countrymen" (1866, later collected in Friendship's Garland), he (along with some "foreigners" who serve to convey his opinions) claims that "it was not the aristocracy which made the Crimean war; it was the strong middle part—the constituencies" (CPW 5.10, 15). Indeed, as Arnold's Arminius writes, "the Russian war and the Russian peace; a war and peace your aristocracy did not make and never would have made,—the British Philistine and his newspapers have the whole merit of it." Such a war did Britain "nothing but harm" as the country was propelled forward into disaster by "the British Philistine, with his likes and dislikes, his effusion and confusion, his hot and cold fits, his want of dignity and of the steadfastness which comes from dignity, his want of ideas and of the steadfastness which comes from ideas" (CPW 5.332).

Even though the British aristocracy may not have been to blame for the Crimean invasion, that same social class nevertheless had to bear the brunt of middle-class disappointment as fostered, detected, and amplified by The Times. A leader of 2 October 1854 reported that

Sebastopol had been taken, with predictions that if such an event had indeed occurred, "ten days will have sufficed to terminate the campaign of the Crimea" (6). Such optimism was proven to be unfounded, however ("Fall" 6; Leader, 6 October 1854, 6; Leader 7 October 1854, 6), and dissatisfaction with the war effort started to grow. British reservations about the Crimean adventure were undoubtedly nurtured by a report written by Thomas Chenery and printed on 13 October 1854, which described "the deficiencies" of the British "medical system" at the front resulting in the British "sick and wounded" having received treatment "worthy only of the savages of Dahomey" (8). Also disheartening was the news of the destruction, through a misinterpretation of orders, of the Light Brigade at Balaclava (Leader, 11 November 1854, 6; Leader, 13 November, 1854, 6; Leader, 1 January 1855, 6). In addition, there was disgruntled commentary on the costly victory at Inkermann (5 November 1854) that asked, "How many more such victories can we afford to win ere we sink overwhelmed by the weight of our own triumphs, vanquished by our own valour, and worn out by our own success?" Indeed, the Allies were "besieged as well as besiegers" (Leader, 14 November 1854, 6) as mismanagement, bad weather, cholera, and bad luck stretched what had been supposed to be a quick, easy campaign into months of torment for the British nation.

Arnold's correspondence shows that he followed newspaper coverage of the Crimean War carefully. In a letter to his wife, probably written during late October or early November 1854, he declared that "the newspaper makes one melancholy" because "renewed bombardment" of the Russians "has not, in fact, done anything," and seemed chagrined that France would "more and more take the position of head of the Alliance, disposing of England as suits her best" (LMA 1.39). In a letter of 6 November 1854, he remarked to Wyndham Slade that "the siege [of Sebastopol] is awfully interesting; one thinks they [the

Allies] must take the place, though, after all; the loss of prestige will be so great if they do not" (LMA 1.40). In a letter of 9 December 1854 to his mother, Arnold asserted that "the war, and the great length of time that has passed since most of the poems . . . [in Poems by Matthew Arnold, Second Series] were written, make me myself regard it [the book] with less interest than I should have thought possible" (LMA 1.41). In a letter written to his wife sometime during the latter half of 1855, he noted that "the situation [at Sebastopol] is altogether disagreeable until the English fleet or army perform some brilliant exploit" (LMA 1.47). In a letter of 12 December 1855 to Mrs. W. E. Forster (his eldest sister, Jane), he stated that "it is hard to think of any volume like that of mine having a sale in England just now, with the war going on, and the one cry being for newspapers" (LMA 1.48).

While most of the work on "Stanzas from the Grande Chartreuse" rightly concentrates on what occurred during Arnold's trip to the famous monastery and how those experiences may have been communicated through the poem,[3] relatively less attention has been paid to portions of the poem that may have been inspired months or years after September of 1851. It is quite possible that The Time's attacks on the English aristocracy during the Crimean War provided Arnold with the perfect example of much from which the persona of the poem was trying to escape by imaginatively joining with the venerable, but antiquated routines of life at the monastery.

It is not unreasonable that The Times, characterized by Arnold as a "Sancho Panza" and the mouthpiece of "the modem spirit" (5.29), was what the persona of "Stanzas", was, referring to as the "eternal trifler" that "breaks" the "spell" when he is trying to conjure up the limited but poten magic of the previous era of the "former men" who have been abandoned to "slumber" in the "silent grave" (128, 151, 155). Storm-blastafrom The Times may also have disrupted Arnold's desire to recover past values and emotions when he was working on that particular section of the poem. Perhaps the persona's (and Arnold's) "tears" at the utter confusion reigning in their age (162) were inspired by thoughts such as these in The Times, on "the British TANTALUS in the Crimea," which "has all the necessaries and comforts of life within sight or reach, but is never permitted to grasp and enjoy them" (Leader, 29 December 1854, 6).

Arnold, like his persona in "Stanzas," may have felt as if he were "Wandering between two worlds, one dead,/ The other powerless to be born" (85-86) when he read passages in The Times impugning "a generation that allows itself to be entirely ruled by the past," led by "the men of the past—the old men of the past—the old men who never were young," who "rise from their graves and undertake to manage for us the new resources of our own age" (Leader, 29 December 1854, 6).

Arnold would almost certainly have agreed with The Time's assessment that the events in the Crimea during the year of 1854 had "overturned . . . faith in many things, shaken many convictions, and dissipated many illusions" (Leader, 1 January 1855, 6), but, as has been shown, he placed the blame for the calamity squarely on the middle class and The Times. He probably felt little sense of triumph, though, when the Thunderer itself finally admitted, in a leader of 8 February 1855, that "there is something quite uncanny about this awful war. Nothing follows suit in it, and it goes wrong from first to last" (6). Indeed, the persona's decision, at the conclusion of "Stanzas," to stay buried within the past at the monastery rather than join the "passing troops in the sun's beam" on their way to war, may be interpreted as a refusal to heed the call exerted by mindless "action" (175-80, 194), much as Arnold had wished that Britain had refused the earlier frenzied summonses of The Times for the nation to rush headlong into a disastrous war.

Lord Raglan, the British Commander-in-Chief, became a prime target in The Time's campaign to stir up public outrage at a war that was destined to become something much less than Waterloo for the British public. Ironically, Raglan, whose life's work, according to Cecil Woodham-Smith, "had been to make himself the second self of the Duke of Wellington" (156-57), was being asked to shoulder a Wellingtonian task that even the Great Duke himself probably could not have managed. After receiving the Duke of Newcastle's dispatch of 28 June 1854, urging an attack on Sebastopol, Raglan conferred with Sir George Brown about the matter. Brown, noting that they both were "accustomed, when in any difficulty" to ask themselves "how the Great Duke would have acted," decided that Wellington would probably not have accepted such a responsibility, but that, since "they [helped by urgings for such an attack in The Times] have made up their minds to it at home," Raglan had better undertake the project, lest they "send someone else out to command the army, who will be less scrupulous" (qtd. in Woods and Bishop 71-72).

Leaders and letters to the editor in The Times during the height of that newspaper's criticism of Lord Raglan provide a possible explanation for why Arnold, in "Stanzas," may have identified Achilles pondering in his tent (115) with Raglan. Arnold could have gotten the idea after reading a leader of 19 January 1855, which characterized the troubles befalling the British forces after the voyage to the Crimea as an "Iliad after an Odyssey"(6). Thinking of Lord Raglan, the successor to Wellington in the public's mind, as Achilles would have been a not unusual association. After all, Wellington himself had been immortalized soon after 1814, when Lavinia, Countess Spencer, enlisted the women of her nation, byway of a public subscription limited only to their participation, to honor Wellington by having Richard Westmacott create a monument to him in Hyde Park in London. Finished in 1822, "London's first nude statue" represented Wellington (with fig leaf added at the insistence of the gentlemen on the statue committee) as Achilles, brandishing sword and shield in defense of his people (Colley 258-59).

Arnold's imagining Raglan as sequestering himself within his tent could have been inspired by the growing concern expressed in The Times about the Commander-in-Chief's apparent isolation from the rank and file in the army. A letter of 12 December 1854, written "From a Field Officer Mentioned for Distinguished Conduct in Lord Raglan's Dispatch," and printed on 3 January 1855, stated that "Lord Raglan (if Lord Raglan be really here, and not in London) is never seen. Whether he knows anything of how things are going on or not I do not know; I am sure he ought to do so." The letter goes on to charge that, before the Battle of Inkermann, "Lord Raglan never once rode over the ground, or knew anything of it until after the Russians attacked us" (7). Another letter of 22 December 1854, written "From a Troop Sergeant-Major of the Hussars," and printed in the 16 January 1855 issue of The Times, observed that "the troop which composes Lord Raglan's escort has not suffered much, as it was not at the horrible engagement of Balaclava, nor on the heights of Inkermann" (9). In a leader of 5 February 1855, Raglan's not allowing himself to be seen by the troops was criticized as an outmoded continuance of Wellingtonian military protocol that should have supplied "a warning" rather than "an example" for a war far removed from 1814 (6).

The very reference to a "tent" in Arnold's "Achilles" allusion may have recalled the memory of a well-known scandal during the Crimean War. During the night after the landing at the Crimea (14 September 1854) it rained quite heavily, and there were no tents for either men or officers. Such a mishap was described by The Times in a leader of 3 October 1854 as "a severe lesson in the hardships of campaigning" (6). The aristocratic leaders were constantly blamed for such problems, but Arnold, given his stance concerning the role played by the press in igniting war-fever throughout the middle class, would probably have had a different view. He could have seen such a blunder as a result of a too hasty and ill-prepared advance into a situation that was the result of a mixture of middle-class ignorance and enthusiasm.

When, then, would Arnold's "Achilles" have been "pondering" in his tent—once he had managed to get one? Arnold, given his previously cited suspicions concerning the French forces unjustly controlling affairs at the Crimea, could have written the line in question as a reaction to Lord Raglan's first setback, not at the hands of the Russians, but of one of the Allies, the French Commander-in-Chief, St. Arnaud, who, contrary to Raglan's wishes, would not accede to a plan to attack Sebastopol directly after an encouraging victory at the Battle of the Alma River (20 September 1854)—when a chance for a decisive end to the war was great (Woods and Bishop 74; Rich 132-34). Arnold could also have been referring to Raglan, the victim of the Clauswitzian fog of war, pondering in his tent after what he thought were his own clear orders resulted in the disastrous charge of the Light Brigade (25 October 1854) during the Battle of Balaclava. That particular wound was re-opened viciously by The Times in a leader of 24 January 1855 that ironically suggested that it and its readership might "suppose that Lord RAGLAN intended the Light Cavalry Brigade to destroy the whole Russian army, artillery, cavalry, and infantry" (6).[4] Finally, Arnold could have conceived of Raglan brooding in his tent during the terrible winter of 1854-55 at the Crimea, when, after a hurricane had destroyed approximately thirty ships bringing precious food, clothing, medical supplies, and money (14 November 1854, and reported in The Times in a leader of 30 November 1854, 6), the British forces were compelled to wage a losing battle against disease, exposure, and starvation.

Whatever the case, Lord Raglan had many reasons to ruminate, and if Lord Raglan was Arnold's "Achilles," there would have been no more suitable, albeit rueful, epitaph than these lines near the conclusion of "Stanzas from the Grande Chartreuse" for a man who was to die on 28 June 1855, broken-spirited, shortly after the publication of that poem:

> We admire with awe
> The exulting thunder of your race;
> You give the universe your law,
> You triumph over time and space!
> Your pride of life, your tireless powers,
> We laud them, but they are not ours. (163-68)

Lord Raglan, seen by many as having been martyred by the modern spirit, was a person whom Arnold would very likely have seen as unjustly brought down by the very real power of confused, reckless, and irresponsible thunderings from The Times and its readers—constituencies that, having displaced the aristocracy and aristocratic values, seemed to hold the future of Britain within their irresolute grasp.

NOTES

1. Sir Edmund Chambers has suggested that "Achilles" might be John Henry Newman, "who, on his return from Rome, founded with Hurrell Fronde the Lyra Apostolica, the motto of which ['They shall know the difference, now I am back.'] was paraphrased from Iliad xviii, 125" (qtd. in Tinker and Lowry 249, n. 3). Tinker and Lowry, on the other hand, see Arnold's allusion to the greatest warrior of the Greeks as a more general reference to "the active . . . life of the times" that seems alien and somewhat useless to the persona of "Stanzas" (249).

Kenneth and Miriam Allott are not even willing to attempt any identification of a particular or general allusion in the linc, writing, "The reference is clumsy: it suggests that `the best' are sulking as Achilles sulked apart until after the death of Patroclus" (Arnold, Poems note to line 115).

2. For background on the complex diplomatic and political causes of the Crimean War, see Gibbs (13-34); Wetzel (1-55); Saab (1-93); Puryear (1-315); Schroeder (1-142); Curtiss (3-199); Rich (1-88); and Bierman (146-63).

3. See Broderick; Dougherty; Wilkenfeld; and Honan (238-44) for close analyses of Arnold's activities at the Grande Chartreuse and their role in "Stanzas."

4. Woodham-Smith provides a masterful analysis of the Light Brigade fiasco.

REFERENCES

Arnold, Matthew. *The Complete Prose Works of Matthew Arnold.* Ed. R.H. Super. 11 Vols. Ann Arbor: U of Michigan P, 1960-77.

——. *Letters of Matthew Arnold 1848-1888.* Collected and Arranged, George W.E. Russell. 2 Vols. London: Macmillan, 1895.

——. *The Poems of Matthew Arnold.* 2nd Edition. Ed. Kenneth and Miriam Allott. New York-Longman, 1979.

Bierman, John. *Napoleon HI and His Carnival Empire.* New York. St. Martin's, 1988.

Broderick, James H. "Two Notes on Arnold's 'Grande Chartreuse.'" *Modem Philology* 66 (1968): 157-62.

[Chenery, Thomas.] "Turkey." *The Times* 13 October 1854: 8.

Colley, Linda. *Britons: Forging the Nation 1707-1837.* New Haven: Yale UP, 1992.

Culler, A. Dwight. *Imaginative Reason: The Poetry of Matthew Arnold.* 1966; rpt. Westport, Gr: Greenwood, 1976.

Curtiss, John Shelton. *Russia's Crimean War.* Durham, NC: Duke UP, 1979.

Davis, Arthur Kyle, Jr. *Matthew Arnold's Letters. A Descriptive Checklist*. Charlottesville: The UP of Virginia, 1968.

Dougherty, Charles T. "What Arnold Saw and Heard at La Grande Chartreuse." *Victorian Poetry* 18 (1980): 393-99.

"The Fall of Sebastopol. Decisive Intelligence." *The Times* 4 October 1854: 6.

Gibbs, Peter. *Crimean Blunder: The Story of War with Russia a Hundred Years Ago*. New York: Holt, 1960.

The History of "The Times". The Tradition Established 1841-1884. London: The Office of The Times, 1939.

Honan, Park. *Matthew Arnold: A Life*. New York. McGraw, 1981.

A Letter "From a Field Officer Mentioned for Distinguished Conduct in Lord Raglan's Dispatch." *The Times* 3 January 1855: 7.

A Letter "From a Troop Sergeant-Major of the Hussars." *The Times* 16 January 1855: 9.

Puryear, Vernon John. *England, Russia, and the Straits Question 1844-1856*. 1931; rpt. Hamden, CT: Archon, 1965.

Rich, Norman. *Why the Crimean Wart?: A Cautionary Tale*. Hanover, NH: UP of New England, 1985.

Saab, Ann Pottinger. *The Origins of the Crimean Alliance*. Charlottesville: UP of Virginia, 1977.

Schroeder, Paul W. *Austria, Great Britain, and the Crimean War The Destruction of the European Concert*. Ithaca, NY. Cornell UP, 1972.

Tinker, C.B., and H.F. Lowry. *The Poetry of Matthew Arnold: A Commentary*. New York: Oxford UP, 1940.

Wetzel, David. *The Crimean War A Diplomatic History*. Boulder, CO: East European Monographs, No. 193,1985.

Wilkenfeld, Roger B. "Arnold's Way in `Stanzas from the Grande Chartreuse.'" *Victorian Poetry* 23 (1985): 413-18.

Woods, Oliver, and James Bishop. *The Story of "The Times."* London: Michael Joseph, 1983.

Index

C

D

E

❑❑❑